Special Edition
Using
Optical
Networks

NIIT

201 W. 103rd Street
Indianapolis, Indiana 46290

CONTENTS

SPECIAL EDITION USING OPTICAL NETWORKS

International Standard Book Number: 0-7897-2581-9

Library of Congress Catalog Card Number: 2001096113

Printed in the United States of America

First Printing: December 2001

04   03   02   01   4   3   2   1

Trademarks

Warning and Disclaimer

Associate Publisher
Dean Miller

Acquisitions Editor
Candace Hall

Development Editor
Gayle Johnson

Managing Editor
Thomas F. Hayes

Project Editor
Karen S. Shields

Copy Editor
Gayle Johnson

Indexer
Erika Millen

Proofreader
Candice Hightower

Team Coordinator
Cindy Teeters

Interior Designer
Ruth Harvey

Cover Designers
Dan Armstrong
Ruth Harvey

Page Layout
Plan-it Publishing

CONTENTS

About NIIT

NIIT is a Global IT Services and IT Training corporation. NIIT has more than 4,900 employees spread across 37 countries and generated more than $270 million in revenue in the financial year 2000.

NIIT is actively involved in creating software solutions and learning solutions for markets worldwide. NIIT's software development procedure is controlled and managed through processes that are 100% ISO 9001-certified and assessed at SEI-CMM Level 5 for the maturity of our software processes—ensuring high-quality solutions that are delivered on-time and on-budget. NIIT's client list includes Hewlett-Packard, IBM, Microsoft, NETg, AT&T, Hitachi, Computer Associates, Red Hat, Oracle, Sony, Sun Microsystems, and Toshiba.

NIIT pioneered IT education and training in 1982. NIIT trains over 350,000 career IT professionals through its network of more than 2,000 training centers in over 26 countries. NIIT has an alumni base of more than 1.5 million IT professionals.

NIIT has one of the world 's largest learning content development facilities staffed with over 900 learning content development professionals. Over the years NIIT has developed a range of curricula for people with diverse requirements—from students seeking careers in computers to IT professionals needing advanced training to global corporate enterprises like Microsoft, Arthur Andersen, PeopleSoft, Computer Associates, Tivoli Systems, Sun Microsystems, The World Bank, Thomson Learning, Pearson Education, and Oracle that require end-to-end learning solutions.

Acknowledgments

This book would not have happened but for Vidya Iyer, who lent her technical expertise and made a valuable contribution to the making of this book.

Writing this book has required a great deal of hard work and focus. There are the people who helped us author this book and we would like to acknowledge their invaluable contributions:

Kumar, for his contribution in coordinating between the different people.

Rajiv, whose timely research helped us complete the book well within schedule.

Nirmala, for her valuable reviews of this book. Our special thanks to her.

Sriram and Badrinarayanan, who created the many visuals for the book.

Gayle Johnson, Sean Dixon, and others at Que publishing whose valuable editing and questioning shaped the book as you finally see it.

Matt Luallen for his invaluable technical edits and comments.

Shantanu Phadnis, for coordinating with the editorial and review teams.

TELL US WHAT YOU THINK!

As the reader of this book, *you* are our most important critic and commentator. We value your opinion and want to know what we're doing right, what we could do better, what areas you'd like to see us publish in, and any other words of wisdom you're willing to pass our way.

As an associate publisher for Que, I welcome your comments. You can fax, e-mail, or write me directly to let me know what you did or didn't like about this book—as well as what we can do to make our books stronger.

Please note that I cannot help you with technical problems related to the topic of this book, and that due to the high volume of mail I receive, I might not be able to reply to every message.

When you write, please be sure to include this book's title and author as well as your name and phone or fax number. I will carefully review your comments and share them with the author and editors who worked on the book.

Fax: 317-581-5831
E-mail: feedback@quepublishing.com
Mail: Dean Miller
          Associate Publisher
          Que
          201 West 103rd Street
          Indianapolis, IN 46290 USA

INTRODUCTION

That you are reading this introduction is proof enough that optical networks are becoming an important part of the high-speed communication sector.

Fiber-optic networks offer a highly scalable and manageable setup. They provide gigabit and terabit speed connectivity with a comprehensive fault-tolerance system.

We welcome you to the world of Optical Networks!

THIS BOOK IS FOR YOU

This book is targeted for an intermediate to advanced audience. A basic knowledge of simple network configurations and networking concepts and theories is desirable, but even if you are new to the world of optical networks, this book provides you with the fundamental knowledge of optical networking you will need to understand the more advanced concepts presented here.

HOW THIS BOOK IS ORGANIZED

This book is divided into three parts. Each part covers a specific topic that you will need to understand to use optical networks effectively in your network. Part I gives you a basic introduction to the features of optical networks. Part II walks you through the different components of optical networks. Part III deals with the concepts of designing, implementing, and managing optical networks in your network, as well as current trends and technologies.

Part I, "An Overview of Optical Networks," introduces the basic concepts optic fibers and how light waves work in a networking environment.

Chapter 1, "Introduction to Optical Networks," introduces you to the types of telecommunication networks present today. You learn the role of optical networks, generations of optical networks, and different transmission media types in telecommunications networks. This chapter also briefly discusses the history of optical networks and serves as a roadmap to the rest of the book.

Chapter 2, "Fiber-Optic Technology," discusses light propagation in optical fibers, types of optical fibers, and solitons. The phenomena of dispersion, attenuation, splicing, and nonlinearities are also introduced.

Chapter 3, "Components of Optical Networks I," introduces you to the components of optical networks, such as couplers, multiplexers, filters, and amplifiers. The operating principles of each of these are explained in detail.

Chapter 4, "Components of Optical Networks II," discusses the operating principles of transmitters, detectors, switches, and converters. The different types of transmitters, such as lasers and Light Emitting Diodes, receivers such as photodetectors, and switches are explained.

Chapter 5, "Modulation and Demodulation," explains the process of modulation and demodulation of digital signals and the schemes used in modulation and demodulation.

Part II, "The Evolution and Architecture of Optical Networks," takes you through a detailed study of the evolution, topologies, and system considerations you must consider when designing an optical network. The different access techniques of optical networks are the highlight of this section.

Chapter 6, "Optical Fiber Fabrication, Power Launching, and Coupling," discusses in detail the different types of optical fibers and their manufacturing techniques. You will also be introduced to fiber connectors and splices. The glass optical fiber types, such as Chalcogenide Optical Fibers and Plastic Optical Fibers, are also dealt with detail. The processes involved in fiber fabrication, such as Outside Vapor Phase Oxidation, Inside Vapor Phase Oxidation, Vapor-Phase Axial Deposition, and Double Crucible Method are explained. The mechanical properties of fibers and fiber joints are considered in detail.

Chapter 7, "System Parameters and Design Considerations," explains the different parameters that affect system performance. You will be introduced to the types of optical amplifiers. The different design parameters to be considered, the penalties in an optical network, crosstalk and its types, and fiber and amplifier spacing are extensively covered in this chapter. This knowledge will help you to design an efficient optical network.

Chapter 8, "Generations of Optical Networks," enables you to understand the different types of first-generation and second-generation optical networks. The architecture and layers of these networks are elaborately discussed. The Fiber Distributed Data Interface, Fiber Channel High Performance Peripheral Interface, Optical Layer Wavelength Division Multiplexing Networks, Optical Time Division Multiplexing Networks, and Code Division Multiple Access Networks are the highlights of this chapter.

Chapter 9, "Synchronous Optical Networks," enables you to identify and understand the different layers of SONET, different types of network configurations, the components of SONET, the frame format structures, and payload mapping.

Chapter 10, "Second-Generation Optical Networks," introduces you to basic wavelength division multiplexing architectures, dense wavelength division multiplexing, and the basics of optical layers.

Chapter 11, "Broadcast and Select Topologies," discusses the different types of broadcast and select networks. You will then be introduced to Media Access Control (MAC), multiplexing, and ways of accessing data. The different types of testbeds used in optical networks are also studied in brief.

Chapter 12, "Routing in WDM Networks," discusses the design of wavelength routing nodes. This includes wavelength conversion, transparency of the network, and network realization. You will be exploring wavelength routing network topologies and understanding the various traffic models. The chapter then describes the techniques of routing and wavelength assignment. You will then learn about wavelength routing testbeds.

Chapter 13, "The Optical Access Network," helps you explore the various architectures of access networks. Passive optical networks are also covered in detail.

Chapter 14, "Optical Switching Networks," explains Optical Time Division Multiplexing and the photonic switching architecture. The types of multiplexing and demultiplexing and the different types of photonic switching networks are also introduced. You then learn the performance of bit interleaving and packet interleaving multiplexing. Deflection Routing and OTDM testbeds are also discussed in brief.

Part III, "Managing Optical Networks," takes you through the most critical functions of any network management. This part aims to equip you with enough knowledge to objectively evaluate your network to know how well it suits your requirements.

Chapter 15, "Virtual Topology Networks," introduces you to the design principles of virtual networks and the difficulties in virtual topology implementation. You are then introduced to the elements of virtual topology. The implementation of virtual topologies in broadcast and select networks and wavelength-routed networks is also explained. The solution for the virtual topology design problem is then explained. You also learn about regular virtual topologies and broadcast and select networks.

Chapter 16, "Managing Optical Networks," discusses performance tuning, power loss management, device management, and gain management in optical networks. You are introduced to various network management functions and deployment techniques in optical communications. Fault detection techniques are also studied in this chapter. Finally, upgrading of safety management and areas of operation of optical networks are introduced.

Chapter 17, "Current Trends and Technologies," introduces you to the present day applications and technologies of optical networks. This includes Optical Add/Drop Multiplexers, Optical Crossconnects, Optical Bidirectional Line Switched Rings, and Optical Gateways. The latest technologies, such as Micro Electro Mechanical Systems, Thermo-Optics, Liquid Crystals, and Acousto Optics, are covered extensively.

The appendixes in this book contain an explanation of Snell's law, Ray theory, and theories in communication. Finally, this book provides you with an appendix that contains a glossary of all the important terms used in optical networks.

CONVENTIONS USED IN THIS BOOK

This book uses various stylistic and typographic conventions to make it easier to use.

Note

When you see a note in this book, it indicates additional information that can help you better understand a topic or avoid problems related to the subject at hand.

Tip

Tips introduce techniques applied by experienced developers to simplify a task or to produce a better design. The goal of a tip is to help you apply standard practices that lead to robust and maintainable applications.

Caution

Cautions warn you of hazardous procedures (for example, actions that have the potential to compromise the security of a system).

Cross-references are used throughout the book to help you quickly access related information in other chapters.

→ To learn more about the limitations of dispersion and nonlinearities on optical communication systems, **see** "Dispersion," **p.37** (Chapter 2) and "Nonlinear Effects," **p.39** (Chapter 2)

PART I

An Overview of Optical Networks

CHAPTER 1

INTRODUCTION TO OPTICAL NETWORKS

In this chapter

TELECOMMUNICATIONS NETWORKS

Communication has always been an important part of human life. In the past, people used smoke signals and light-emitting devices as a means of communication. Then they transmitted information by sending signals over wires. With the advent of telephones, telecommunications witnessed profound changes, in both a quantitative and qualitative sense. The word *telecommunication* means "communication by electronics." Here, communication could mean voice or data. The telecommunications industry, once dominated by the voice-centric world, is now moving toward the data-centric world. Today, telecommunication is recognized as a powerful business resource.

The following are some situations in which telecommunication affects our daily lives:

- Airline and railway reservation systems let you book tickets through telephone calls or direct PC connections.

- Large stock-trading firms use computer applications to buy and sell stock and to track stock prices.

- Mail-order catalog services accept orders using telephone numbers. At the telephone centers, orders are accepted and entered directly into computers, thereby making effective transactions.

Before we go into the details of telecommunications networks, you should understand the concept of communicating between two points using the basic communication model.

This model, shown in Figure 1.1, has three components: a source, a sink, and information. The information flows from the source, called the sender, through a transmission medium to the sink, called the receiver.

Figure 1.1
The three components in a communication model.

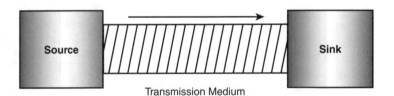

Transmission Medium

Let's now apply this model to telecommunications networks. There are typically three parts in a telecommunication network. The first part is the access part, which connects the end user to the network. The second part is the equipment that carries the data from one end to another. The third and most important part is the transmission part, which results in the actual communication.

TRANSMISSION MEDIA

Transmission media allow data to be transmitted from one point to another. The data is in the form of electronic signals represented as 0s and 1s. These signals are transmitted using some form of transmission media. Transmission media can be classified into two broad categories—bounded media and boundless media. *Bounded media*, also called *cable media*, includes cable types such as coaxial cable, twisted-pair cable, and fiber-optic cable. *Boundless media* includes all forms of wireless communication.

COAXIAL CABLE

Coaxial cable was the first cable type used in networks. A coaxial cable is also called *coax*. It consists of two conductors that share a common axis. These cables are easy to install and can carry very high-frequency signals without causing signal loss. However, they are difficult to manage because they are highly sensitive to electromagnetic interference.

> **Note**
>
> *Electromagnetic interference* is noise due to nearby electrical devices. It disrupts the components' operation, thereby leading to the deterioration of the signals traversing the medium.

TWISTED-PAIR CABLE

Twisted-pair cable became the dominant cable type for all network designs that employed copper cables. The significant factor in this cable's being predominantly used is its low cost. The two types of twisted-pair cable are shielded and unshielded. *Shielded twisted pair (STP)* cable consists of one or more twisted pairs of cables enclosed in a copper shielding. On the other hand, *unshielded twisted pair (UTP)* cable does not include a shield, so there is a risk that the frequency part of the signal will leak out. However, this cable is suitable for voice communications.

> **Note**
>
> Several twisted pairs can be combined in a single cable to make a multipair UTP cable.

FIBER-OPTIC CABLE

The latest to join the bounded transmission media bandwagon is fiber-optic cable. These cables are ideal for data transmission over longer distances. This type of cable can accommodate extremely high bandwidths. Moreover, it presents no problems with electromagnetic interference.

> **Note**
>
> *Bandwidth* is the measure of a medium's capacity to transmit data.

In this medium, the signal transmission is in the form of light. An optical fiber is made up of two strands of glass. The small inner tube, called the *core*, controls the flow of the light. Another layer called the *cladding* prevents the escape of light and shields the core. At present, many variants of optical fiber are optimized for different rates of transmission and distances. The incredible capacity of optical fiber certainly makes for more effective communications.

A revolution in telecommunications networks began when fiber-optic technology made its first move to improve network quality. Today, fiber optics has become the nucleus of telecommunications networks.

TRANSMISSION CAPACITY A single fiber has an enormous amount of bandwidth. Thus, to make efficient use of the fiber, it is essential to channelize its bandwidth, thereby increasing its capacity. The two methods by which a fiber's capacity can be allocated are baseband transmission and broadband transmission. *Baseband* allocates the entire capacity of the fiber to one communication channel. *Broadband* lets two or more channels share the fiber's bandwidth. *Multiplexing* is a technique that combines two or more data channels for transmission on a common medium. In other words, multiplexing lets broadband media support multiple data channels. *Demultiplexing* is the recovery of the original channels from a multiplexed signal.

There are primarily two techniques by which a fiber's transmission capacity can be increased—*time-division multiplexing (TDM)* and *wavelength-division multiplexing (WDM)*. TDM provides a way to increase the bit rates for each channel. That is, it divides the channel into time slots, and the receiver recovers and restructures the original data. However, the sender and the receiver need to agree on the time-slot assignments. This requires higher-speed electronics. TDM transmits the multiplexed signals in baseband mode. Figure 1.2 illustrates time-division multiplexing.

Figure 1.2
Increasing a fiber's transmission capacity using time-division multiplexing.

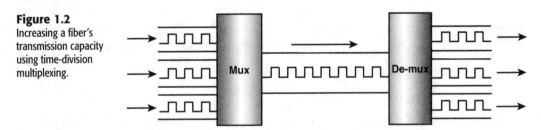

On the other hand, WDM enables an increase in transmission capacity by using multiple channels at different wavelengths over the fiber. WDM supports broadband mode. Interestingly, in WDM, a TDM signal can be one of the data channels. Thus, TDM and WDM are complementary approaches. Figure 1.3 illustrates wavelength-division multiplexing.

The current optical technology is particularly suited to multiwavelength techniques. In WDM networks, each optical transmitter or receiver is tuned to transmit or receive on a specific wavelength, and many signals operating on distinct wavelengths share each fiber.

Figure 1.3
Multiple channels in
wavelength-division
multiplexing.

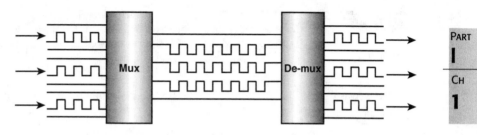

These wavelengths usually do not interfere with each other. However, if they are not suffi-ciently far apart, there is a good chance that the wavelengths will interfere with each other, resulting in undesirable effects. Dispersion is one such effect. It becomes an important limit-ing factor in transmission systems that cater to longer distances and higher bit rates. *Dispersion* occurs when different components of the signal travel at different velocities in the fiber. In particular, *chromatic dispersion* occurs when signals at different wavelengths travel with different velocities and reach the receiver at different times.

As today's systems become more and more scalable to multiple wavelengths and higher bit rates and distances, nonlinear effects pose a serious challenge to the performance of optical communication systems. Advances in optical amplifiers and the distributed feedback lasers allow the wavelengths to be more closely spaced. 16, 32, and 40 channel systems are now common. These are referred to as *Dense WDM (DWDM)*. Currently a combination of TDM/WDM gives a capacity of 100Gbps per fiber. In the near future, it is expected that TDM will allow up to 40Gbps per channel and WDM will allow 80 wavelengths per fiber.

→ To learn more about the limitations of dispersion and nonlinearities on optical communication systems, **see** "Dispersion," **p.37** (Chapter 2) and "Nonlinear Effects," **p.39** (Chapter 2)

APPLICATIONS Optical networks use lightwaves to communicate, as opposed to conven-tional electronic communication, which uses electrons. The major advantages of fiber optics over other cable media are high capacity and longer-distance transmission capabilities.

Some of the applications of fiber-optic cables are

- Linking chips and circuits inside computers.
- Establishing connections between computers that are used for computer-aided design.
- Operating the network at very high speeds over long distances.
- Transmitting data in environments that have electromagnetic interference.
- Meeting the Internet's bandwidth requirements, where large numbers of users flock to the Web.
- Managing high-speed networks in hospitals, where storage facilities for film-based images such as X-rays are indispensable. Also, fiber-optic cables allow easy access to these images, unlike conventional wired media.
- Videoconferencing, which involves high bandwidth and low latency with reasonable loss rates.

> **Note**
>
> *Latency* is the amount of time a packet takes to travel from source to destination. Latency and bandwidth together define a network's speed and capacity.

PROS AND CONS   The following are the advantages of fiber-optic cable over other cable media:

- The fibers in optical networks are resistant to electromagnetic interference.
- Light pulses in fibers are carried much farther than with copper wires, which carry electrical signals.
- Light encodes more information, resulting in more data transmission.
- Fiber-optic signals cannot be tapped as easily as wire signals can, ensuring higher security.
- Fiber-optic networks provide additional security compared to copper-based networks by eliminating the interference of radio frequencies.
- Fiber-optic cables are bidirectional, unlike electrical circuits, which always require a pair of wires connected into a complete circuit.

Despite their advantages, optical fibers do have some disadvantages:

- Setting up an optical network involves special skills, and managing it requires a greater level of expertise.
- If a fiber breaks, it becomes difficult to identify the location of the damage.
- Repairing a broken fiber is difficult, because special equipment is required to join the split ends.

> **Note**
>
> Large networks use combinations of different cable media. However, this mixed transmission media could be difficult to manage, because it might require a higher level of proficiency.

→ To learn more about the transmission of data in optical fibers, **see** "Fiber-Optic Technology," **p.25** (Chapter 2)

WIRELESS MEDIA

Wireless communication is the ultimate choice as a transmission medium. Microwave, synchronous satellites, and cellular are some forms of wireless communication. However, this system needs a complex wired infrastructure as its backbone. This boundless medium is a realm of its own and is not within the scope of this book.

TYPES OF TELECOMMUNICATION NETWORKS

Telecommunication networks can be broadly classified into two categories—private networks and public networks.

PRIVATE NETWORKS

Networks that are set up in private enterprises are called *private networks*. The private enterprise owns the tools and links that make up these networks.

Networks with a group of computers sharing resources and network communication devices within a small geographical area are called *local-area networks (LANs)*. LANs usually connect personal computers within a building or buildings. LAN users not only share data and devices, but also communicate with each other through e-mail and chat sessions. Moreover, data transmission is faster in LANs. The transmission facilities in such networks are provided by the organization itself. However, there is a limit to the number of computers that can be attached to this type of network.

Wide-area networks (WANs) interconnect LANs that span a broader geographical area. The largest WAN is the Internet, which uses the Internet Protocol to provide services to the users. These networks, however, transfer data at relatively lower speeds.

Networks that span a town or a city are called *metropolitan-area networks (MANs)*. In terms of geographical area, MANs are larger than LANs and smaller than WANs. MANs act as high-speed networks and are generally owned by network service providers. Networks that connect continents with undersea optical fiber cable are called *undersea networks*.

PUBLIC NETWORKS

Networks that are owned by telecommunications service providers are called *public networks*. Telecommunications service providers are government-regulated organizations that operate the network and provide telecommunications services to the public. In an enterprise WAN, the links are usually leased from a public telecommunications carrier. In other words, WANs use transmission facilities provided by public networks for data communication.

> **Note**
>
> A *leased line* is a link between two points set up by a telecommunications carrier. Leased lines are always active, unlike normal dial-up connections. They are typically used by businesses to connect geographically distant offices.

The following are the four main parts of any public network:

- Central office
- Access network
- Local-exchange network
- Interexchange network

The *central office (CO)* is the main part of the public network. COs are located in almost all regions from where a telecommunications carrier operates and where switching is performed.

> **Note**
>
> *Switching* is the process of filtering and forwarding packets of data from one point to another.

An *access network* is the part of the telecommunications network that connects the CO to individual homes and businesses. It consists of remote nodes (RNs) and network interface units (NIUs). The CO is connected to a number of RNs. Each RN in turn is connected to a number of NIUs. An NIU can be located in a home or can serve several homes. The network between the CO and the RN is called the *feeder network*. The network between the RN and the NIUs is called the *distribution network*.

A *local-exchange network* is the part of the public network that connects all the COs in a metropolitan area.

An *interexchange network* interconnects cities or major traffic hubs. However, these different networks can be owned and operated by different units.

Figure 1.4 shows the four parts of a public network.

Figure 1.4
The various parts of a public network.

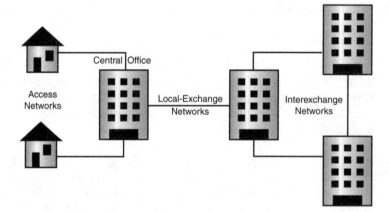

OPTICAL NETWORKS

The telecommunications industry has undergone unprecedented technological change due to the rapid growth of the Internet and the World Wide Web. With the evolution of more bandwidth-intensive networking applications, the demand for high-bandwidth networks emerged. To meet this demand, new technologies were deployed. Optical networks were one such technology. An *optical network* is a telecommunications network with optical fiber as the transmission medium. This network architecture is designed in such a way that it makes full use of the unique features of optical fibers. Today, optical fiber has become the preferred means of data transmission, because it offers much higher bandwidth and is less bulky than copper cables.

WHAT ARE OPTICAL NETWORKS?

The term *optical network* does not imply a purely optical framework. An optical network is more than a set of fibers. Fibers cannot become a network unless they are interconnected in a structured architecture. This usually involves complex combinations of both optical and electronic devices. The optical infrastructure present in such networks is called a *transparent optical network*. Such an infrastructure provides basic communication services to a number of other independent networks. Each in turn provides a particular service to a group of users. The transparent optical network is held together by electronic devices. These devices can be classified into two basic categories: *optical network nodes (ONNs)* and *network access stations (NASs)*. The ONNs or *nodes* connect the fibers within the optical network, and the NASs or *stations* connect the optical network to the nonoptical systems in the electronic domain. The electronic domain is the equipment that is outside the purely optical segment of the network.

For data to be transmitted over an optical fiber, the data, which is in electronic form, must be converted into an optical format. This process of converting data from electronic form to an optical signal is called *modulation*. The process of extracting the transmitted data at the other end by converting the optical signal back to electronic form is called *demodulation*.

Note

The process of modulation and demodulation of optical signals can be compared to the working of the Modems. The difference between a normal modulation and modulation of an optical signal is that the normal modulation converts the digital signal to analog signals. Both these signals are electrical signals. In the case of the modulation of optical signals, the electrical signals are converted to optical signals.

Figure 1.5 shows the conversion of signals in a fiber-optic cable. The electronic form of data is translated into light pulses by a transmitter, usually a laser, and is transmitted to the other end of the fiber cable. Here, the light pulses are detected by the receiver, usually a photodetector, and are converted back to electrical signals. Thus, for every transmission signal, there are two basic components—the digital signal in electronic form and the optical signal.

Figure 1.5
Modulation and demodulation of signals in a fiber-optic cable.

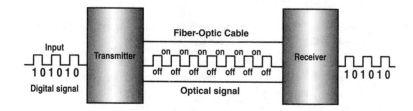

The nodes provide functions that control the optical signals, whereas the stations provide the terminating points for the optical signal. The stations and nodes contain the network's optoelectronic and photonic components, respectively. These components can be lasers, detectors, couplers, filters, switches, amplifiers, wavelength converters, and so on. These components, together with the fibers, produce the required optical signals.

The stations represent the interface between the electronic domain and the optical domain. They perform the basic functions of getting the light into the fibers by using lasers and getting it out with photodetectors. On the other hand, the nodes use the photonic components to perform functions such as optical power combining, splitting, filtering, wavelength multiplexing, demultiplexing, and routing.

Figure 1.6 shows an optical domain containing stations and nodes.

Figure 1.6
A transparent optical network with stations and nodes.

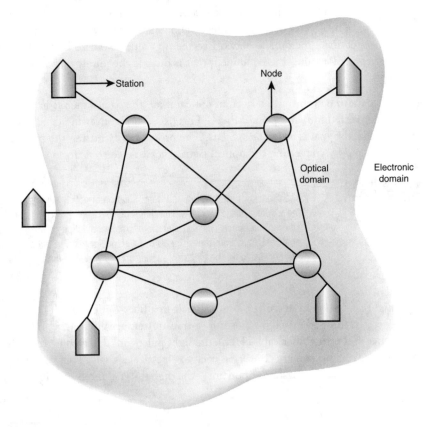

→ To learn more about the various components of optical networks and their functions, **see** Chapter 3, "Components of Optical Networks I," **p.43**

GENERATIONS OF OPTICAL NETWORKS

Fibers in optical networks were initially used only as a transmission medium. Later, researchers realized that optical fibers can provide more functions than just point-to-point transmissions. Switching and routing functions that were previously performed by electronics are now included in the optical part of the network.

FIRST-GENERATION OPTICAL NETWORKS

Networks in which optical fibers function solely as a transmission medium serving merely as a substitute for copper cable are called *first-generation optical networks*. In these networks, the processing of data is performed by electronics. In first-generation optical networks, the electronics at a node handle not only the data planned for that node, but also the data that passes through that node. These networks are extensively set up in all kinds of public networks, except in residential access networks. Examples of first-generation optical networks are *SONET (synchronous optical network)* and *SDH (synchronous digital hierarchy)*. SONET is a transmission standard adopted in North America for optical communications transport. It is a core technology in which many signals of different capacities are carried through a synchronous optical hierarchy. If the system fails at one location, transmission takes place in the opposite direction, because the system is bidirectional. SDH is a similar standard adopted in Europe and Japan. In addition, *asynchronous transfer mode (ATM)* is a metropolitan-area standard that is commonly deployed in the integration of voice and data networks.

→ To learn more about first-generation optical networks, **see** "First-Generation Optical Networks," **p.142** (Chapter 8)

SECOND-GENERATION OPTICAL NETWORKS

The more the data transmission rate increases in a network, the more difficult it becomes for electronics to process the data. If this data that is passed through a node is routed through the optical domain, the burden on the electronics at the node is considerably reduced. This view marked the beginning of second-generation optical networks. WDM networks were developed based on this model. These networks are deployed in interexchange networks, undersea networks, local-exchange networks, and access networks.

WDM network architecture can be broadly classified into two categories—broadcast and select architecture and wavelength routing architecture. In *broadcast and select networks*, different nodes transmit data at different wavelengths. Figure 1.7 shows a part of the broadcast and select network. Here, each node is equipped with a laser transmitter, which can transmit light at a fixed wavelength. It also contains an optical receiver, which can be tuned to the wavelength of any transmitter. The signals are broadcast to all the nodes by a centrally located passive device—in this case, a star coupler. The coupler combines these signals from all the nodes, and the combined stream is split and delivered to the output ports. A filter is employed at each node at the receiving end to select the wavelength. By selecting the appropriate wavelength, each receiver can accept the signal transmitted by the corresponding transmitter, thereby establishing a transparent connection. However, there is a limit to the number of nodes that are present in these networks, because the power of the transmitted signal from one node must be split among all the receivers in the network. Therefore, this form of network is suitable for LANs and MANs such as access networks.

Figure 1.7
The transmission of signals in a broadcast and select network.

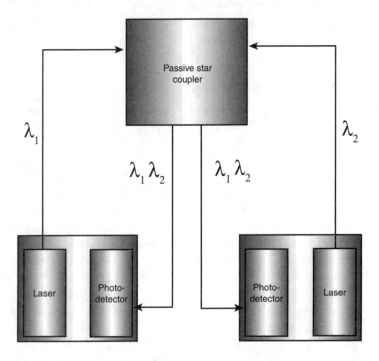

Wavelength routing networks are a more practical architecture employed today. In these networks, the nodes can transmit signals of different wavelengths to different output ports, thus enabling reuse of the wavelengths (see Figure 1.8). This architecture also avoids sending signals to unwanted receivers in the network. These networks are suitable for WANs, such as local exchange and interexchange networks, and MANs. A number of test-bed efforts on broadcast and select networks and wavelength routing networks have been developed by research laboratories.

However, WDM networks with a large number of closely spaced wavelengths can lead to fiber nonlinearities. Furthermore, in order to use the bandwidth most efficiently, it is best to deploy optical receivers, which use coherent optical transmission techniques.

→ To learn more about optical transmission techniques in receivers, **see** "Receivers," **p.78** (Chapter 4)

Alternative techniques were explored to access the huge bandwidth, which lead to time-division multiplexing (TDM) in optical networks. These networks are called *optical time-division multiplexing* (OTDM) networks. The simplest form of an OTDM network is a broadcast and select network. Here, each node obtains different time slots to transmit its data. Optical packet-switched networks are another form of OTDM network that are widely deployed in LANs. In OTDM networks, optical packet switches replace the conventional electronic packet switches at the nodes. Figure 1.9 illustrates a packet-switched OTDM network. A node receives a packet, interprets its header, and sends it to the appropriate output port. When two packets from different ports need to go out through the same output port, one of the packets is buffered, or sent out through another port. Each node ideally performs all functions in the optical domain. However, certain functions, such as processing the header and controlling the switch, are performed in the electronic domain because of the limited processing capabilities in the optical domain.

Figure 1.8
Transmitting signals of different wavelengths in a wavelength routing network.

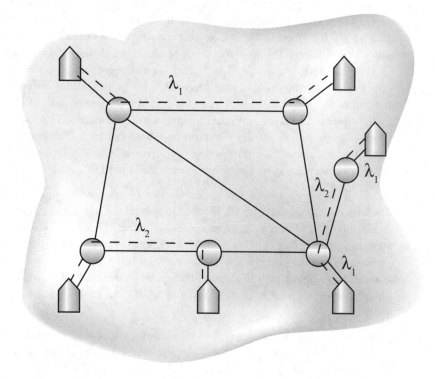

Figure 1.9
The transmission of a packet by a node in a packet-switched network.

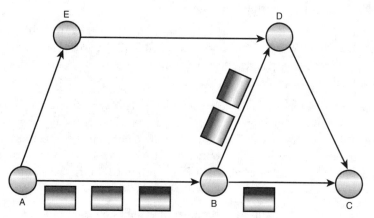

However striking the fiber-optic technology might be, very often the cost of managing an optical network is far greater than the cost of the equipment deployed in the network.

HISTORY

The idea of a high-speed optical transmission system was thought of as early as 1958. This was when the laser was introduced. The first prototype of a transmission system was demonstrated in the mid-1960s. A practical optical system was developed after the production of the first low-loss fibers in 1970. Constant refinements of optical transceivers and reducing fiber losses enhanced the effectiveness of optical transmission systems from the early '70s to the late '80s. The first optical fiber cable using electronic repeaters was laid in 1988. The advent of Erbium-doped fiber amplifiers (EDFAs) diminished limitations caused by fiber attenuation. Over the years, long-distance optical transmission using EDFAs has rapidly gained attention. In laboratory experiments in which dispersion effects are eliminated using solitons, limits on transmission distances have been reduced. During the late '70s to mid-1990s, the capacity of fiber transmission approximately doubled each year. The late '90s saw a significant increase in transmission bit rates due to WDM techniques.

Standards for the deployment of optical fibers for high-speed digital transmission were developed in the late '80s, which resulted in SONET. SDH is another similar international standard promoted by the International Telecommunications Union-Telecommunication Standardization Sector (ITU-T). These standards pertain to transmission links carrying synchronous bit streams terminated by electronic switches. Soon after SONET and SDH were introduced, the concept of broadband integrated services digital network (B-ISDN) became widely acknowledged as a means of supporting all kinds of multimedia services in a common network.

A packet-switched transport service is most appropriate for many integrated services applications. Therefore, in the '90s, ATM was a preferred transport service for B-ISDN. The Internet protocol suite, together with ATM, has been refined to keep pace with the incredible growth of Internet applications.

In the mid-1980s, lightwave networks gained popularity, but technological barriers to the deployment of large-scale networks remained until the arrival of the fiber amplifier. During the pre-EDFA era, systems efforts were focused on the broadcast and select network, which is a simple architecture appropriate for LANs or MANs.

The first prototype of a broadcast and select network is Lambdanet. Broadcast and select networks rely on rapid tuning of optical transceivers over a wide range of wavelengths. Therefore, they do not scale well to large sizes, primarily because they dissipate optical power, making poor use of the optical spectrum. To eliminate the constraints of broadcast and select networks, mesh topologies were proposed. In these networks, the optical spectrum was reused using wavelength routing.

When wavelength routing was proposed, the multihop concept was suggested to obtain high connectivity without requiring expensive tunable optical transceivers. In the late '80s to mid-1990s, activities in optoelectronic and photonic technology strengthened, and the deployment of new network architectures was reinforced. Multiwavelength technology matured, and activities continued in areas involving nonlinear optical devices. Potential applications include optical packet switching and optical computing.

Several optical network test beds were deployed in the United States, Europe, and Japan, involving multiwavelength technology. These test beds incorporate the necessary management requirements for making these networks equipped and reliable.

Thus, the second-generation optical network can be thought of as constituting an optical layer that offers services to the higher layers in the network.

→ To learn more about the optical layers, **see** "Second-Generation Optical Networks," **p.158** (Chapter 8)

SUMMARY

Telecommunications means "communication by electronics." Like any communication model, a telecommunications network has three parts—the access part, the equipment part, and the transmission part. An optical network is a telecommunications network with fiber as the transmission medium. First-generation optical networks use fibers as a mere replacement of copper cables. In these networks, the processing of data is done by the electronics part of the network. Gradually, data transmission led to demand for high bandwidth due to various reasons. It became more difficult for electronics to process data. Then, researchers realized that processing of data could be routed through the optical domain so that the burden on the electronics part of the network could be significantly reduced. This is one of the key drivers for second-generation optical networks. The WDM network architecture can be classified into two categories—broadcast and select architectures and wavelength routing architectures.

CHAPTER

2

FIBER-OPTIC TECHNOLOGY

In this chapter

LIGHT PROPAGATION IN OPTICAL FIBERS

Light is a form of electromagnetic radiation that propagates as a transverse wave. Light is channeled in glass fibers by a property known as *total internal reflection*. Total internal reflection is discussed in detail in the following sections. Glass fibers are a light-carrying communication medium that provides high-speed transmission over long distances.

→ To learn more about the different types of glass used in the manufacture of optical fibers, **see** "Glass Fibers," **p.108** (Chapter 6)

TYPES OF OPTICAL FIBERS

Today, optical fibers are the most widely used communication medium. Optical fibers are also known as fiber-optic cables or glass fibers. A fiber-optic cable consists of a cylindrical glass core that carries light signals (see Figure 2.1). It is covered with a cladding, which confines signals within the core. The core and the cladding are made of silica and are protected by a plastic sheath. During the manufacture of the fiber, dopants are introduced into the core and the cladding to make the refractive index of the core slightly greater than that of the cladding.

Figure 2.1
A fiber-optic cable has a core and a cladding made of silica and a protective plastic sheath for insulation.

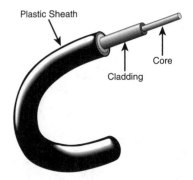

Plastic Sheath

Core

Cladding

Note

Dopants are the elements added to a semiconductor material during manufacture to increase its conductivity. Commonly used dopants include arsenic, antimony, bismuth, and phosphorous.

Note

The *core* is the central part of the fiber-optic cable through which light travels. It is composed of materials that have higher indices of refraction than the cladding so that light passes only through the core.

Note

Cladding provides a protective outer covering for the core. It consists of one or more layers of materials that have lower indices of refraction.

There are two basic types of optical fibers—multimode and single-mode.

MULTIMODE FIBER

Multimode fibers are those that can propagate light in more than one mode. Multimode fibers have a larger core radius than the wavelength of the transmitted light. They can further be classified into multimode step-index fibers and multimode graded-index fibers. However, in general, the term multimode fibers refers to step-index fibers. A step-index fiber has a core of approximately 50μm in diameter. Figure 2.2 shows a cross section of a multimode fiber. The fiber's refractive index increases (or steps up) from the cladding to the core and is a step function.

Figure 2.2
A multimode fiber with a large core can propagate light in many modes.

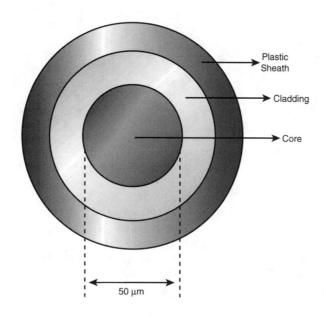

Plastic Sheath

Cladding

Core

50 μm

> **Note**
>
> A medium's *refractive index* is the ratio of the speed of light in free space to the speed of light in the medium.

> **Note**
>
> Multimode fibers were used to build first-generation optical networks.

Now let's look at the phenomenon of light propagation in multimode fibers using the ray theory approach. The lightwaves within the fiber travel in straight lines. However, they get reflected and refracted at the interface between the core and the cladding, thus bending around the corners of the fiber.

→ To learn more about ray theory, **see** Appendix A, "Theories Related to Optics," **p.303**

Consider a step-index fiber having a core of radius a. The refractive index of the core and the cladding are n_1 and n_2, respectively. As stated earlier, the core has a greater refractive index than the cladding. The radius of the cladding is denoted by b. The air surrounding the cladding has a refractive index of n_0. A light ray from the core is incident on the core-cladding boundary. Here, a part of the ray is reflected into the core as a *reflected ray*, and the remaining part passes into the cladding as a *refracted ray*. Figure 2.3 illustrates the reflection and refraction of lightwaves at the core-cladding boundary.

Figure 2.3
The core and the cladding's different indices of refraction cause portions of incident light to be partially reflected and refracted.

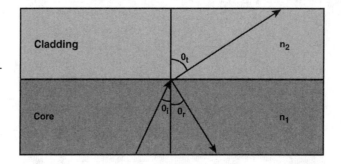

Here, θ_i is the angle of incidence, θ_r is the angle of reflection, and θ_t is the angle of refraction.

Note

The angle between the incident ray and the normal to the core-cladding boundary is called the *angle of incidence*. The angle between the reflected ray and the normal to the interface is the *angle of reflection*, and the angle between the refracted ray and the normal is the *angle of refraction*.

Now, according to the ray theory:

$$\theta_i = \theta_r$$
$$n_1\sin\theta_i = n_2\sin\theta_t \text{---(1)}$$

Equation (1) is called Snell's law.

From Snell's law, it is evident that as θ_i increases, θ_t also increases. When

$$\theta_i = \sin^{-1} n_1 \div n_2$$

θ_t becomes $\pi \div 2$ radians.

→ To learn more about Snell's law, **see** "Theories Related to Optics," **p.303** (Appendix A)

In this case, the transmitted ray lies on the boundary. For larger values of θ_i, there is no refracted ray, and all energy from the incident ray is totally reflected. This phenomenon is called *total internal reflection*. The smallest angle of incidence for which total internal reflection occurs is called the *critical angle*, denoted by θ_c. The critical angle is given by

$$\theta_c = \sin^{-1} n_1 \div n_2$$

This total internal reflection results in guided rays, which carry optical signals to the other end of the fiber. *Guided rays* are lightwaves that undergo total internal reflection at the core-cladding boundary. In other words, light is propagated in an optical fiber due to a series of total internal reflections bouncing back and forth between the walls of the core. Figure 2.4 illustrates the propagation of light rays in a fiber due to total internal reflection.

Figure 2.4
Light is coupled efficiently if launched at the acceptance angle, allowing total internal reflection.

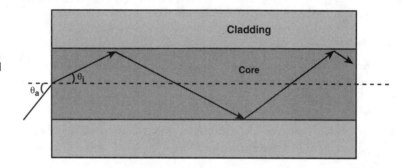

The largest possible angle of incidence for guided rays is called the *acceptance angle*, θ_a, and it is given by

$$\sin^{-1}\sqrt{n_1{}^2 - n_2{}^2}$$

The guided rays entering the fiber are well within the acceptance core, as shown in Figure 2.5.

Figure 2.5
Light propagation in step-index fibers with the incident ray launched at the acceptance angle to confine light within the core.

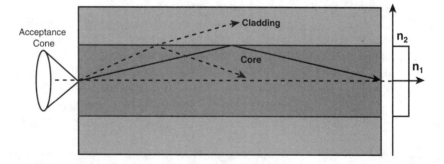

Also, the numerical aperture (NA) of the fiber is given as

$$NA = \sin\theta_a = \sqrt{n_1{}^2 - n_2{}^2} \ \text{------------------------(2)}$$

Note

The *numerical aperture* is a measure of the fiber's light-gathering power. The value of NA lies between 0 and 1. If NA=0 (when $\theta_a=0°$), the fiber gathers no light. If NA=1 (when $\theta_a=90°$), the fiber gathers all light that falls into it.

Although θ_c is the critical angle, light need not propagate for all angles greater than θ_c. Light might not propagate for some of these angles due to the destructive interference of the incident ray and the reflected ray at the core-cladding boundary. For other angles, the interference is constructive, leading to the propagation of lightwaves. These angles are referred to as *modes* in a fiber.

Note

Destructive interference occurs when two lightwaves in opposite phases superimpose each other, thus canceling the waves.

The relation between the number of modes supported by a multimode fiber and the normalized frequency V is given by

$$V = k_0 a \sqrt{n_1^2 - n_2^2} \text{------------------(3)}$$

Here, $k_0 = 2\pi \div \lambda$ is the free-space propagation constant, where λ is the wavelength of the transmitted light. In a multimode fiber, the number of modes m is approximately given by

$$m \sim V^2 \div 2 \text{----------------------------------(4)}$$

The guided rays entering the fiber at a slightly different angle of incidence take shorter or longer paths from one end to another, resulting in energy dispersion over a larger interval of time. This is called *intermodal dispersion*. From equations (2), (3), and (4), it is easy to understand that intermodal dispersion becomes worse for large numerical apertures. You will learn more about intermodal dispersion in future sections.

To reduce the effect of intermodal dispersion, graded-index fibers were introduced. A graded-index fiber, similar to all multimode fibers, also has a refractive index, which gradually decreases from the center of the core to the core-cladding boundary. This means that the rays traverse longer paths as they approach the cladding. These rays encounter regions of lower refractive index when they are away from the core and therefore travel faster. On the other hand, the rays that traverse shorter paths through the center of the core encounter regions of higher refractive index and therefore travel slower. This reduces intermodal dispersion by several orders of magnitude. Today, all multimode fibers are graded-index fibers. Figure 2.6 shows the light propagation in a graded-index fiber.

Figure 2.6
Graded-index fibers with light rays curved at the core-cladding interface due to the gradual change in the refractive index.

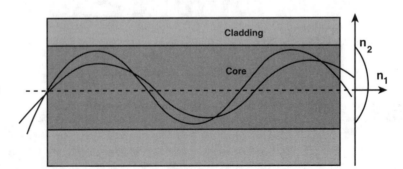

SINGLE-MODE FIBER

You have seen that graded-index fibers significantly reduce the effects of intermodal dispersion. However, to eliminate intermodal dispersion, fibers with a smaller core radius that are comparable to the light's wavelength need to be used. By reducing the core radius, you can capture a single mode in the fiber. Such fibers are called *single-mode fibers*. Figure 2.7 shows a cross section of a single-mode fiber.

Figure 2.7
A single-mode fiber with a small core diameter for propagation of one mode of light.

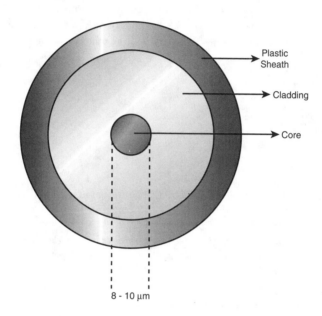

Unlike multimode fibers, single-mode fibers have only one mode in which lightwaves propagate. Single-mode rays travel shorter distances because they are more or less parallel to the fiber's axis (see Figure 2.8).

Figure 2.8
Light propagating in a single-mode fiber. This is used mainly in long-haul communication, because there is no interference from adjacent modes.

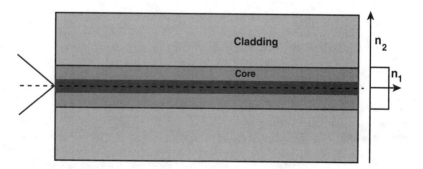

Ray theory cannot be used to study the behavior of light in a single-mode fiber. Therefore, I will use wave theory to explain light propagation in a single-mode fiber.

Light can be considered an electromagnetic wave that tends to spread out as it travels. It is made up of mutually perpendicular fluctuating electric and magnetic fields. When light travels in the fiber, a layer of light energy surrounds the core. Some of the lightwaves' energy penetrates the cladding for a short distance. This penetration of light energy is called an *evanescent wave*. The evanescent wave's energy flow is parallel to the core's surface and is in the same direction as the flow of energy.

Let's start with Maxwell's equations, the fundamental equations governing electromagnetic phenomena. The electric and magnetic field vectors of an electromagnetic wave at any point in space and time can be denoted by $\mathbf{E(r,t)}$ and $\mathbf{H(r,t)}$, where $\mathbf{r}$ is the position vector and t is the time.

$\mathbf{E}$ and $\mathbf{H}$ are related by

$$\nabla \times \mathbf{H} = \delta \mathbf{D} \div \delta t$$
$$\nabla \times \mathbf{E} = \delta \mathbf{E} \div \delta t$$
$$\nabla . \mathbf{H} = 0$$
$$\nabla . \mathbf{E} = 0$$

The vectors $\mathbf{D}$ and $\mathbf{B}$ are the electric flux density and magnetic flux density, respectively.

Note

Electric and *magnetic flux densities* are the number of electric and magnetic field lines in a given surface.

Now

$$\mathbf{D} = \varepsilon_0 \mathbf{E} + \mathbf{P}$$
$$\mathbf{B} = \mu_0 \ (\mathbf{H} + \mathbf{M}) \text{---(1)}$$

where

ε_0 is the electric permittivity of a vacuum.

μ_0 is the electric permeability of a vacuum.

$\mathbf{P}$ is the electric polarization.

$\mathbf{M}$ is the magnetic polarization.

Note

The orientation of the lightwaves in a particular direction due to the electric field generated is called *electric polarization*. Similarly, *magnetic polarization* is the alignment of the lightwaves in a specific direction due to the magnetic field.

> **Note**
>
> Lightwaves are said to be linearly polarized when they contain waves that vary in only one specific plane.

M=0 because the medium is nonmagnetic.

Therefore, equation (5) becomes

$$\mathbf{B}=\mu_0\mathbf{H}$$

Maxwell's equation takes into account the material properties of the electromagnetic waves. It considers not only the electric and magnetic field intensities, but also the flux densities.

The relationship between **P** and **E** in fiber optics is the origin of two main effects—dispersion and nonlinearity. These effects are predominant in silica fibers. Moreover, many devices, such as switches, isolators, and filters can be constructed by modifying this relationship. This relationship also depends on the nature of the medium. Let's analyze light propagation by considering the five characteristics of a medium and their effect on **P** and **E**. Assume that the core and the cladding are locally responsive, isotropic, linear, homogeneous, and without loss.

LOCALLY RESPONSIVE MEDIUM

In this medium, the response to the applied electric field is local. Here, $\mathbf{P(r)}$ at $\mathbf{r=r_1}$ depends only on $\mathbf{E(r_1)}$. In other words, the values of $\mathbf{E(r_1)}$ for $\mathbf{r \neq r_1}$ do not affect $\mathbf{P(r_1)}$. This property provides a good response in silica fibers in the wavelength range of interest in optical communication.

ISOTROPIC MEDIUM

An *isotropic medium* is one in which the electromagnetic properties are the same in all directions. In an isotropic medium, **E** and **P** are vectors with the same orientation. A perfectly cylindrical optical fiber is an isotropic medium. However, if the symmetry of this fiber is destroyed, it is no longer isotropic and is said to be *birefringent*. A medium is birefringent if its refractive indices along two different directions are different.

LINEAR MEDIUM

In a linear isotropic medium:

$$\mathbf{P(r,t)}= \varepsilon_0 \int \chi(\mathbf{r},t-t')\mathbf{E}(\mathbf{r},t')dt' \text{----------------------(6)}$$

In equation (6), χ is the linear susceptibility of the medium. If $\mathbf{P_f}$ and χ_f denote the Fourier transforms of **P** and χ, respectively, equation (6) can be rewritten in terms of Fourier transforms as

$$\mathbf{P_f(r,\omega)}=\varepsilon_0\chi_f(\mathbf{r},\omega)\mathbf{E_f}(\mathbf{r},\omega)$$

> **Note**
>
> *Susceptibility* is the degree to which a piece of equipment is affected by the radiated electromagnetic energy.

→ To learn more about Fourier transforms, **see** "Fourier Transforms," **p.309** (Appendix B)

> **Note**
>
> A *Fourier analysis* is particularly well-suited for communications equipment design and for predicting the performance of a given design. In Fourier transforms, a periodic waveform of arbitrary shape is described as a summation of sine waves having specific amplitudes and phases. The sine waves have frequencies that correspond to the harmonics of the waveform being defined.

In this case, the induced polarization can be viewed as the output of a linear system with impulse response $\varepsilon_0\chi(\mathbf{r},t)$ $\varepsilon_0\chi_f(\mathbf{r},\omega)$ and input $\mathbf{E}(\mathbf{r},t)$. Note that the value of $\mathbf{P}$ at time t depends not only on the value of $\mathbf{E}$ at t, but also on the values of $\mathbf{E}$ before t. Thus, $\chi_f(\mathbf{r},\omega)$ is a function of ω leading to chromatic dispersion (this is discussed later, in the section "Dispersion"). If the medium's response is instantaneous, its Fourier transform is constant, and the chromatic dispersion vanishes.

> **Note**
>
> When a function describes an output waveform that is excited by a unit impulse input, it is called an *impulse response*. A *unit impulse* is a short surge of electrical, electro-magnetic, or magnetic energy having infinite amplitude and zero width with unit area.

HOMOGENEOUS MEDIUM

A homogeneous medium has the same electromagnetic properties at all its points. Here, χ is independent of the position vector $\mathbf{r}$, so χ_f is also independent of $\mathbf{r}$. Therefore, χ is only a function of time. In general, optical fiber is not a homogeneous medium, because the core might have a graded-index profile. However, in a step-index fiber, the core and the cladding regions are individually homogeneous.

LOSSLESS MEDIUM

The loss of silica fiber in propagation is negligible and is assumed to be zero. However, there is no significant change even if the nonzero loss of silica is taken into consideration. A material's refractive index can be defined in terms of susceptibility as follows:

$n^2(\omega)=1+\chi_f(\omega)$

Therefore, the refractive index is a function of angular frequency ω. This dependence results in chromatic dispersion in optical fibers.

PART
1
CH
2

Note

The frequency at which a system's phase changes is called the *angular frequency*.

With these assumptions and from Maxwell's equations, the wave equations for **E** and **H** can be derived as

$$\nabla - E_f + \omega^2 n^2(\omega) E_f \div c^2 = 0$$
$$\nabla - H_f + \omega^2 n^2(\omega) H_f \div c^2 = 0$$

Although single-mode fibers support transmission over long distances, they introduce the problem of coupling light into the small core. However, a narrow beam of light with a high concentration of light energy can be generated by a semiconductor laser. Table 2.1 compares single-mode and multimode fibers.

TABLE 2.1   COMPARISON OF OPTICAL FIBERS

Single-Mode Fiber	Multimode Fiber
Small numerical aperture	Large numerical aperture
Coupling is difficult	Easy coupling
Due to only one mode, intermodal dispersion is not present	Light waves are dispersed into numerous paths, or modes, as they travel through the cable's core, causing signal distortion at the receiving end, which results in an unclear and incomplete data transmission; reduced intermodal dispersion in graded-index fibers
Used for long-distance applications	Used for comparatively short-distance applications
The diameter of a single mode fiber is 8.3 – 10 microns	The common diameters of multimode fibers are in the 50 to 100 micron range; (the most common size is 62.5 microns)
The wavelength of operation of a single mode fiber is typically in the range of 1300-1320 nanometers	The wavelength of operation of a multimode fiber is typically in the range of 850-1300 nanometers

Figure 2.9 shows a comparison of light propagation in a single-mode and multimode fiber.

Figure 2.9
A comparison of light propagation in single and multimode fibers.

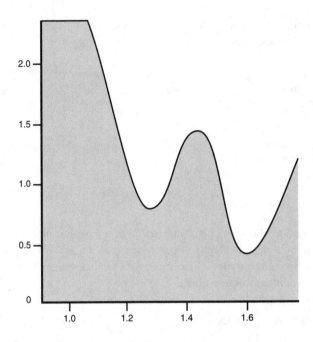

TRANSMISSION IMPAIRMENTS IN FIBER

Several important phenomena limit system performance—attenuation, dispersion, and non-linear effects.

ATTENUATION

Light signals become weaker as they travel through a transmission medium. The measure of the loss of signal strength is called *attenuation*. When attenuation is greater, the receiver has difficulty receiving the signal. In such situations, repeaters are used to regenerate the signal.

> **Note**
>
> A *repeater* is a device that repeats or regenerates weak signals from one point to another.

Fiber attenuation is the amount of optical power transmitted through an optical fiber. It is usually expressed in dB/km. Fiber attenuation leads to a reduction in transmitted signal power, and it depends on the light's wavelength. Let P_o be the output optical power propagation at the end of the fiber of length L. Let α be the fiber's attenuation constant. P_i is the input optical power launched into the fiber. In general, losses in fiber can be expressed by the following equation:

$$dP \div dz = -\alpha P \text{-----------------------------------(7)}$$

Here, P is the optical power propagating down the fiber at some point z.

Now, integrating equation (7), we obtain the following equation:

$$P_o = P_i e^{-\alpha L} \text{---(8)}$$

Here, L is the length in kilometers.

From equation (8), the fiber attenuation can be calculated as follows:

$$-\alpha_{dB} L = 10 \log_{10} P_o \div P_i$$
$$\alpha_{dB} = -10 \div L \log_{10} P_o \div P_i$$

Here, α_{dB} is the fiber attenuation. Attenuation is also a function of wavelength, as shown in Figure 2.10.

Figure 2.10
Attenuation loss caused by improper fabrication and fiber material properties as a function of wavelength.

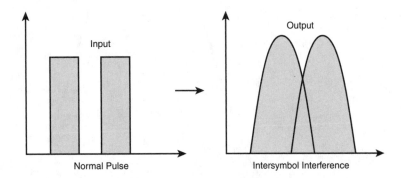

Two mechanisms, material absorption and Rayleigh scattering, primarily cause attenuation.

Material absorption occurs as a result of absorption of silica and the residual materials within the fiber. The absorption of pure silica is negligible in the 0.8µm to 1.6µm band. The absorption of the impurities in silica, however, has made the optical fiber a remarkable communication medium. The most serious impurity effect is due to water ions, which cause the peak region on the attenuation curve at 1390nm, as well as several minor peaks.

Rayleigh scattering occurs because the medium is not uniform, leading to fluctuations in the density of the medium. The scattering causes the general shape of the attenuation curve. The loss due to scattering decreases with increasing wavelength. Therefore, operating at higher wavelength significantly reduces fiber loss.

DISPERSION

You know that the data transmitted through an optical fiber is made up of light pulses. However, there is a limit to the number of pulses that can be sent per second. As a light pulse propagates through a fiber, elements such as numerical aperture, the core diameter, and the wavelength pose limitations on the fiber's bandwidth. This limitation is due to the *pulse spreading* or *pulse broadening* effect, shown in Figure 2.11. A light pulse traversing the fiber starts off as a narrow square-shaped wave. It then becomes wider as some components of the light pulse move faster than others. As the pulse broadens, it interferes with neighboring pulses on the fiber, leading to intersymbol interference (ISI). ISI is the overall effect of dispersion on system performance. Dispersion is a phenomenon in which different components of the transmitted signal travel at different velocities. In digital transmission, dispersion limits the rate of data transmission, the distance, and the fiber's capacity. In analog transmission, dispersion can cause composite second-order distortion.

Figure 2.11
The pulse-spreading effect, caused by many modes propagating within the fiber.

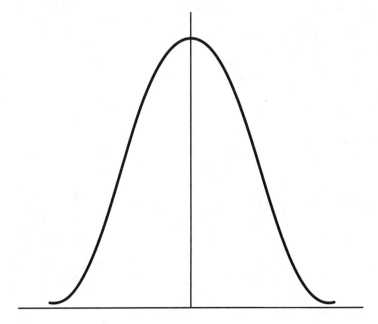

There are two forms of dispersion—*intermodal* and *chromatic*. Intermodal dispersion is caused when multiple modes of the same signal propagate along the fiber at different velocities. In other words, intermodal dispersion is the pulse-spreading effect caused by the time delay between the lower-order modes and higher-order modes. Intermodal dispersion occurs in only multimode fibers.

> **Note**
>
> *Lower-order modes* are the rays that propagate through the fiber close to the optical axis in a straight line. *Higher-order modes* are those that propagate at greater angles.

Chromatic dispersion is a phenomenon in which different wavelengths of light travel through the fiber at different speeds. Chromatic dispersion arises because of material dispersion and waveguide dispersion. *Material dispersion*, the principal component of chromatic dispersion, is the pulse-spreading effect due to the refractive index of silica. Different wavelengths propagate at different velocities, because this refractive index is a wavelength-dependent quantity. The second component, *waveguide dispersion*, is caused by the light traveling in both the core and cladding at different speeds at the same time. Waveguide dispersion is significant in fibers that have more-complex index profiles rather than simple step-index fibers.

Note

Index profiles are obtained by varying refractive indices in the core and the cladding. They are used depending on the application. Some of the index profiles used are step-index and graded-index.

Material dispersion and waveguide dispersion can have opposite signs, depending on the transmission wavelength. In the case of single-mode step-index fiber, these two effectively cancel each other at 1310nm, yielding zero dispersion. This makes very high-bandwidth communications possible at this wavelength. However, the disadvantage is that at 1310nm, although dispersion is minimized, attenuation is lost.

NONLINEAR EFFECTS

After the problem of dispersion was solved, nonlinear effects had a significant impact on the performance of optical communication systems. In an optical fiber, the refractive index depends on the signal's optical intensity. The following are the four important nonlinear effects in multiwavelength systems:

- Self-Phase Modulation and Cross-Phase Modulation (SPM/XPM)
- Stimulated Raman Scattering (SRS)
- Stimulated Brillouin Scattering (SBS)
- Full-Wave Mixing (FWM)

SELF-PHASE MODULATION AND CROSS-PHASE MODULATION

Self-Phase Modulation (SPM) is caused because the fiber's refractive index has a component that is dependent on intensity. This nonlinear refractive index leads to variations in the signal's phase. These variations depend on the intensity of the pulse. The accumulated phase shifts with varying intensities represent SPM. This produces a spectral pulse-broadening effect down the fiber. The variations in the signal's phase result in variations in frequency around the signal's central frequency. Each part of the pulse undergoes phase shifts by a different amount at each point in time, depending on its intensity at that time. SPM might degrade the performance of an optical system, because the receiver depends on the phase information. For shorter pulses, the additional frequency components generated by SPM together with the effects of material dispersion also lead to pulse broadening.

Cross-Phase Modulation (XPM) is a shift in the signal's phase caused by nonlinear interactions between the signals. In other words, XPM is caused by variations in the intensity of signals propagating at different wavelengths. It depends on the aggregate power in all signals. XPM, together with SPM and dispersion, leads to pulse broadening, thereby limiting system performance.

STIMULATED RAMAN SCATTERING

Stimulated Raman Scattering (SRS) is caused by the interaction of light with molecular vibrations. Light incident on the molecules creates scattered light at a longer wavelength than that of incident light. A portion of the light traveling at each frequency in a *Raman-active fiber* is downshifted across a region of lower frequency. This light generated at the lower frequencies is called the *Stokes wave*. The range of frequencies occupied by the Stokes wave is determined by the *Raman gain spectrum*, which covers a range of about 40THz below the frequency of the input light. In silica fiber, the Stokes wave has a maximum gain at a frequency of about 13.2THz less than the input signal. The fraction of power transferred to the Stokes wave grows rapidly as the power of the input signal is increased. Under very high input power, SRS causes almost all of the power in the input signal to be transferred to the Stokes wave. In multiwavelength systems, the shorter-wavelength channels lose some power to each of the higher-wavelength channels within the Raman gain spectrum. To reduce the amount of loss, the power on each channel needs to be below a certain level.

STIMULATED BRILLOUIN SCATTERING

Stimulated Brillouin Scattering (SBS) is similar to SRS, except that sound waves rather than molecular vibrations cause the frequency shift. Other characteristics of SBS are that the Stokes wave propagates in the opposite direction of the input light, and SBS occurs at relatively low input powers for wide pulses, but has a negligible effect on short pulses. The intensity of the scattered light is much greater in SBS than in SRS, but the frequency range of SBS (on the order of 10GHz) is much lower than that of SRS. Also, the gain bandwidth of SBS is only on the order of 100MHz. To counter the effects of SBS, the input power must be below a certain threshold. Also, in multiwavelength systems, SBS might induce crosstalk between channels. Crosstalk occurs when two counterpropagating channels differ in frequency by the Brillouin shift, which is approximately 11GHz for wavelengths of 1550nm. However, the narrow-gain bandwidth of SBS makes crosstalk fairly easy to avoid.

FULL WAVE MIXING

Full-Wave Mixing (FWM) occurs when two wavelengths operating at frequencies f_1 and f_2 mix to cause signals at $2f_1-f_2$ and $2f_2-f_1$. These extra signals, called *sidebands*, can cause interference if they overlap with frequencies used for data transmission. Likewise, mixing can occur between combinations of three or more wavelengths. You can reduce the effect of FWM in WDM systems by using unequally spaced channels.

SOLITONS

Well before the advent of fiber-optic communications, it was known that a special type of solitary wave, or *soliton*, can exist in certain types of media that are both dispersive and nonlinear. Although each of these effects tends to distort and broaden a propagating pulse, the right combination of dispersion and nonlinearity produces a narrow and stable pulse that propagates over long distances without any distortion, with one effect compensating for the other. This is the ideal situation for long-distance communication.

Solitary waves or solitons are narrow pulses with high peak powers and special shapes. The most commonly used soliton pulses are called *fundamental solitons*. Most pulses undergo spreading in time due to group velocity dispersion when propagating through optical fiber. However, soliton pulses take advantage of nonlinear effects in silica—specifically, SPM—to overcome the pulse-broadening effects of group velocity dispersion. Thus, these pulses can propagate for long distances with no change in shape.

You can deduce a soliton's form by modifying the wave equation. If you include a nonlinear and time-dispersive refractive index, the wave equation becomes

$$\delta^2 E \div \delta z^2 - 1 \div c^2 \delta^2 (n^2 E) \div \delta^2 t = 0$$

By assuming a quadratic dependency of β on ω (corresponding to a linear dependence of group velocity on ω), and assuming that the nonlinearities and dispersive effects are weak, and dropping terms that are negligible, it can be shown that the complex envelope $u(z,t)$ of a soliton satisfies the nonlinear Schrodinger equation:

$$\delta u \div \delta z = j \div 2 \; \text{sgn}(\beta_2) \delta^2 u \div \delta t^2 - j \; u\;^2 u \text{------------(9)}$$

A soliton of equation (1), called the fundamental soliton solution, is

$$u(z, t) = U_0 e^{jaz} \text{sech}((t - \beta_1 z) \div T_0) \text{------------------(10)}$$

where $a = \beta_2 \div T_0^2$, T_0 is the pulse width, and β_1 and β_2 are the first and second derivatives of β with respect to ω. Figure 2.12 shows the shape of a soliton represented by equation (10).

Figure 2.12
A fundamental soliton used mainly in dispersive and nonlinear media used for long-distance communications.

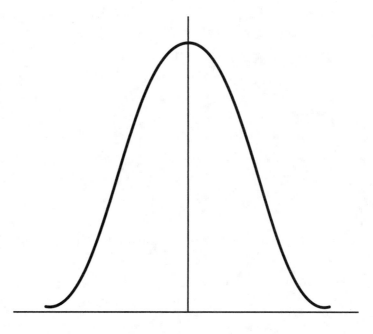

The fundamental soliton is stable in the sense that if a pulse approximating a soliton in shape and amplitude is launched on a fiber, it tends toward a soliton as it propagates and thereafter retains the soliton form. Furthermore, solitons propagating in opposite directions pass through each other. To maintain solitons over long distances, fiber amplification is required.

SUMMARY

A fiber-optic cable carries data in the form of lightwaves and thus provides high-speed transmission over long distances. There are two basic types of fibers—multimode and single-mode. Multimode fibers propagate more than one mode of light. The rays take a longer route as they pass through the fiber. They can further be classified into multimode step-index fibers and multimode graded-index fibers. The phenomenon of light propagation in multimode fibers can be studied by using the ray theory approach.

The guided rays entering the step-index fiber result in energy dispersion over a larger interval of time. This is called intermodal dispersion. Graded-index fibers reduce the effects of intermodal dispersion significantly. However, to eliminate intermodal dispersion, single-mode fibers must be used. The phenomenon of light propagation in single-mode fibers can be studied using wave theory. Attenuation, dispersion, and nonlinearities are phenomena that limit the performance of optical communication systems. Solitons are solitary waves that exist in certain types of media that are both dispersive and nonlinear.

CHAPTER 3

COMPONENTS OF OPTICAL NETWORKS I

In this chapter

COUPLERS

Coupler is the general name given to all devices that combine light into a fiber or split light out of a fiber. These devices can be constructed using two methods. One method fuses fibers in the middle, which causes light to split or combine in appropriate ratios. An alternative method is to fabricate a coupler using the properties of waveguides in fiber optics. An ideal coupler has low cross talk and low excess loss caused by fusing.

Note

Excess loss is the difference between the sum of all output signals and the sum of all input signals. *Loss* is the amount of light signal that is lost in a connector (which connects two fibers temporarily), in a splice (which connects two fibers permanently), or in a long length of fiber. It is expressed in *decibels* or *dB*. For example, a 10dB loss denotes a reduction in power by 10 times.

Note

Cross talk is the undesirable effect of a transmission on one channel interfering with the transmitted signal on another channel.

Couplers are the building blocks for optical devices. For example, couplers are used to construct optical switches and Mach-Zehnder interferometers, which are used as optical filters and multiplexers/demultiplexers, respectively. These devices are explored in detail later in this chapter.

TYPES OF COUPLERS

The various types of couplers discussed in this section are splitters, combiners, and directional couplers.

A *splitter* is a coupler that divides the optical signal on one fiber into two or more fibers. The most common splitter is the 1×2 splitter, which is shown in Figure 3.1. The *splitting ratio* is the amount of power for each output. For a 1×2 splitter, the common splitting ratio is 50:50. However, splitters with any splitting ratio can be manufactured.

A *combiner* is another type of coupler. Its function is opposite that of a splitter. It combines optical signals from different fibers onto one fiber. The most common combiner is a 2×1 combiner, which is shown in Figure 3.2. A combiner when used in the reverse direction can be used as a splitter. In addition, an input signal for a combiner suffers a loss of about 3dB when the optical signals are combined.

A *directional coupler* is also called a 2×2 coupler. It is generally a 2×1 combiner followed immediately by a 1×2 splitter, as shown in Figure 3.3. The role of a 2×2 coupler is to propagate the signals from two input fibers onto two output fibers. A directional coupler can be created in two ways. One way is to fuse two fibers in the middle. The other way is to fabricate the coupler based on the fact that if two waveguides are placed adjacent to one another, coupling is possible, provided that the propagation constants of the two waveguides are equal.

Figure 3.1
You can use a 1×2 splitter to split a signal.

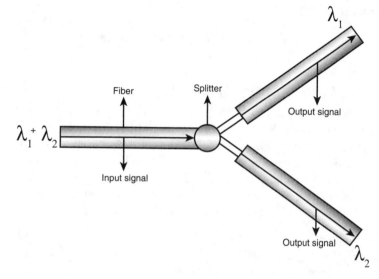

Figure 3.2
You can use a 2×1 combiner to combine two signals.

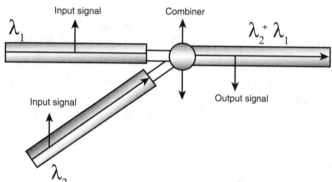

Figure 3.3
Two signals are coupled by a 2×2 directional coupler.

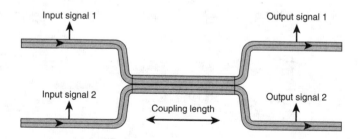

Note

A *waveguide* is a device that confines and directs the propagation of electromagnetic waves, such as radio waves, infrared rays, and visible light. Waveguides take many shapes and forms. Typical examples include hollow metallic tubes, coaxial cables, and optical fibers.

> **Note**
>
> A *constant* is the rate of change of time and displacement for a sinusoidal wave in a given direction. This kind of constant is known as the *propagation constant*.

WAVELENGTH CHARACTERISTIC OF COUPLERS

An important characteristic of couplers that must be taken into consideration is that they are wavelength-sensitive. You can make a coupler wavelength-independent by carefully designing it in such a way that it takes a fraction of the power from input 1 and places it on output 1 and places the remaining power on output 2. In the same way, a fraction of the power from input 2 is distributed to output 2 and the remaining power to output 1. The coupling length l can be adjusted such that half the power from each input appears at each output. For example, a 3dB 2×2 coupler is wavelength-independent.

The two types of losses present in a 3dB 2×2 coupler are *return loss* and *insertion loss*. Return loss is incurred when a signal from the input port is passed to the output port and a small amount of signal that is reflected in the opposite direction is passed back to the coupler's input ports. Therefore, the amount of power passed to the output is in the range below the input power. Insertion loss is incurred when light passes from a fiber into a coupler. The axes of the fiber and the coupler must be perfectly aligned to avoid this loss.

An example of a wavelength-independent coupler is an *n*×*n* passive star coupler, which is a generic form of the 3dB 2×2 coupler. It is constructed by connecting a number of 3dB 2×2 couplers that have *n* inputs and *n* outputs such that the power from each input is divided equally among all the outputs, as shown in Figure 3.4.

Figure 3.4
An n×n passive star coupler.

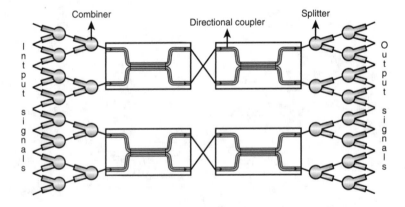

A coupler can be made wavelength-dependent when its coupling coefficient depends on the signal's wavelength. Such couplers are used to combine signals at 1310nm and 1550nm into a single fiber without loss. If it is a 2×2 coupler, the 1310nm signal from input 1 is passed to output 1, and the 1550nm signal from input 2 is passed to output 2. The same coupler can be used to split two signals coming in on a common fiber. For example, a wavelength-dependent coupler is used in an erbium-doped fiber amplifier.

> **Note**
>
> Every color in a light beam traveling in the fiber is associated with a particular wavelength. All fiber-optic systems use light in the infrared region, which is invisible to the human eye. Wavelengths are expressed as nanometers (nm), meaning one one-billionth of a meter.

> **Note**
>
> The coupling coefficient is a function of the width of the waveguides, the refractive index of the waveguiding region and the substrate, and the distance between the waveguides.

THE PRINCIPLE USED IN COUPLER OPERATION

When two waveguides are placed adjacent to each other, light couples from one waveguide to the other, provided that the propagation constants of the waves in the two guides are the same. Depending on the interaction region's length, the coupling might be partial or complete. By assuming that there is no loss in the coupler, the power relation is given by the following equations:

$$E_{o1} = a11 \ E_{i1} + a12 \ E_{i2}$$
$$E_{o2} = a21 \ E_{i1} + a22 \ E_{i2}$$

where E_i and E_o are the electric fields at the input and output of a directional coupler. For an ideal symmetric coupler, the power transfer matrix is

$$A = [aij]$$

According to coupled-mode theory, the general form of the electric fields E_{o1} and E_{o2} at the output of the directional coupler can be expressed in terms of the electric fields at the inputs E_{i1} and E_{i2} as follows:

$$E_{o1}(f) \ cos(kl) \ isin(kl) \ E_{i1}$$
$$E_{o2}(f) = e^{-i\beta l} \ isin(kl) \ cos(kl) \ E_{i2}$$

where

l denotes the coupling length.

β denotes the propagation constant.

k denotes the coupling coefficient, which is a function of the width of the waveguides, the refractive index of the waveguiding region and the substrate, and the distance between the waveguides.

The power transfer function from input i to output j is defined as follows:

$$T_{ij}(f) = E_{oj}^2 \ / \ E_{ii}^2$$

The assumption that there is no loss in combining the signals is incorrect. Although the electric fields at the two outputs have the same magnitude, they have a relative phase shift of $\pi/2$. This relative shift plays an important role in designing optical devices.

MACH-ZEHNDER INTERFEROMETERS

The functioning of a Mach-Zehnder interferometer (MZI) is based on the interferometric properties of light and the Mach-Zehnder method. The Mach-Zehnder method states that when two coherent light sources consist of more than one wavelength, the regions of maxima and minima differ for each wavelength. The regions for each wavelength can be calculated if the wavelengths, the phase of the signals, and the refractive index are known. Therefore, a mix of wavelengths can be separated into its component wavelengths, which implies that MZIs can be used as filters, multiplexers, and demultiplexers.

Figure 3.5
The design of a Mach-Zehnder interferometer.

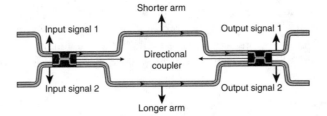

MZIs consist of two 3dB directional couplers interconnected through two waveguides having different path lengths, as shown in Figure 3.5. The substrate is made of silicon, and the waveguides are made of silica, which has a high refractive index.

Consider the operation of MZI in terms of input 1. After the input signal passes the first directional coupler, the power of the input signal is split between the two arms of MZI, where the wavelength of the signal in one arm has a phase shift of $\pi/2$ with respect to the other. The signal in the lower arm lags behind the signal in the upper arm because of the difference in length, δl, between the arms. It also has a phase shift of $\pi/2$. In the second directional coupler, the signal in the lower arm undergoes a phase delay of $\pi/2$ in going to the first output with respect to the signal in MZI's upper arm. The signals in the first output that are in phase add up, and the signals in the second output that are out of phase cancel each other out. If only one input is active and the path difference between the two arms of MZI is expressed as δl, the power-transfer function according to coupled-mode theory for MZI is given by the following equations:

$$T_{11}(f) = \sin^2(\delta l/2)$$
$$T_{12}(f) \cos^2(\delta l/2)$$

Therefore, the path difference δl is the key parameter for the transfer function of MZI.

ISOLATORS AND CIRCULATORS

Isolators are passive components that allow the transmission of light in one direction and that block all the lightwaves reflected in the opposite direction. For example, isolators play an important role in optical amplifiers and lasers to prevent unwanted reflections from entering these devices. The operation of an isolator is based on the principle of a polarizer, which passes only the vertical state of polarization (SOP) for a lightwave.

> **Note**
>
> *Polarization* of an electromagnetic wave is a property that describes the orientation and amplitude of the electric field.

> **Note**
>
> *State of polarization (SOP)* refers to the distribution of light energy between two polarized modes.

A polarization-independent isolator is shown in Figure 3.6. It works by transmitting an input signal with a random SOP on the fiber into a polarizer, which splits the signal into two polarized components. The vertical component is transmitted through the polarizer, and the horizontal component is deflected. Each of these components passes through a Faraday rotator, whose main function is to rotate the SOP by 45°. This rotator is followed by a half-wave plate, which rotates the SOPs by another 45° in the clockwise direction for waves traveling from left to right and in the counterclockwise direction for waves traveling from right to left. Therefore, the rotator and the half-wave plate convert the horizontal component to vertical and vice versa. The two separate components are again combined by another polarizer and are transmitted to the output fiber. For reflected waves in the reverse direction, the half-wave plate and the Faraday rotator cancel each other's effect. The waves remain unchanged and are not combined at the input. It is important to note that the main parameters for an isolator are its insertion loss, and isolation loss. The insertion loss is in the forward direction and must be minimized. The isolation loss is in the backward direction and must be maximized.

Figure 3.6
An isolator.

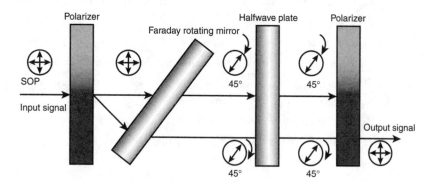

A *circulator* is similar to an isolator, except that it has multiple ports. Figure 3.7 shows a three-port circulator. The principle of operation is similar to an isolator. It operates in a cyclic fashion by first transmitting an input signal from port 1 to port 2, next from port 2 to port 3, and then from port 3 to port 1.

Figure 3.7
A three-port circulator.

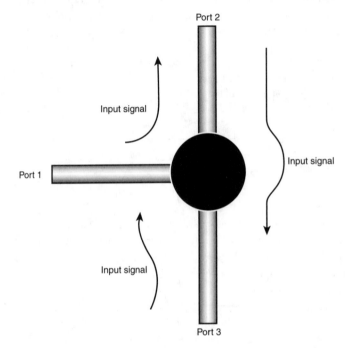

OPTICAL FILTERS

Optical filters are essential for building many applications in optical transmission systems. For example, they are used to multiplex and demultiplex wavelengths in a wavelength-division multiplexing (WDM) system, to filter noise in optical amplifiers, and to route wavelengths in wavelength-routing networks.

A simple filter selects one wavelength and rejects the others. The properties that an ideal filter must possess are as follows:

- It must have low insertion losses.
- The loss that is incurred must be independent of the input signals' state of polarization.
- The wavelength shift must be less than the space between two parallel waveguides per unit degree change in temperature in a WDM system.
- It must be able to reduce cross talk from adjacent signals.
- The cost of making optical filters must be minimal.

There are two ways to reduce the cost of making optical filters. The first is to fabricate them by making waveguides on substrates such as silica, silicon, and polymers. However, these devices are polarization-dependent due to the geometric properties of waveguides. The filters must be carefully designed to reduce polarization-dependent loss (PDL). The second method is to use fibers, because it is easy to transmit and couple light into and out of these devices from or into other fibers.

All filters and multiplexers use the property of interference in optical waveguides, except for a few such as gratings, which use the diffraction property in waveguides.

TYPES OF FILTERS

This section explores the different types of filters.

GRATINGS

A grating is a device that disperses light in many directions using the phenomenon of reflection or diffraction among numerous optical signals originating from the same source. Gratings are used to increase the capacity of fiber-optic networks using wavelength-division multiplexing.

TYPES OF GRATINGS   There are basically two types of gratings—transmission and reflection. These two gratings are very similar to diffraction grating; they differ only in the surfaces. Therefore, it is important for you to understand what diffraction grating is before I define the two types of gratings.

A *diffraction grating* is a collection of reflecting or transmitting elements separated by a certain distance. It can be thought of as a collection of diffracting elements, such as a pattern of transparent slits (or apertures) in an opaque screen or collection of reflecting grooves on a substrate.

A *reflection grating* consists of a grating superimposed on a reflective surface, whereas a *transmission grating* consists of a grating superimposed on a transparent surface. A lightwave incident on a grating has its electric field amplitude or phase (or both) modified upon diffraction.

OPERATING PRINCIPLES   This section explores in detail the operating principles of transmission and reflection grating with respect to multiplexing and demultiplexing techniques in an optical network.

Multiple narrow slits are placed at equal distances on a plane called the *grating plane*. When light is incident on the grating plane, it is diffracted in discrete directions. You can picture each grating groove as a secondary source of light. Consider a plane parallel to the grating plane at which the transmitted light from all the slits interferes. This plane is called the *imaging plane*. The usefulness of a grating depends on the fact that there exists a unique set of discrete angles. Along these angles, for a given spacing between grooves, the diffracted light from each facet is in phase with the light diffracted from any other facet. This causes them to combine constructively on the different points on the imaging plane. Optical fibers can be placed at different points on the imaging plane to collect light at different wavelengths. Gratings also act as demultiplexers.

Diffraction by a grating is illustrated in Figure 3.8. It shows a ray of light of wavelength λ incident at an angle α and diffracted by a grating along angles β_m. These angles are measured from the grating normal, which is the dotted line perpendicular to the grating surface at its center. The sign convention used for these angles depends on whether the light is diffracted on the same side or the opposite side of the grating. It also depends on the grating type.

Figure 3.8
A ray of light diffracted by the diffraction grating.

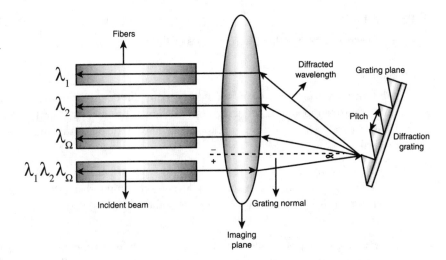

Figure 3.9 shows a reflection grating, in which the light is diffracted on the same side of the grating plane. Figure 3.10 shows a transmission grating in which light is diffracted on the opposite side of the grating plane.

Figure 3.9
A reflection grating, in which the incident and diffracted rays lie on the same side of the grating.

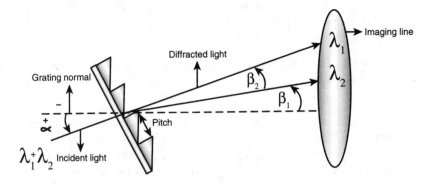

The geometrical path difference between light from adjacent grooves (slits) is seen to be $d\mathrm{Sin}\ \alpha + d\mathrm{Sin}\ \beta$. However, when $\beta < 0$, the second term is actually negative. The principle of interference states that only when this difference equals the wavelength λ of the light, or an integral multiple of λ, is the light from adjacent grooves in phase, leading to constructive interference. At all other angles β, there is a certain measure of destructive interference between the wavelets originating from the grooves. These relationships are expressed by the following *grating equation:*

$$m\lambda = (d\sin\alpha + \sin\beta)$$

where m is the *grating order*. The grating equation can also be written as follows:

$$Gm\lambda = (d\sin\alpha + \sin\beta)$$

Figure 3.10
A transmission grating, in which the incident and diffracted rays lie on either side of the grating.

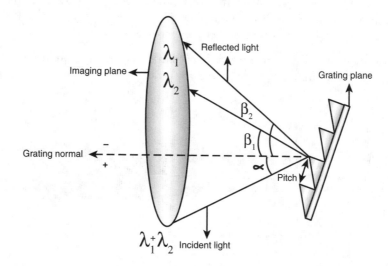

In the given equation, G = 1/d is the groove frequency, or pitch, or number of grooves per millimeter of the grating plane. This pitch plays an important role in designing a grating so that light energy is maximized at the interference points.

FIBER GRATINGS

Fiber gratings are all-fiber devices that are used in a variety of applications, including filters and add/drop multiplexers. Fiber gratings have an edge over all other optical filtering devices because of their low loss, ability to couple easily with other fibers, and insensitivity to polarization. They are also inexpensive to make.

You can write gratings on the fiber by doping a silica fiber with germanium so that it becomes photosensitive, exposing this fiber to a periodic pattern of ultraviolet (UV) rays. This produces a corresponding periodic variation in the fiber's refractive index.

Another method by which fiber gratings can be written is by using phase masks. A *phase mask* is a diffractive optical element that, when illuminated by a light signal, splits the light signal based on the diffractive orders. These, in turn, interfere with one another to write the gratings on the fiber. Fiber grating are classified into two types—short-period and long-period.

SHORT-PERIOD FIBER GRATINGS Short-period gratings are also called fiber Bragg gratings. They are based on the Bragg effect and act as a wavelength selective filter. To understand the operating principles of fiber Bragg gratings, you must understand what a Bragg grating is.

Any periodic disturbance in the propagation medium acts as a Bragg grating. This disturbance is usually the result of the periodic variation of the refractive index of the medium. This Bragg grating can be constructed on a fiber or by propagating an acoustic wave.

Fiber Bragg grating is manufactured by writing the grating into a fiber containing photosensitive material. After that, exposing this fiber to a periodic pattern of UV light results in a corresponding variation in the fiber's refractive index.

To learn about the operating principle of fiber Bragg grating, consider two light waveguides propagating in the same direction with the propagation constants β_0 and β_1, as shown in Figure 3.11.

Figure 3.11
Using a simple fiber Bragg grating with closely spaced periods as a filter.

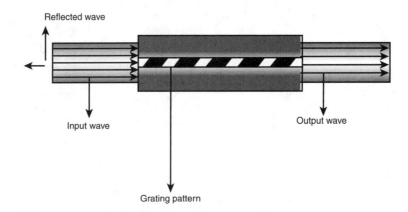

Reflected wave

Input wave

Output wave

Grating pattern

Energy couples from one waveguide to another if they satisfy the Bragg phase-matching condition:

$$\beta_0 - \beta_1 = 2\pi/\Lambda$$

where Λ is the period of the grating. In a reflecting filter, the incident waveguide with propagation constant β_1 is reflected in the opposite direction. However, the incident waveguide couples with the reflected waveguide coming in the opposite direction with the same wavelength provided:

$$\beta_0 - -(\beta_0) = 2\ \beta_0 = \pi/\Lambda$$

Let $\lambda_0 = 2n_{eff}\Lambda$, where λ_0 is the Bragg wavelength. With reference to this equation, the reflecting waveguide's intensity decreases if the wavelength of the incident wave is varied from the Bragg wavelength. However, if several wavelengths are transmitted into the fiber Bragg grating, only the wavelength corresponding to twice the measure of the grating period is reflected.

IMPLEMENTATION IN AN ADD/DROP MULTIPLEXER The properties of fiber Bragg gratings, such as low wavelength shift for a temperature range of more than 100° C, minimized adjacent channel cross talk, and low loss, make them very attractive for use in other optical devices. Consider an add/drop multiplexer, shown in Figure 3.12. It consists of a three-port circulator with a fiber Bragg grating and coupler. The circulator operates by transmitting light coming in on port 1 out to port 2 and light coming in on port 2 out to port 3. Multiple wavelengths of light traveling from left to right on the fiber entering port 1 of the circulator are transmitted out to port 2. These waves are then incident on the fiber Bragg grating, which reflects a specific wavelength—say, λ_3. This is then reflected to port 2 of the circulator and is routed to port 3, where it gets dropped, and the remaining wavelengths are passed through the fiber Bragg gratings to the output. It is also possible to add the dropped wavelength by having a coupler that adds the dropped wavelength, as shown in Figure 3.12. The principle of add/drop multiplexing comes into play. Many add/drop multiplexers can be designed using gratings with a combination of circulators and couplers.

Figure 3.12
An add/drop multiplexer using a fiber Bragg grating.

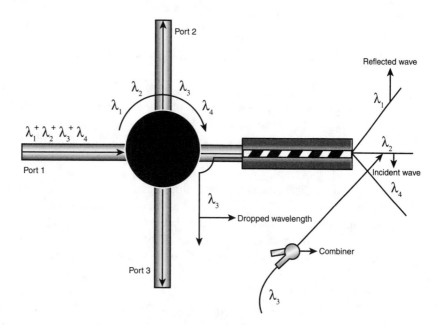

LONG-PERIOD FIBER GRATINGS Long-period fiber gratings, shown in Figure 3.13, can couple light between two propagating modes of an optical fiber. They have the same properties as short-period gratings. They are used as nonreflecting band-rejection filters, bandpass filters, optical sensors, and gain flatteners for the erbium-doped amplifier. They are constructed by imprinting a long-period grating into an optical fiber and exposing the fiber core surface to UV light from the side that has an amplitude of period Λ. An alternative way to fabricate them is to focus the fiber to UV light and turn the laser beam on and off periodically. This writes the desired pattern.

Figure 3.13
Using a simple long-period grating as a filter.

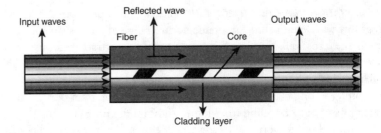

As mentioned, long-period gratings have the same properties as short-period gratings, but they operate on a somewhat different principle. The energy of the waveguides in the fiber core traveling from left to right couples with the energy of the forward propagating waveguide of the fiber covering layers. For energy to couple successfully, the phase-matching condition is as follows:

$$\beta_o - \beta_1{}^P = 2\pi/\Lambda$$

where

β_o is the propagation constant of the waveguide in the fiber core.

$\beta_1{}^P$ is the propagation constant of the waveguide in the Pth layer.

In long-period grating, the difference in propagation constants between the incident and reflected modes is quite large, leading to a small value of grating period approximately equal to 0.5 μm. If $\beta = 2\pi n_{eff}/\Lambda$, the wavelength λ is given by the following:

$$\lambda = \Lambda(n_{eff} - n_{eff}{}^P)$$

Here, n_{eff} and $n_{eff}{}^P$ are the refractive indices of the fiber core and the pth layer of the fiber covering, respectively. Knowing the refractive indices of the various layers of the fiber helps you design the grating with a value of Λ that is suitable for causing coupling of energy out of the desired wavelength. This causes the grating to have wavelength-dependent loss, which can be minimized by controlling the UV exposure time during construction.

ARRAYED WAVEGUIDE GRATINGS

The *arrayed waveguide grating (AWG)* or phased array is another form of wavelength router. It is a generalization of the Mach-Zehnder interferometer, which was discussed earlier. It can be used as an n×1 wavelength multiplexer where n signals are combined into a single output signal. It can also be used in the reverse as a 1×n demultiplexer where a signal is split depending on its phase shift into n signals.

AWG consists of two multiport couplers connected by a phased array of waveguides, as shown in Figure 3.14. The input and output waveguides, the multiport couplers, and the arrayed waveguides are all typically fabricated on a silica substrate. The incident waveguides are also silica or Germanium-doped silica fibers. The phased array connecting the two couplers is a collection of multiple wavelengths with path length differences between them.

Figure 3.14
Arrayed waveguide gratings.

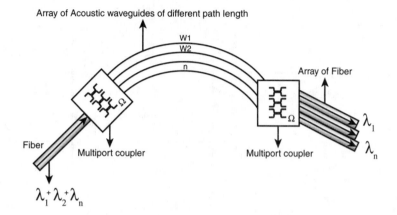

Array of Acoustic waveguides of different path length

W1
W2
n

Array of Fiber

Fiber

Multiport coupler

Multiport coupler

λ_1
λ_n

$\lambda_1^+\lambda_2^+\lambda_n$

An AWG grating is based on the principle of interferometry. Consider a fiber F carrying multiple wavelengths, λ_1, λ_2, ..., λ_n, as shown in Figure 3.14. Let the light of all wavelengths be incident on coupler S1, which is coupled to an array of waveguides, W_1, W_2, ..., W_n. The optical path difference of each waveguide in the phased array introduces a wavelength-dependent delay in the phase of the incident waveguides in coupler S2, where an array of fibers is coupled. The phase difference of each wavelength interferes constructively in such a manner that each wavelength contributes the maximum at one of the output fibers.

The salient features of AWGs are as follows:

- Efforts are being undertaken to make AWGs polarization-independent.
- AWGs are temperature-sensitive, so to eliminate wavelength shifts, thermoelectric coolers with a negative thermal coefficient are used.
- AWGs are said to operate in the wide temperature range of 0° to 85°C.
- AWGs have good wavelength control.
- Insertion loss is in the range of <3dB, and the cross talk level is better than –35dB.
- AWGs are suitable for integration with photodetectors.

FABRY-PEROT FILTERS

A Fabry-Perot filter is used as a filter in many applications and also in lasers. This filter is also called a Fabry-Perot interferometer or etalon.

The Fabry-Perot filter consists of a cavity formed by two highly reflective mirrors placed parallel to each other, as shown in Figure 3.15. The device operates on the principle that the input signal is incident on the left mirror at right angles to its surface. After one pass through the cavity, a part of the light beam leaves the cavity through the right mirror, and a part of it is reflected back. The left mirror reflects the reflected light. The round trip around the cavity by the reflected part of the signal has a wavelength that is an integral multiple of the length traveled. Therefore, all wavelengths transmitted through the right side will add in phase. Such wavelengths are called the cavity's *resonant wavelengths*.

Figure 3.15
The structure of a
Fabry-Perot filter.

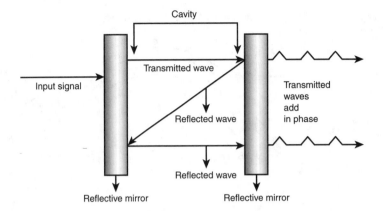

TUNABILITY OF A FABRY-PEROT FILTER   A Fabry-Perot filter can be tuned to select different wavelengths in different ways. One way is to change the cavity length. Another way is to vary the refractive index within the cavity. The Fabry-Perot filter can also be tuned mechanically by moving one of the mirrors so that the length of the cavity constantly varies. However, the main drawback is that it is unreliable. A precise mechanism is needed to keep the moving mirrors parallel to each other.

MULTILAYER DIELECTRIC THIN-FILM FILTERS OR INTERFERENCE FILTERS

A multilayer thin-film resonant cavity filter can be used as a multiplexer or demultiplexer in many applications. It is constructed by fabricating the mirrors surrounding the cavity using multiple reflective dielectric thin-film layers, as shown in Figure 3.16. A thin-film multicavity filter can be built by depositing several layers of dielectric thin films onto a glass substrate.

Figure 3.16
A simple multilayer
interference filter with
thin-film dielectric
layers.

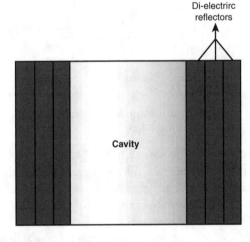

The principle of operation is illustrated in Figure 3.17. Several signals are input to the filter. The thickness of the layers and the dielectric property of the thin-film layers causes multiple reflections to occur between the layers and the cavity. It also allows a selected wavelength that has constructive interference to pass through to the right and reflects the remaining wavelength back through the glass substrate. In Figure 3.17, the wavelengths λ_1 and λ_2 are input to the filter. Due to multiple reflections, λ_1 is transmitted and λ_2 is reflected. This filter can be cascaded as an array by depositing on both sides of a glass substrate and can be used in wavelength multiplexing and demultiplexing. In this optical device, the light signal is reflected from filter to filter with a single wavelength passed and the others reflected and passed on to the other filters.

Figure 3.17
A multilayer interference filter.

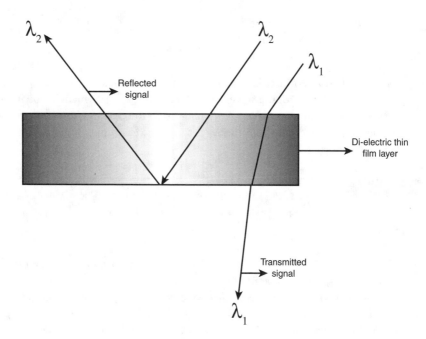

ACOUSTO-OPTIC TUNABLE FILTERS

The *acousto-optic tunable filter (AOTF)* is the only filter that can select multiple wavelengths at the same time. This feature is very useful in constructing several other optical devices, such as optical switches and wavelength routers.

The AOTF is constructed based on the interaction of sound and light. It is constructed on a lithium niobate ($LiNbO_3$) substrate. The basic AOTF implements a switching operation by turning the polarization of the input wave. Figure 3.18 shows a polarization-independent model using a polarization beam splitter (PBS), which reflects one mode and refracts another. An input is fed into the upper-left fiber and is split by PBS into two polarized components—the transverse magnetic (TM) and transverse electric (TE) components, which correspond to the vertical and horizontal components of the substrate surface. The TM component then transmits to the upper output and exits.

Figure 3.18
An acousto-optic
tunable filter.

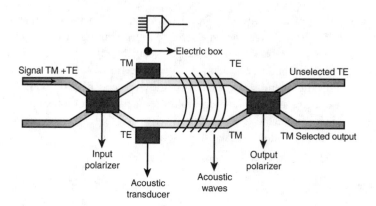

An acoustic transducer creates acoustic waves that propagate in the same direction as the lightwaves. These acoustic waves form a moving grating, which can be in phase with an optical wave so that it couples. The signal from the TM mode is converted into the TE mode so that the output PBS directs it to the lower output. The unselected signal exits at the upper port.

> **Note**
>
> An *acoustic transducer* converts an electric signal to sound or acoustic waves (as in a loudspeaker) and vice versa (as in a microphone).

AOTF AS A DEMULTIPLEXER   A combination of an all-pass polarizer, an AOTF, and a polarizing beam splitter can be used to split a wavelength from a mix. This arrangement is based on the fact that beam splitters reflect one polarization mode and refract another. It is also based on the principle that AOTFs rotate the polarization mode of a specific wavelength from TE to TM mode. The operation of this demultiplexer is shown in Figure 3.19.

Figure 3.19
Using an AOTF as a
demultiplexer.

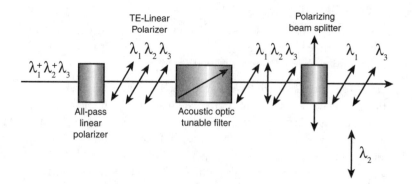

MULTIPLEXERS AND DEMULTIPLEXERS

The main function of an optical multiplexer is to receive optical wavelengths from many fibers and converge them into a single beam that is coupled into a single fiber. An optical demultiplexer functions in the opposite way: It receives from a fiber a beam consisting of multiple optical frequencies. It then separates the beam into its frequency components, which are coupled in individual fibers. A few optical devices, such as filters and Mach-Zehnder interferometers, act as multiplexers or demultiplexers. Figure 3.20 shows the classification of multiplexers and demultiplexers under wavelength-selective and non-wavelength-selective devices.

Figure 3.20
Classification of multiplexing and demultiplexing devices.

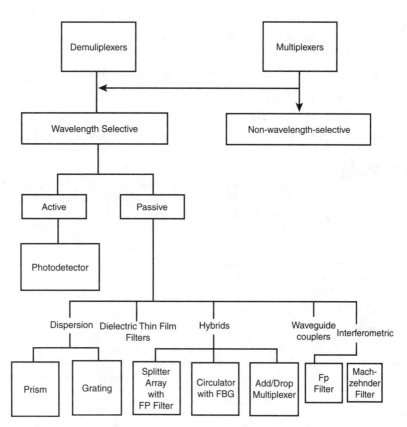

OPTICAL AMPLIFIERS

Optical amplifiers play an important part in the revolution created by optical communication networks and have contributed to their expansion. Optical signals are prone to losses in the fibers as they propagate through them. After traveling a certain distance, they become too weak to be noticed. These signals have to be strengthened to enable propagation. Before the advent of amplifiers, regenerators were used to photodetect the signal, electronically amplify it, and then retransmit the signal using laser beams. Optical amplifiers eliminate the need for regenerators. They project a bandwidth of more than 100GHz.

The salient features that an ideal optical amplifier must possess are as follows:

- Provide high gain (30dB or more).
- Have a wide spectral bandwidth to allow several wavelengths to be transmitted.
- Provide uniform gain to maintain relative strengths of spectral components.
- Allow bidirectional operation—that is, gain in both directions.
- Add minimal noise.
- Have no cross talk. In other words, no interference should occur between spectral components.
- Have low insertion loss by maximizing the amplification gain.
- Have a wide, dynamic range so that the gain does not saturate with high input power.
- Use laser diodes for pumps.
- Have good conversion efficiency—that is, pump power converted to amplifier gain.

> **Note**
>
> The amount of amplification that takes place is known as *gain,* which is usually expressed in decibels (dB). It is calculated as one-tenth of the logarithm of the output power divided by the input power.

Amplifiers are used in three different ways in a fiber transmission system:

- Power amplifiers
- Line amplifiers
- Preamplifiers

Power amplifiers boost the signal's power before it is launched on the fiber, thereby extending the signal's transmission distance, as shown in Figure 3.21.

Figure 3.21
Using a power amplifier before a transmitter.

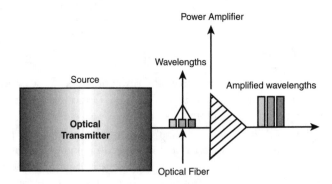

Line amplifiers, as shown in Figure 3.22, are placed at strategic locations along a transmission system to restore the signal to its initial power level. This compensates for the loss suffered by the fiber.

Figure 3.22
Using a line amplifier to amplify the signal along the transmission system.

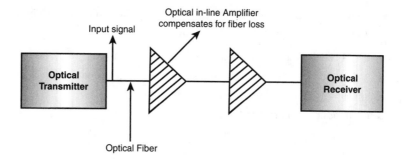

Preamplifiers improve receiver sensitivity, as shown in Figure 3.23.

Figure 3.23
Using a preamplifier to amplify the signal before it is received.

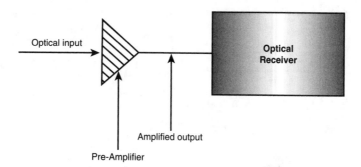

The important feature for a power amplifier is high gain. Preamplifiers require a low noise figure (3dB) because the entire amplifier output is immediately detected. Line amplifiers require both.

Amplifiers based on stimulated emission and nonlinear effects are classified into semiconductor amplifiers and fiber amplifiers. We will consider a few in each category in the following section.

Types of Optical Amplifiers

The distance between the transmitter and the receiver, the type of fiber used for transmission, and other factors in an optical network might vary. Several types of optical amplifiers are required to give the best output for each set of conditions. The following sections briefly discuss the various types of optical amplifiers, their operations, and their functions.

Erbium-Doped Fiber Amplifier

The erbium-doped fiber amplifier (EDFA), shown in Figure 3.24, provides efficient optical amplification of about 1.5µm. It is transparent to modulation formats (analog/digital, linear/nonlinear) and can be used as a power amplifier, inline amplifier, or preamplifier. It provides many advantages over other amplifiers:

- It has compact and reliable high-power semiconductor pump lasers.
- It is an all-fiber device, which makes it insensitive to polarization and easier to couple light in and out of these fibers.
- It introduces no cross talk.

Figure 3.24
An EDFA.

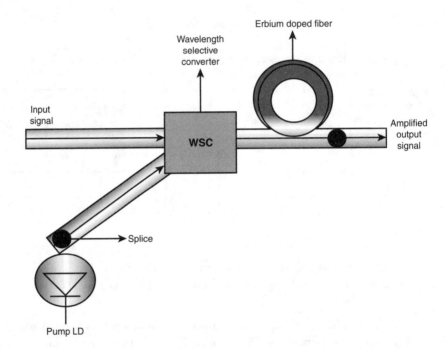

An EDFA design consists of a few meters of optical fiber doped with a rare-earth element called erbium. The semiconductor pumps the energy and injects power into doped fiber to excite the erbium ions. This pump is typically coupled into the transmission fiber using a wavelength-selective coupler (WSC). Generally, amplification occurs by transfer of power from the pump wave to the signal wave as it propagates down the erbium-doped fiber.

Before we explore the working principles of EDFA, I will define the energy levels of an atom as described in the principles of quantum mechanics. Electrons in an atom exist at various energy levels. The lowest energy level is called the ground state. Whenever electrons decay from a higher energy level to a lower energy level, they emit a photon (a particle of light). There are two types of photoemission—spontaneous and stimulated.

In *stimulated emission*, consider two energy levels of an atom—E1 and E2. The electromagnetic field causes the atoms to decay from one energy level to another only if the electric signal has energy equivalent to $hfc = \delta E$, where h denotes Planck's constant and δE is the difference in energy levels. The transition from E1 to E2 results in the absorption of power from the electric signal, and the transition from E2 to E1 results in the emission of photons. This means that if a photon interacts with an atom in an excited state, it causes the electron to return to a lower energy level and emits a photon. The photon that induces emission of the new photon is called the stimulating photon. Therefore, stimulated emission results in two photons having the same energy and being in phase with each other. For stimulated emission to occur, the number of atoms in the higher energy level (E2) must be greater than the number of atoms in the lower energy level (E1). This is called *population inversion*.

In *spontaneous emission*, if an electron spontaneously decays from one energy state to another, photons are emitted that have different phases and directions.

The EDFA uses a three-energy-level system, as shown in Figure 3.25. The levels E1, E2, and E3 are called the ground, metastable, and pump levels, respectively. The erbium atom population in the three energy levels is denoted by N1, N2, and N3. When the system has no pump energy or signal, it is said to be in the thermal equilibrium state, where N1>N2>N3. When energy is pumped, the atom population gets excited and oscillates between the levels, simultaneously emitting photons at frequencies determined by the energy levels. The wavelengths associated with the transition state are 980nm and 1530nm. The wavelength of each energy transition state is given by $\lambda = hc/\delta E$, where h denotes Planck's constant and δE is the difference in energy levels.

Figure 3.25
The energy levels used by an EDFA.

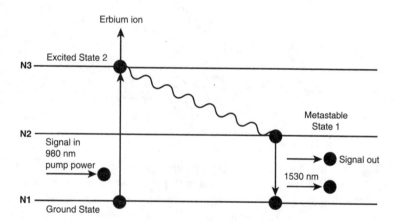

For an EDFA, the two pump wavelengths that are pumped into the fiber are 980nm and 1480nm. So, if 980nm of the pump power is pumped into the erbium-doped fiber, the atoms in ground state E1 jump to state E3. These excited atoms from level E3 quickly decay to the metastable state E2 through the process of spontaneous emission. This transition occurs at a much faster pace than the pace at which the atoms transited from ground to metastable state. The transition from state E1 to state E2 is nonradiative, so energy is lost to the fiber medium. The atom population accumulates in state E2, so N2>N1. This is called population inversion. The transition rate from level E2 to E1 is very slow compared to other transitions, leading to a longer lifetime for atoms in the E2 state. The wavelength band for transition from E2 to E1 is in the 1530nm range.

Generally, the transition of atoms from E2 to E1 uses either of the two types of photoemission—spontaneous and stimulated. In spontaneous emission, an atom drops spontaneously to the ground state, emitting a photon in the 1530nm range. This produces noise, which is an unavoidable side effect of this emission. In the case of a stimulated emission, an incident photon in the 1530nm range stimulates the emission of another photon at the same wavelength, direction, phase, and polarization. If the incident photon is from the incident signal, it produces the required amplification. However, if the incident photon is a result of spontaneous emission, the result is amplified spontaneous emission (ASE), which is the root cause of noise caused by amplification in fiber transmission.

SEMICONDUCTOR OPTICAL AMPLIFIERS

A *semiconductor optical amplifier (SOA)* is an alternative to fiber-based amplifiers such as EDFAs and Raman amplifiers. A SOA is constructed using two specially built slabs of semiconductor materials placed on top of each other, with another material between them forming the active layer (see Figure 3.26).

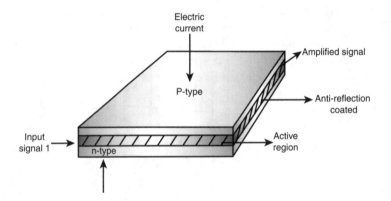

Figure 3.26
The design of a semiconductor optical amplifier.

This principle is similar to the functioning of a basic laser. The SOA is made using a pn-junction. The pn-junction consists of a p-type semiconductor and an n-type semiconductor. The p-type semiconductor is constructed using dopants so that the semiconductor contains an excess number of holes, which have a positive charge. Similarly, the n-type semiconductor is constructed using a dopant, which results in an excess number of electrons in the semiconductor, which have a negative charge.

Note

A semiconductor consists of two energy levels—*valence band* and *conduction band*. The valence band is the ground state, and the conduction band is a higher energy band.

When p-type and n-type semiconductors are placed adjacent to each other, holes from the p-type semiconductor migrate to the n-type semiconductor, and electrons from the n-type semiconductor migrate to the p-type semiconductor. Therefore, the p-type semiconductor has a region that has an increased number of electrons, and the n-type semiconductor has a region that has an increased number of holes. The middle region that has both charges is called the *depletion region*.

An electrical voltage is passed through the device to excite the holes and the electrons present in the junction. As illustrated in Figure 3.27, positive voltage is applied to the p-type region, and negative voltage is applied to the n-type region. This is known as forward-biasing a pn-junction. The excited electrons in the n-type semiconductor get transited to the p-type semiconductor, thereby increasing the population of electrons in the conduction band of the p-type semiconductor. The holes in the p-type semiconductor get transited to the n-type semiconductor, thereby increasing the population of holes in the valence band of the n-type semiconductor. Population inversion occurs, and the excited electrons of the conduction band fall back to the nonexcited valence band, emitting photons as they lose energy. These photons trigger stimulated emission as they travel along the device. Therefore, there are now two photons for the same particle of light, which in turn amplifies the light signal.

Figure 3.27
Using a pn-junction in a SOA.

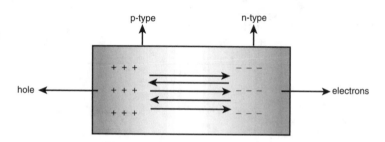

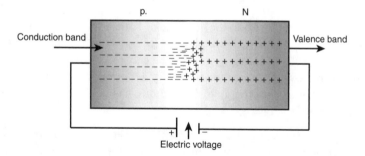

Semiconductor amplifiers provide high gain, large bandwidth, and lower current consumption. A major drawback of SOA is that major coupling loss is incurred between SOA and the optical fiber.

Semiconductor amplifiers do not currently offer as much amplification as EDFAs (1540nm). However, they can be designed to amplify around 1300nm regions.

RAMAN AMPLIFIER

Recent advances in grating technology and the use of the Raman effect in optical fibers led to the development of Raman amplifiers. These amplifiers are easier to design than EDFAs.

A Raman amplifier uses the fundamental properties of silica fibers and high-powered laser pumps to amplify signals (see Figure 3.28). This means that transmission fibers can be used as a medium for amplification.

Figure 3.28
The design of a Raman amplifier.

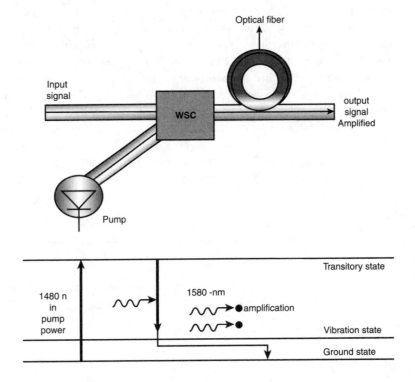

Raman amplifiers are based on the principle of Raman scattering, which states that if incident light consisting of particles or photons (with energy proportional to the frequency) strikes the molecules of a sample, most of the encounters are elastic, and the photons are scattered with the same energy and frequency. However, on certain occasions, the molecules take up energy or give up energy to the photons, which are thereby scattered with diminished or increased energy.

The pump generates a large pump wave with a lower wavelength than that of the signal to be amplified along with the input signal into the fiber. The pump wave gives up its energy by creating new photons at the signal wavelength, along with some residual energy that is absorbed in the form of vibrational energy. Therefore, the light signal has additional photons representing it, and it gets amplified.

Raman amplifiers offer several advantages compared to EDFAs:

- Minimum noise.
- They can be constructed easily, because signal amplification is achieved in the optical fiber itself, and the design is simple. There is no need for a special medium.

- They depend on the wavelength of the pump wave.
- They exhibit broad bandwidth by combining the Raman amplification effect of several pump waves on the same wavelength band.

SUMMARY

The various components used in optical networks are couplers, isolators, circulators, filters, multiplexers, and amplifiers.

Couplers are devices that combine light into or split light out of a fiber. The various types of couplers are splitters, combiners, and directional couplers. These are used as basic components in many optical devices.

Isolators allow the transmission of light in one direction and block all the lightwaves reflected in the opposite direction. A circulator is a three-port device that enables light to be transmitted through any of the ports in the direction of flow. A filter selects one wavelength and rejects the others.

The main function of an optical multiplexer is to receive many optical wavelengths from many fibers and converge them into a single beam that is coupled into a single fiber. An optical demultiplexer receives from a fiber a beam consisting of multiple optical frequencies. The demultiplexer then separates the beam into its frequency components, which are coupled in individual fibers. The different types of filters can also be used as multiplexers and demultiplexers in many optical networks.

Optical amplifiers are used to amplify weak signals. Amplifiers are used in three different places in a fiber transmission system: as preamplifiers, as power amplifiers, and as inline amplifiers. The two types of amplifiers are fiber amplifiers and semiconductor optical amplifiers. They play an important role in the future of telecommunications, because they eliminate the need for electrical signal regeneration and also provide bandwidths of more than 100GHz.

PART

I

CH

3

CHAPTER 4

COMPONENTS OF OPTICAL NETWORKS II

In this chapter

TRANSMITTERS

The optical transmission system converts digital or electrical signals into optical signals. The optical signals are then transmitted over optical fibers. This chapter discusses the various components used in optical transmission, such as lasers and light-emitting diodes.

LASERS

Laser is an acronym for Light Amplification by Stimulated Emission of Radiation. We will discuss the basic principles of lasers and how they are used in optical communication.

BASIC LASER PRINCIPLES

Lasers work due to the interaction of light and an atom's electrons. Electrons in an atom exist in various energy levels. The lowest energy level is called the *ground state*. Whenever electrons fall from a higher energy level to a lower energy level, a photon is emitted. This release of energy is called *photoemission*.

There are two types of photoemission—*spontaneous* and *stimulated*. If an electron spontaneously decays from one energy state to another, photons are emitted. This is called spontaneous emission. If a photon interacts with an atom in an excited state, it causes the electron to return to a lower energy level and emit a photon. The photon that induces emission of the new photon is called the *stimulating* photon, and the process is called stimulated emission. This results in two photons having the same energy and being in phase with each other.

For stimulated emission to occur, the number of atoms in the higher energy level must be greater than the number of atoms in the lower energy state. This theory is called *population inversion*. It is vital for laser action to take place.

Some substances can exist in higher energy states for a longer time. They are said to be in the quasi-stable state. Population inversion can be achieved by energizing these substances.

CONSTRUCTION OF A TYPICAL LASER

A typical laser (see Figure 4.1) consists of three important components—gain medium, pumping source, and resonant cavity. The space between the two mirrors forms the resonant cavity. The lasing medium, which occupies the cavity, is called the gain medium, and the pumping source is the device used to excite electrons.

Figure 4.1
Construction of a typical laser.

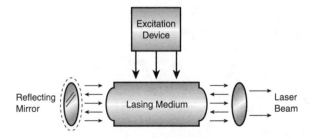

The lasing medium usually consists of a quasi-stable substance. The pumping source excites the electrons in the lasing medium. As a result of this, electrons start decaying to a lower energy state and emit photons. These photons further stimulate other electrons to release energy, resulting in the emission of new photons. The mirrors at both ends reflect the photons to induce further stimulated emission. This builds up to produce a high-intensity light called a laser.

The lasing medium acts like an optical amplifier, increasing the intensity of light passing through it. The gain for the amplifier is the factor by which light intensity is increased by the amplifying medium. This factor also depends on the wavelength of incoming light, the extent to which energizing the gain medium occurs, and the length of the gain medium.

Light amplification is not a laser's only purpose. The mirrors cause the light emerging from the lasing medium to reflect for more amplification. This is called *positive feedback*. An amplifier that works on the concept of positive feedback is called an *oscillator*. Of the two mirrors, one reflects the light completely, and the other reflects the light partially. Light that is not reflected is transmitted through the partially reflecting mirror. This light constitutes the laser beam.

LASER CHARACTERISTICS

Lasers are monochromatic and coherent sources of light. The emitted lightwaves have the same frequency (monochromatic) and are in phase with each other (coherent). The light's wavelength is related to the energy released. Based on the lasing material, absorption and emission of light of particular wavelengths are possible. The following sections discuss laser properties.

LINE WIDTH   The spectral width of a laser beam is called its *line width*. This affects the amount of light dispersion passing through the fiber.

FREQUENCY   Variations in laser frequency are of three types: *mode hopping*, *mode shift*, and *wavelength chirp*. Mode hopping is due to an unexpected rise in laser frequency because of a change in the injected current above the threshold value. Mode shift causes a change in the laser frequency due to changes in temperature. Wavelength chirping happens due to differences in the injected current.

LONGITUDINAL MODES   Lasing happens only at wavelengths that are an integral multiple of the cavity length. The set of integral multiples of the cavity length is called the cavity's set of *longitudinal modes*. The number of wavelengths that the laser can amplify is the number of longitudinal modes of a laser beam. Based on this, lasers can be classified as single longitudinal mode (SLM) lasers or multiple longitudinal mode (MLM) lasers. Generally, single longitudinal modes are preferred because the other modes result in dispersion of the light beam.

TUNING   A laser can be tuned to different wavelengths. This phenomenon, called *laser tuning*, depends on the tuning time and tuning range. The tuning time is the time it takes for the laser beam to tune from one wavelength to another. The tuning range is the range of wavelengths that are tuned by the laser. A laser can be tuned continuously or tuned to selected wavelengths.

TYPES OF LASERS

The following sections discuss the different types of lasers employed in optical networks.

SEMICONDUCTOR LASER DIODES   Semiconductor lasers are the most basic type of laser. A basic knowledge of semiconductor theory is required to understand the workings of a semiconductor laser diode. Semiconductors are small, highly efficient photon sources. Such semiconductor photon sources find application in displays, optical storage, communications, and other optical processes. In a semiconductor, electrons are present in either the valence band or the conduction band. Electrons that are not free from the atom occupy the valence band. Free electrons occupy the conduction band. Holes are created when electrons migrate from the valence to the conduction band. During this migration, the electrons combine with the holes and produce photons.

Doping is the process of adding impurities to increase the number of holes or electrons in a semiconductor. A p-type semiconductor has a majority of holes, and an n-type semiconductor has a majority of electrons. The number of holes in the p-type semiconductor and the number of electrons in the n-type semiconductor can be increased by doping them with the appropriate impurities. Figure 4.2 shows the structure of a semiconductor diode laser.

Figure 4.2
A semiconductor diode laser.

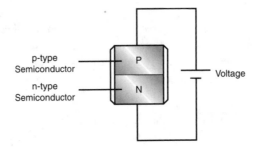

A semiconductor diode is similar to a normal laser, except for the addition of a pn-junction. The mirrors at both ends of the laser are perpendicular to the pn-junction. An electric voltage is applied to the pn-junction, causing electrons of the n region to interact with the holes in the p region and produce photons. These photons further stimulate the emission of more photons and produce high-resolution lasers. The frequency of the laser beam depends on the length of the cavity between the mirrors. By changing the semiconductor material, light of different frequency ranges can be produced.

Semiconductor lasers differ from ordinary lasers in the following respects:

- The population inversion caused between the valence and conduction bands results in increasing the gain of the lasing material.
- The laser beam's gain spectrum is very high.
- The cavity between the mirrors is on the order of 100 microns. This increases the longitudinal mode spacing.

FABRY-PEROT LASERS   The Fabry-Perot (FP) laser, shown in Figure 4.3, consists of the Fabry-Perot cavity as the gain medium and the two faces of the cavity, called *facets*. The facets are parallel to each other. One part of the light is transmitted at the right facet, and the rest is reflected. The reflected wave is again reflected. The transmitted lightwaves for the resonant wavelength of the Fabry-Perot cavity are all in phase, and they add up to increase the amplitude.

Figure 4.3
The Fabry-Perot laser.

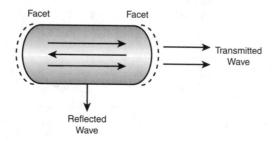

Lasers oscillate if both the gain of the amplifier and the reflectivity of the mirrors are large. The point at which the laser begins to oscillate is called the *lasing threshold*. After the lasing threshold value is reached, the laser tends to function only as an oscillator. Spontaneous emission of electrons occurs at all wavelengths present in the amplifier's bandwidth. This results in amplification with positive feedback, which is the general characteristic of an oscillator. The feedback of light comes from the two reflecting ends of the cavity, so the feedback is called localized feedback.

The wavelength must always be within the bandwidth of the gain medium, and an integral multiple of the wavelength must be twice the length of the Fabry-Perot cavity for the laser to oscillate. A laser's longitudinal modes are the wavelengths, which are integral multiples of twice the length of the cavity. Because the Fabry-Perot laser has several longitudinal modes, it belongs to the MLM laser type described earlier. The spectral width of the laser beam in the Fabry-Perot laser is very large.

Optical networks require low-spectral-width lasers to work at high speeds. Thus, an SLM laser, which outputs a low-spectral-width laser beam, is beneficial. SLM can be achieved by suppressing all longitudinal modes other than the main node. The level to which this suppression is done is called the *side-mode suppression ratio*. The various SLM implemented lasers are discussed in the following sections.

DISTRIBUTED FEEDBACK LASERS   A laser that uses a corrugated waveguide and that functions in a single longitudinal mode is called a *distributed feedback (DFB)* laser. This laser is used for high-speed transmissions. It is generally very expensive. It is called a distributed feedback laser because light feedback happens in a distributed manner with the help of a set of reflectors.

This laser operates as follows: The incoming light undergoes a series of reflections. These reflected waves form the resultant transmitted wave through a process called in-phase addition. This is achieved only if Bragg's condition is satisfied. In other words, the wavelength of the cavity must be twice the period of corrugation. A number of wavelengths satisfy this condition. However, the strongest transmitted wave has a wavelength that is exactly equal to twice the corrugation period. This particular wavelength gets amplified more compared to the rest. All the other wavelengths are suppressed to make the laser oscillate in a single longitudinal mode. If the corrugation is inside the cavity's gain region, it is called a distributed feedback laser. If it is outside the cavity's gain region, it is called a Distributed Bragg Reflector (DBR) laser.

The disadvantage of a DFB laser is that due to the series of reflections that occur, there are variations in wavelength and power. This deviation can be rectified by using a photodetector and a thermoelectric cooler. The thermoelectric cooler avoids variations in wavelength by maintaining a constant temperature. The photodetector avoids optical power leakage in the laser.

DFB lasers are difficult to fabricate compared to FP lasers. Hence, they are more expensive. FP lasers are used only for short-distance transmissions, but DFB lasers are used for long-distance transmissions.

EXTERNAL CAVITY LASERS   Lasers can be made to operate in a single longitudinal mode using an external cavity. This external cavity is in addition to the primary cavity. A diffraction grating that consists of a wavelength-selective mirror is used in the external cavity. The end of the cavity that faces the grating is coated with an antireflecting material. The external cavity allows only certain wavelengths to have more reflectivity and exhibit lasing. Generally, the external cavity grating is selected in such a way that only one wavelength satisfies the condition to operate in a single longitudinal mode.

Filters such as the Fabry-Perot filter or the Bragg's grating filter can also be used in external cavity lasers. Because the cavity length of an external cavity laser is large, it cannot be modulated at high speeds. Figure 4.4 shows the structure of an external cavity laser.

Figure 4.4
The external cavity laser.

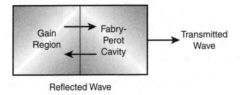

Reflected Wave

TUNABLE LASERS   Typically, lasers can be tuned to particular wavelengths. They are generally tuned to make them function in a single longitudinal mode. There are different types of tunable lasers. The following sections discuss each of them in detail.

MECHANICALLY TUNED LASERS   This laser is tuned by a physical adjustment of the cavity portion to make the laser operate in a single longitudinal mode. The Fabry-Perot cavity is used as an external cavity to filter unwanted wavelengths. This tuning method also increases the gain of the semiconductor laser. The external cavity that is used stabilizes the wave frequency.

This laser is tuned by injecting current; therefore, it is called an injection-current-tuned laser. A DFB laser with a diffraction grating is used to select the required wavelength. The diffraction grating contains a waveguide. The waveguide's refractive index varies. Wavelengths that match the grating's refractive index and period pass through the waveguide if they satisfy the following condition:

$$D = \lambda \div 2n$$

where

D is the period of the grating.

λ is the wavelength.

Injecting current through the laser changes the grating's refractive index. This helps tune the laser to selected wavelengths.

ACOUSTO-OPTICALLY AND ELECTRO-OPTICALLY TUNED LASERS As the names suggest, these lasers are tuned using sound waves and electric current. Tunable filters are used as the external cavity. The refractive index of the external cavity is varied using sound waves or electric current. The tuning range is restricted, because the transmitted wave has a range of frequencies. Therefore, these lasers cannot be tuned continuously. However, the tuning time of these lasers is faster than that of mechanically tuned lasers.

LASER ARRAYS In some cases, tunable lasers are replaced with laser arrays. A laser array consists of a group of tuned lasers. Each laser transmits light of a particular wavelength. If these wavelengths are modulated individually, multiple transmissions are possible. However, laser arrays have a major disadvantage. The number of wavelengths available in the laser array is limited. If one of the lasers does not meet the requirements, the entire array is of no use.

VERTICAL CAVITY SURFACE EMITTING LASERS These lasers work by making the length of the cavity small to increase the mode space. This ensures that only one longitudinal mode is available in the gain medium, thereby making it function as an SLM laser. A vertical cavity with mirrors on the top and bottom surfaces of a semiconductor is used—hence the name vertical cavity surface emitting laser. Figure 4.5 shows the structure of a VCSEL.

Highly reflective mirrors are required in this type of laser to provide oscillation. This is because of the cavity's short length. Using alternating dielectrics with low and high refractive indexes solves this problem. This helps in high reflection as well as wavelength selection.

VCSEL has a major disadvantage. The resistance created due to injected current heats up the device, and thermal cooling is required to bring it down to room temperature.

PART

I

CH

4

Figure 4.5
A vertical cavity surface emitting laser.

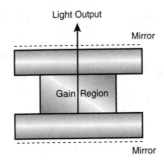

MODE-LOCKED LASERS   If the phases of all the waves in a laser are equal, the laser is said to be mode-locked. A mode-locked laser is used to produce narrow optic pulses.

Mode lock is achieved by modulating the laser's gain. This is achieved by performing amplitude or frequency modulation. Modulation is done in such a way that the laser oscillates in a single longitudinal mode. The gain can be modulated using an external modulator in the cavity.

LIGHT-EMITTING DIODES

Light-emitting diodes (LEDs) are generally used as an alternative to the more-expensive lasers. LEDs have a pn-junction that is forward-biased. This causes the electrons in the p region to combine with the holes in the n region and produce photons. This emission of photons is spontaneous. Due to spontaneous emission, light coming out of the LED has a wide spectrum. Therefore, LEDs cannot produce a high-intensity beam like a laser can.

In applications where a narrow spectral width is required, DFB lasers are generally used. If cost is a drawback, LED slices can be substituted for DFB lasers. An LED slice is obtained by placing a narrow passband optic filter in front of the LED. This filters the spectrum that the LED emits. Many filters can be used to make the LED common and shareable for many users.

RECEIVERS

A receiver converts optic signals back into electric signals. The components of an optical receiver are the optical amplifier, photodetector, and front-end amplifier. An optical amplifier can optionally be placed before the photodetector. Figure 4.6 diagrams an optical receiving system.

Figure 4.6
An optical receiving system.

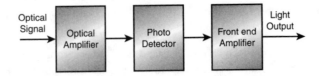

PHOTODETECTORS

Photodetectors are based on the principle of quantum mechanics. Electrons in the valence band absorb the photons, which are incident on the semiconductor. These electrons get excited and return to the conduction band, leaving a vacancy or hole in the valence band. If a voltage is applied to the semiconductor, the electron-hole pairs combine and give rise to photocurrent. The energy of the resulting photon must equal the order of the resulting photocurrent. Mathematically, the energy of the incident photon is represented as follows:

$$E = hf_c = hc \div \lambda \text{ --------------(1)}$$

where

f_c is the frequency of the photon.

h is Planck's constant.

c is the velocity of light.

λ is the wavelength.

The value of λ at which the energy of the incident photon is at least equal to the bandgap energy of the semiconductor is called the *cutoff wavelength*. The ratio of the energy of the optical signal absorbed to the photocurrent generated is called the *efficiency* of the photodetector (η). Photodetectors are constructed in such a way that the efficiency is always close to the value 1. This efficiency is attained using a semiconductor slab of suitable thickness in the photodetector.

PART

I

CH

4

Note

Bandgap energy is the energy difference between the valence and conduction bands.

Now, calculate the efficiency of the photodetector. Power absorbed by the semiconductor is denoted as

$$P_{abs} = (1 - e^{-\alpha\lambda})$$

where

l is the thickness of the semiconductor slab.

α is the material's absorption coefficient.

The efficiency of the photodetector η is calculated as follows:

$$\eta = P_{abs} \div P_{in} = 1 - e^{-\alpha\lambda}$$

where P_{in} is the power of the incident optic signal.

The value of the absorption coefficient depends on the wavelength. The semiconductor is transparent to wavelengths greater than the cutoff wavelength.

The responsivity of the photodetector is given as follows:

$$R = I_p \div P_{in}$$

where

I_p is the average current generated by the photodetector.

P_{in} is the power of the incident optic signal.

If the fraction n of the incident photons is absorbed and the receiver generates photocurrent, the responsivity of the photodetector becomes

$$R = en \div hf_c$$

where e is the electronic charge.

Substituting the value of hf_c from equation (1) results in the following:

$$R = en\lambda \div hc = n\lambda \div 1.24$$

Therefore, the responsivity is expressed in terms of the wavelength. The photodetector is designed to achieve an efficiency close to 1, so the responsivity of the photodetector is also close to 1.

A semiconductor slab has some disadvantages. The electrons in the conduction band start recombining with holes in the valence band before they enter the external circuit. This does not provide high efficiency. Therefore, the electrons must be forced out of the semiconductor. This is ensured using a photodiode, which consists of a pn-junction with a reverse-bias voltage applied to it. Figure 4.7 shows the working of the photodiode.

Figure 4.7
The operating principle of a photodiode.

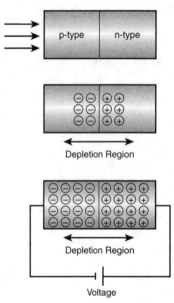

The pn-junction creates an electric field. By applying a reverse-bias voltage, electrons near the depletion region move into the n-type region. This prevents recombination of electrons with holes in the p region. The holes near the depletion region drift to the p region, and the photocurrent is generated.

PIN PHOTODIODE

A pin photodiode, shown in Figure 4.8, consists of an intrinsic semiconductor switched between p-type and n-type semiconductors. The intrinsic semiconductor covers the depletion region, and its width is greater compared to p-type and n-type semiconductors. The majority of light absorption occurs in the depletion region. A semiconductor material can be placed in the region to provide the required wavelength. This wavelength is larger than the cutoff wavelength of the semiconductor, and there is no light absorption in this region. A pin photodiode can also be constructed with two junctions of different semiconductor materials. This is called a heterostructure or double heterojunction.

Figure 4.8
A pin photodiode.

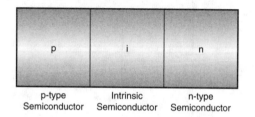

| p-type
Semiconductor | Intrinsic
Semiconductor | n-type
Semiconductor |

AVALANCHE PHOTODIODE

In photodetectors, a photon can produce only one electron. If an intense electric field is generated, more electrons can be made to excite from valence band to conduction band. The resulting electron-hole pairs are called secondary electron-hole pairs. These pairs, in turn, generate more electron-hole pairs. This multiplication is called *avalanche multiplication*, and the photodiode is called an *avalanche photodiode*.

> **Note**
>
> The multiplication gain of the avalanche photodiode is the mean value of the number of secondary electron-hole pairs generated by the primary electron.

The value of multiplication gain can be increased to a large extent and can also become infinite in a condition called *avalanche breakdown*.

FRONT-END AMPLIFIERS

There are two types of front-end amplifiers—high-impedance and transimpedance. Figures 4.9 and 4.10 show the circuits for these two types of front-end amplifiers.

PART

I

CH

4

Figure 4.9
A circuit for a high-impedance front-end amplifier.

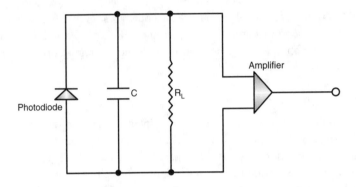

Figure 4.10
A circuit for a tran-simpedance front-end amplifier.

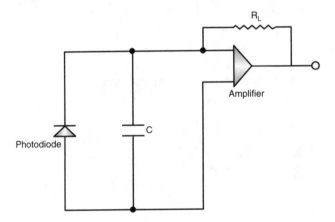

There are two considerations for designing the amplifier. The thermal noise that gets added to the photocurrent is inversely proportional to the load resistance R_L. Therefore, R_L must be made small to reduce the thermal noise current. On the other hand, the bandwidth of the photodetector is also inversely proportional to the output load resistance R_p. Therefore, the front-end amplifier is selected based on a trade-off between photodiode bandwidth and the noise current.

In the case of a high-impedance front-end amplifier:

$$R_p = R_L$$

R_L is always made small to reduce the thermal noise current.

In the case of a transimpedance front-end amplifier:

$$R_p = R_L \div (A + 1)$$

where A is amplifier gain.

The photodiode bandwidth is increased by a factor of A + 1. The thermal noise is higher than in the case of a high-impedance front-end amplifier. Nevertheless, it is used in most optical networks because the increase in thermal noise current is quite low.

SWITCHES

Switches are vital components in any network. Before the invention of optical switching components, electronic switches were used in optical networks. These switches helped process the data by converting optic signals to electronic signals in a fiber-optic medium. This process is called optoelectronic conversion. This process was essential because these switches performed only electronic switching. The optoelectronic conversion is an internal process, wherein the switch converts the signal to electronic pulses and switches these signals, and then re-converts the signals to optical signals.

However, these switches are not very effective for the large bandwidth of the optical fiber medium. This led to the discovery of specialized optical switches that could function without optoelectronic conversion.

There are two kinds of switching—*relational* and *logical*. Relational switching provides a relation between the input and output control signals. The contents of the signal that pass through the switching element do not affect this relation. The directional coupler (discussed in Chapter 3, "Components of Optical Networks I") belongs to this type. Relational devices are said to be data-transparent, because they are independent of the input data and signal contents. However, the drawback is that switching of independent data elements is not possible. Relational devices are mainly used in circuit-switching applications.

In logical switching, the signals that carry data in the device apply some Boolean functions on the inputs. Switching is generally faster than the signal's bit rate. However, the maximum bit rate is always limited. Therefore, logical switches are flexible compared to relational switches.

TYPES OF SWITCHES

The following sections discuss the different types of switches employed in optical networks.

FIBER CROSS-CONNECTS

Cross-connect elements switch optical signals from an input port to the output port. They are generally not sensitive to wavelengths. Cross-connect elements have two input ports and two output ports. Optic signals are transferred from the input ports to the output ports in two states—cross state and bar state. The cross state transfers the optic signal from the lower input port to the upper output port. The bar state transfers the optic signal from the upper input port to the upper output port and from the lower input port to the lower output port.

DIRECTIVE SWITCHES

A directive switch consists of a directional coupler that has two optical waveguides. The waveguides are placed parallel and close to each other. The light inputs sent to the two waveguides couple with each other along the boundary of the waveguides. The coupling strength is based on factors such as separation between the waveguides, wavelength of light, and the confinement factor. The *confinement factor* is a fraction of the power traveling the core of the waveguide. Complete coupling is possible only if the two waveguides are similar. If electrodes are placed over the waveguides, coupling of light can be reduced to a maximum level. This sets the cross-state applied voltage to zero and the bar-state switching voltage to a nonzero value. Some examples of directive switching are given in the following sections.

REVERSED DELTA-BETA COUPLER   In a reversed delta-beta coupler, the electrode applied to prevent coupling is split into two sections. An equal voltage is applied to the two electrodes to achieve cross state. This switching technology is applicable for a wide range of wavelengths.

BALANCED BRIDGE INTERFEROMETER SWITCH   This device consists of an input 3-dB coupler, two waveguides, electrodes, and a final 3-dB coupler. The two waveguides are separated so as to avoid coupling, and the electrode is placed over one of the interferometer arms. The input 3-dB coupler splits light passing through the first waveguide. The second coupler does the same, crossing the light over the second waveguide to achieve cross state. By applying a voltage across the electrode, a phase difference of 180° is created between the interferometer's arms. The two inputs combine with the final 3-dB coupler out of phase.

The intersecting waveguide switch is another kind of directional switch, in which the waveguides are arranged compactly.

MECHANICAL SWITCHES

These types of switches employ mechanical methods for switching. Although inexpensive, they have low insertion losses and low cross talk. They are generally used in optical crossconnects. The following are some of the mechanical methods that are used:

- A mirror is moved in the optical path to control the switching state.
- A directional coupler is used. By stretching the optic fiber, the coupling ratio of the coupler is changed, and this causes switching.

ELECTRO-OPTIC SWITCHES

Switching is achieved by applying voltage to the electrodes of a dielectric coupler. Varying the refractive index of the material in the coupling region changes the coupling ratio. The most commonly used material in an electro-optic switch is lithium niobate (LiNbO3). The advantage this material offers is that it integrates the switches to form a large switch. This switch also changes its state quickly. The time taken for switching depends on the capacitance of the electrodes used. Figure 4.11 shows the structure of an electro-optic switch.

THERMO-OPTIC SWITCHES

This kind of switch consists of a Mach-Zehnder interferometer, which is constructed with a waveguide. The waveguide's refractive index is dependent on the temperature. If the interferometer's refractive index is varied, this causes the phase difference between the two arms of the interferometer to vary. This gives rise to the switching of signals from input to output ports. Thermo-optic switches exhibit disadvantages such as low cross talk and slow switching speed.

Figure 4.11
An electro-optic switch converts the electrical signal to an optical signal.

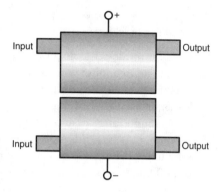

SEMICONDUCTOR OPTICAL AMPLIFIER AS A SWITCH

A semiconductor optical amplifier can also be made to function as a switch by varying the bias voltage applied to it. If bias voltage is provided, it amplifies the signal. In the absence of bias voltage, or if the bias voltage is reduced, there is no population inversion. This causes the amplifier to absorb the input signal. Thus, it works like an on-off switch, amplifying in the on state and absorbing in the off state.

LARGE SWITCHES

Large switches can be constructed by cascading small switches. The factors that have to be considered when building large switches are specified next.

THE NUMBER OF SMALL SWITCHES   The cost of making a large switch depends on the number of small switches involved in the construction of the large switch. The other factors that affect the construction of large switches are splicing, packaging, and fabrication.

LOSSES IN SWITCHES   The amount of loss varies across switches. The loss occurring in a switch depends on its input and output port. In a large switch, the loss is uniform, because it is calculated by taking the minimum and maximum losses for switching elements.

THE NUMBER OF CROSSOVERS   Some large switches are constructed by integrating small switches and fabricating them on a single substrate. Semiconductor optical amplifier (SOA) switches and thermo-optic switches are examples of this type. Power loss and cross talk result if the paths of the waveguides cross. Crossovers also reduce the switch's efficiency. Therefore, steps have to be taken to prevent crossovers.

Note

In integrated optics, the connections are made in a single layer using waveguides. When the paths of the two waveguides cross, there is power loss and cross talk. This crossing of waveguides is called a *crossover*.

BLOCKING CHARACTERISTICS   Switchesare classified into two types—*blocking* and *nonblocking*—based on their blocking characteristics. If it is possible to connect an unused

PART
I

CH

4

input port to an unused output port, the switch is said to be a nonblocking switch. If no such interconnection is possible, the switch is a blocking switch.

Nonblocking switches are further classified into wide-sense nonblocking and rearrangeable nonblocking. In wide-sense nonblocking, any unused input port can be connected to any unused output port without rerouting existing connections. If there is no variation in the existing connection in a nonblocking switch, it is called rearrangeable nonblocking. This type of switching is better than wide-sense nonblocking because it requires a lesser number of small switches to construct the large switch. However, this is also considered a drawback at times, because many applications do not allow the existing connection to be re-created. Some architectures that are available for building large switches are cross-bar, Benes, Spanke-Benes, and Spanke.

WAVELENGTH-ROUTING SWITCHES

A wavelength-routing switch routes the signals from input ports to output ports based on their wavelengths. This process has three stages. First, wavelengths are demultiplexed at the input port. Second, each wavelength is switched individually. Finally, the wavelengths are multiplexed at the output port.

Wavelength-routing switches are classified into two types—*nonreconfigurable* and *reconfigurable*. If the switching stage that happens between demultiplexing and multiplexing is absent, the switch is nonreconfigurable. If the routing function is electronic, the switch is reconfigurable.

NONRECONFIGURABLE WAVELENGTH-ROUTING SWITCHES This switch consists of two stages—demultiplexing and multiplexing. During the demultiplexing stage, each wavelength that comes from the input port is separated. Later in the multiplexing stage, these wavelengths are combined and sent to a single output. The output of the demultiplexer is directly connected to the input of a multiplexer. The routing matrix determines the route each wavelength has to travel from the input port to the output port.

Note The routing matrix is established through internal connections between the multiplexer and the demultiplexer.

The waveguide grating router is an example of a nonreconfigurable wavelength-routing device. Signals of different wavelengths are each routed to a different output port. Signals of the same wavelength are sorted to different input ports.

RECONFIGURABLE WAVELENGTH-ROUTING SWITCHES This switch is also known as wavelength selective cross-connect. The switching process involves three stages. The wavelength in every incoming fiber is demultiplexed using a grating. The output is directed to the switching medium, which consists of an array of optional switches. All signals that have a particular wavelength are directed to the same switch. They are then directed to the multiplexers, which recombine the wavelengths in the output.

PHOTONIC PACKET SWITCHES

Photonic packet switches belong to the category of logical devices because the switching function is based on the input signal's data. When multiple packets request a resource in a switch, the problem of contention arises. This is overcome by buffering, which is done using delay lines.

> **Note**
>
> A *delay line* is a long fiber with propagation delays.

The contention resolution by delay lines (CORD) architecture, shown in Figure 4.12, is used to overcome contention due to packet switching. In this architecture, each delay line is a buffer for a single packet. If two packets compete for the same output port, one packet is switched to a delay line, and the other packet is directed to the output. After the packet leaves the output, the delayed packet is directed to it.

Figure 4.12
The CORD architecture.

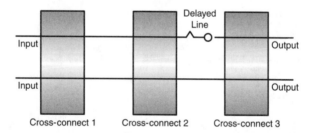

THE STAGGERING SWITCH This is more or less an all-optical switch. Although the switching is done electronically, the path of the data is purely optical. It consists of two rearrangeable nonblocking switching stages connected by delay lines. These delays are unequal. Figure 4.13 shows the staggering-switch architecture.

Figure 4.13
The staggering-switch architecture.

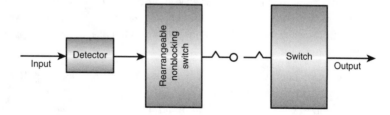

WAVELENGTH CONVERTERS

The function of a wavelength converter is to convert data from the incoming wavelength to an outgoing wavelength. The following are the uses of wavelength converters:

- If the wavelength of the data entering the network is unsuitable, the wavelength converters convert it to the required wavelength.

- Wavelength converters improve the usage of wavelengths available in the network.
- They are required at the boundaries between networks to allot the required wavelengths to the respective networks.

Classification of wavelength converters is done based on the wavelength range they operate. The following are the four types of wavelength converters:

- **Fixed-input, fixed-output**—This device receives a fixed-input wavelength and sends a fixed-output wavelength.
- **Variable-input, fixed-output**—This device receives an input that contains various wavelengths, but the output is always of a fixed wavelength.
- **Fixed-input, variable-output**—This device receives a fixed wavelength as input, but sends an output containing different wavelengths.
- **Variable-input, variable-output**—This device receives input of different wavelengths and sends output of varying wavelengths.

A wavelength converter provides the following features:

- It is transparent to bit rates and signal formats.
- It takes much less time to set up the output wavelength.
- It can convert both short and long wavelengths.
- It is easy to implement.

WAVELENGTH CONVERSION

The two methods employed for wavelength conversion are optoelectronic conversion and all-optical conversion.

THE OPTOELECTRONIC APPROACH

The converter used in this method is a variable-input, fixed-output type. In this method, the input signal is first converted to an electronic signal using a photodetector. The electronic signal is then regenerated and fed as input to a tunable laser. The laser is tuned for variable-output wavelength.

Three types of regeneration can be applied to the electronic signal. The simplest type of regeneration is called 1R generation. With 1R, the photodetector converts the photons in the input signal to electrons. An RF amplifier amplifies the signal and sends it to the laser. There are some disadvantages with this type of regeneration, such as addition of noise, dispersion, and nonlinear effects.

The second type of regeneration is called 2R regeneration. Here, the regeneration is applied to digital data only. The signal is sent through a logical gate to reshape it, but the timing is not changed.

The third and the most advanced type of regeneration is 3R regeneration. This involves reshaping and retiming the signal. This type of regeneration is free of noise and other effects such as dispersion and nonlinearities.

This type of conversion has a disadvantage. The signal must be at a specific bit rate, so the transparency of signal modulation is lost.

THE ALL-OPTICAL APPROACH

This type of conversion belongs to the all-optical type, where the signal always remains in the optic domain. The all-optical conversion method has two approaches—optical gating and wave mixing.

OPTICAL GATING   This type of wavelength conversion uses variable-input and fixed-output or variable-output devices. The incoming signal changes the device characteristics according to its intensity. This change is passed to an unmodulated probe signal in the device. The wavelength of the unmodulated probe signal is generally different from that of the incoming signal. At the output, the probe signal has the same data as that of the input signal. If the probe signal is fixed, a fixed output is produced. If the probe signal is tunable, a variable output is produced. The following sections describe the different optical gating approaches.

WAVE MIXING   Wave mixing is the nonlinear optic response of a medium containing more than one wave. It gives rise to another wave. The intensity of the resultant wave is relative to the product of other interacting waves. Wave mixing has various advantages. It helps maintain phase and amplitude and allows the conversion of a set of input wavelengths to another set of output wavelengths. Some wave-mixing techniques are discussed in the following sections.

PART

I

CH

4

FOUR-WAVE MIXING   Four-Wave Mixing (FWM) is achieved in WDM systems by three optical waves with frequencies fa, fb, and fc that give rise to a fourth wave. This concept is a third-order nonlinear interaction. The frequency of the fourth wave, fd, is given by the following equation:

$$fd = fa + fb + fc$$

FWM can also be obtained in other devices, such as semiconductor waveguides and semiconductor optical amplifiers.

DIFFERENCE FREQUENCY GENERATION   This type of wavelength conversion is based on a second-order nonlinear interaction. Two optical waves, the signal wave and the pump wave, undergo nonlinear interaction in the medium. By using this method, excess noise is not added to the signal, and it is fast and bidirectional. However, there are some drawbacks, such as low efficiency, polarization sensitivity, and difficulty of phase mixing.

CROSS-GAIN MODULATION

In this approach, shown in Figure 4.14, conversion is based on the nonlinear effect of SOAs. The SOA's gain depends mainly on its input power. The gain changes according to the variations in input power. Although cross-gain modulation is very simple, it has some disadvantages. The carrier density inside the SOA changes, resulting in a change in refractive index. This results in a large amount of pulse distortion.

Figure 4.14
Cross-gain modulation.

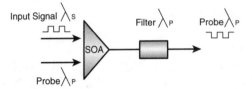

CROSS-PHASE MODULATION

This works on the principle of phase change effect for wavelength conversion to be carried out. The carrier density of the amplifier changes with respect to the input signal. This changes the probe signal's phase. The resulting phase modulation is converted into intensity modulation. This is achieved using the Mach-Zehnder interferometer. This interferometer consists of two arms of equal length and an SOA. The signal and probe are sent to both ends of the device. The probe signal is unmodulated if there is no signal. If the signal is available, a phase change is created in the amplifier. The output at the probe signal is usually intensity-modulated. If the signal power is low and the probe power is high, a large phase shift can be developed. Figure 4.15 depicts cross-phase modulation.

Figure 4.15
Cross-phase modulation.

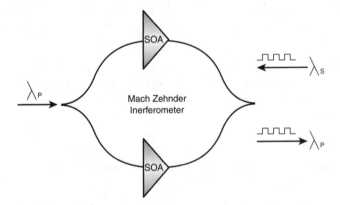

SUMMARY

Transmitters and receivers play a very important role in optical communication. A transmitter converts digital signals into optic signals. The most widely used transmitters are lasers and LEDs. A laser is a high-intensity beam of light resulting from the interaction of light with electrons of an atom. Some of the lasers used in optical networks are semiconductor diode laser, Fabry-Perot laser, distributed feedback laser, and tuned laser. The receiver converts the optic signals back to their electronic form. An optical receiving system consists of components such as optical amplifier, photodetector, and front-end amplifier. The different types of photodetectors are pin photodiode and avalanche photodiode.

Switches also convert the optic signals back to their electronic forms. They are classified into relational switching and logical switching. The different types of switches employed in optical networks are electro-optic switches, thermo-optic switches, large switches, wavelength-routing switches, and photonic packet switches. Wavelength converters are used to convert data from the incoming wavelength to an outgoing wavelength. Wavelength conversion is of two types—optoelectronic and all-optical. The all-optical approach is used in optical gating and wave mixing.

CHAPTER 5

MODULATION AND DEMODULATION

In this chapter

MODULATION

Modulation is the process of converting a signal to a form that is suitable for the transmission medium. In optical networks, the digital signal is converted to an optical signal.

MODULATION SCHEMES

Various schemes are employed to modulate signals. These schemes depend on the application, the availability and limitations of the components, and the medium of transmission. These schemes are discussed in the following sections.

ON-OFF KEYING

On-Off Keying (OOK) is a type of modulation that turns the carrier signal on for a 1 bit and off for a 0 bit. The data signal must be coded because of the difficulty in determining the difference between a 0 bit and a 1 bit.

Consider the difference between sending the message 10 and the message 110 using OOK. To send the first message, you simply turn the switch on to send 1 and then turn it off to send 0. To send the second message, you again turn the switch on to send the first 1. The switch must also be on to send the second 1. If you turn the switch off between the first 1 and the second 1, this is interpreted as a 0. So the switch must be left on for the second 1 and then turned off for the final bit, 0. In both cases, the actions performed for the two messages are the same. The switch is turned on and then turned off. The only difference between the two is that the switch might be left on longer to send two 1s than to send a single 1. Therefore, to successfully interpret signals in this system, the receiver must measure the time the switch was left on to determine whether this act represented a single 1 or two 1s. For the receiver to distinguish a single 1 from a pair of 1s, the sender and receiver must agree on a precise amount of time that will be used to send all single symbols. The information transmitted using OOK is shown in Figure 5.1.

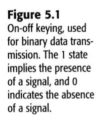

Figure 5.1
On-off keying, used for binary data transmission. The 1 state implies the presence of a signal, and 0 indicates the absence of a signal.

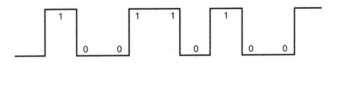

The switching rate of the light source limits the system's data rate.

PULSE MODULATION SCHEME

The carrier signal is used as a pulse train. Square pulses, raised cosine pulses, or sine function pulses can be used. The characteristics of the pulse train that can be varied are its amplitude and width. The two types of pulse modulation schemes are Pulse Amplitude Modulation (PAM) and Pulse Width Modulation (PWM).

To increase the transmission bandwidth, other complex schemes, such as Quadrature Pulse Amplitude Modulation (QPAM) and Pulse Code Modulation (PCM), are used. QPAM is discussed in detail in a moment.

> **Note**
>
> There is no standard definition for raised cosine functions. As the name suggests, you add a constant to change the average value of the cosine function. Raised cosine functions are used in signal processing in Fourier transforms.

PULSE AMPLITUDE MODULATION PAM, shown in Figure 5.2, is a modulation scheme that generates a sequence of pulses whose amplitude is proportional to the amplitude of the sampled analog signal at the sampling instant. The amplitude of the samples is modulated by the sampled frequency.

Figure 5.2
PAM, in which the amplitude of the input signal is sampled at the sampling frequency.

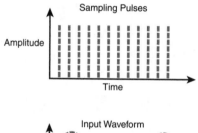

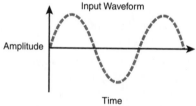

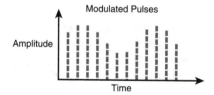

PULSE-WIDTH MODULATION With PWM, a pulse alternates periodically between a high value and a low value. Figure 5.3 shows PWM. Here, the input sinusoidal signal is modulated by a sawtooth wave, and the output is in the form of pulses. The pulse width is less at the positive peak and increases as the input signal reaches the negative peak. The signal is reproduced at the receiving end using a pulse width demodulator.

Figure 5.3
The PWM scheme, in which the amplitude of the signal is determined by the width of the pulse.

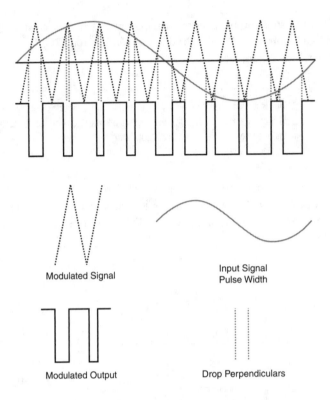

Modulated Signal

Input Signal
Pulse Width

Modulated Output

Drop Perpendiculars

QUADRATURE PULSE AMPLITUDE MODULATION   With QPAM, two sinusoidal carriers, one exactly 90° out of phase with the other, are used to transmit data over a given physical channel. Each carrier can be modulated independently, transmitted over the same frequency band, and separated by demodulation at the receiver, because the carriers occupy the same frequency band and differ by a 90° phase shift. For a given bandwidth, QPAM enables data transmission at twice the rate of standard PAM without any degradation in the bit error rate (BER).

Note

BER is the rate at which the signal is transmitted over the link so that the number of error bits is kept to a minimum.

PHASE-SHIFT KEYING

Phase-Shift Keying (PSK) is a technique for switching phases in response to the signal. Quadrature versions of PSK are called QPSK or 4-PSK.

In radio channels, PSK modulation is useful because the decoder does not need to keep track of the intensity of the received signal. For greater noise immunity in these applications, a differential modulation scheme is used, in which the changes are encoded.

KEYING SCHEME

In PSK, either the frequency or the phase of a carrier signal is keyed in response to patterns of 1s and 0s. Frequency-Shift Keying (FSK) is the process of keying between two different frequencies. In FSK, the two binary states, logic 0 (low) and logic 1 (high), are each represented by an analog waveform. Logic 0 is represented by a wave at a specific frequency, and logic 1 is represented by a wave at a different frequency. A modem converts the binary data from a computer to FSK for transmission over telephone lines, cables, optical fiber, or wireless media. The modem also converts incoming FSK signals to digital low and high states that the computer can understand.

The most important keying scheme is the OOK modulation scheme. OOK modulation uses signal formats such as Non-Return to Zero (NRZ), Return to Zero (RZ), and short-pulse format.

NON-RETURN TO ZERO FORMAT   In the NRZ type of signal format, shown in Figure 5.4, the bandwidth used by the signal is smaller than that of other signal formats. The 0 bit does not have a pulse, and the 1 bit pulse forms a bit interval. If the bit pulses occur continuously, there is a corresponding number of bit intervals. For example, if there are two continuous 1 bit pulses, there will be two bit intervals. One disadvantage of using this format is that a lengthy string of 1 or 0 bits fails to make transitions. This format is generally used for high-speed communication.

Figure 5.4
The NRZ coding format, in which the pulse does not return to zero level during the 1 bit pulse.

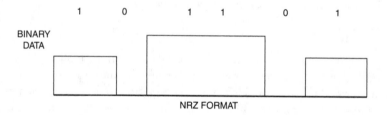

RETURN TO ZERO FORMAT   In the RZ signal format, shown in Figure 5.5, the 0 bit does not have a pulse, and a 1 bit forms half the bit interval. The bandwidth used here is twice that of the NRZ signal format. Unlike with NRZ, lengthy strings of 1 bits produce transitions.

Figure 5.5
The RZ format, in which the signal returns to zero during a portion of the 1 bit pulse.

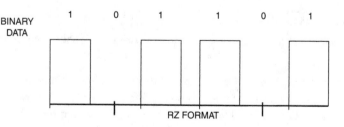

SHORT-PULSE FORMAT   In short-pulse format, shown in Figure 5.6, the 0 bit has no pulses, and the 1 bit forms only a fraction of the bit interval. Short-pulse format reduces the effects of chromatic dispersion. This format is also used to reduce the dispersion properties of solitons in optical communication.

Figure 5.6
Short-pulse format, in
which the 1 bit forms
only a fraction of the
bit interval.

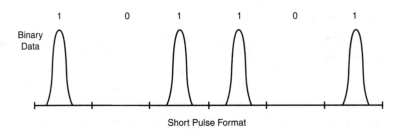

Short Pulse Format

The OOK modulation is successful only if transitions occur in the signal and a DC balance is maintained. This is achieved using line coding or scrambling.

> **Note**
>
> *DC balance* is achieved if the average transmission power of transmitted data is constant.

LINE CODING

Line coding is the process of encoding data into bits. These bits undergo modulation and are then transmitted. At the receiving end, the bits are mapped to the original data. The encoding is carried out in such a way that there is DC balance and transitions occur in the signal. This type of line code is called *binary block line code*.

SCRAMBLING

In *scrambling*, bits are transferred from one data stream to another. A random sequence of bits of a known bit sequence is produced at the transmitting end by a scrambler. At the receiving end is a descrambler, which recovers data from the scrambled stream. The mapping in scrambling is one-to-one. Scrambling has some disadvantages, such as DC imbalance and generation of long strings of 1s and 0s. However, these effects are reduced by mapping in such a way that the required DC balance is achieved and short strings of 1s and 0s are provided.

DEMODULATION

Demodulation is the process of recovering the original signal from the modulated input signal.

After modulation, signals are transmitted through the optic fiber and undergo dispersion and attenuation, which add noise to them. The receiver takes up the transmitted data only if it has an acceptable BER. There are two types of demodulation techniques—*direct detection* and *coherent detection*.

DIRECT DETECTION

Direct detection is based on the availability of light in the bit interval. A 0 bit is transmitted if there is no light, and a 1 bit is transmitted if light is available. Let's consider detection in two cases—the ideal receiver and the practical receiver. In an ideal receiver, it is assumed that no noise gets added during transmission. However, practically this is impossible, because there are various forms of noise, which gets added to the data during transmission. You will now derive the value of the BER for ideal and practical direct-detection receivers.

IDEAL RECEIVER

The BER of an ideal receiver is called the quantum rate. The stream of photons arriving at the receiver can be considered a Poisson random process. Usually, no errors are related to 0-bit transmission, because it is assumed that no photons are received during 0-bit transmission. Photons are received only when the 1 bit is transmitted.

➡ To learn more about Poisson's process, **see** "Poisson Distribution," **p.307** (Appendix B)

The rate at which photons arrive at the receiver is given by the following equation:

$$P \div hfc$$

where

P is the signal power.

h is Planck's constant.

fc is the carrier frequency.

If B is the bit rate, the number of photons received during the 1 bit is given as $P \div hfcB$.

The probability that n photons are received at a bit interval of $1 \div B$ is given by the following equation:

$$e^{-P \div hf_c B} \ (P \div hfcB)^n \div n!$$

The probability that no photons are received is given by the following equation:

$$e^{-P \div hf_c B}$$

If an equal number of 1 bits and 0 bits are considered, the BER is given by the following equation:

$$BER = e^{-P \div hf_c B} \div 2$$

PRACTICAL RECEIVER

Receivers are not ideal, because when they receive the transmitted bits, various noise currents are created along with the resulting photocurrent: thermal noise, shot noise, and noise due to spontaneous emission in optical amplifiers.

THERMAL NOISE CURRENT   This current is created due to random movement of electrons at a finite temperature. It can be considered a Gaussian random process.

➡ To learn more about Gaussian's process, **see** "Theories in Communication," **p.305** (Appendix B)

The variance of the thermal noise current is given by the following equation:

$$\sigma^2{}_{thermal}=4k_B T \div R (B_e)$$

where

R is resistance.

T is temperature.

k_B is Boltzmann's constant.

B_e is the receiver's electrical bandwidth.

The receiver's electrical bandwidth must be at least half the value of the optical bandwidth to avoid signal distortion. At the receiving end, transistors, present in the front-end amplifier, create the thermal noise current. The noise is defined by the noise figure, which is the factor by which the thermal noise present at the amplifier input is enhanced at the amplifier output. The variance of thermal noise current using a front-end amplifier is given by the following equation:

$$\sigma^2{}_{thermal}=4k_B T\, F_n B_e \div R_L$$

where Fn is the noise figure.

SHOT NOISE CURRENT   The photodetector at the receiving end generates electrons randomly even if the intensity of input light remains constant. This current is called the *shot noise current*. It is a component of the resulting photocurrent. The photocurrent is given by the following equation:

$$I = I + i_s$$

where

I is constant current.

i_s is the value of the current, arrived at using the Gaussian random process.

The variance of shot noise current for a pin receiver is given by the following equation:

$$\sigma^2{}_{shot} = 2eI$$

where

$$I = RP$$

R is the responsivity of the photodetector.

If the electrical bandwidth of the receiver is B_e, the variance is given by the following equation:

$$\sigma^2{}_{shot} = 2eI\, B_e$$

If the load resistance of the photodetector is RL, the photocurrent is given by the following equation:

$$I = I + i_s + i_t$$

The thermal current, i_t, has a variance given by the following equation:

$$\sigma^2_{thermal} = 4k_B T\, B_e \div R_L$$

The photocurrent can now be considered a Gaussian random process with variance given by the following equation:

$$\sigma^2 = \sigma^2_{thermal} + \sigma^2_{shot}$$

The variance of the thermal noise current is always larger than that of the shot noise current. Shot noise current also results from an avalanche photodiode (APD). This current is caused by the avalanche multiplication gain G_m.

→ To learn more about photodetectors, **see** "Photodetectors," **p.79** (Chapter 4)

The photocurrent is given by the following equation:

$$I = R_{APD}P$$

where R is the responsivity of the APD.

The variance of current due to APD is given by the following equation:

$$\sigma^2_{shot} = 2eG_m^2 F_A(G_m)RPB_e$$

where $F_A(G_m)$ is the excess noise factor of the APD. It increases as the gain increases.

NOISE DUE TO SPONTANEOUS EMISSION   The optical amplifier in the receiving end gives rise to noise current due to spontaneous emission. Figure 5.7 shows an optical amplifier.

Figure 5.7
An optical amplifier is placed before a receiver to amplify the received signal.

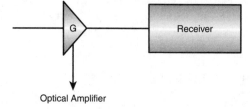

Optical Amplifier

The noise power due to spontaneous emission for each polarization mode is given by the following equation:

$$P_N = n_{sp}hf_c(G-1)B_o$$

where

G is amplifier gain.

B_o is optical bandwidth.

n_{sp} is the spontaneous emission factor based on population inversion occurring in the amplifier. There are two polarization modes in a single-mode fiber, so the noise power becomes twice P_N.

At the receiving end, the optical preamplifier is generally placed before a pin photodiode.

The current generated by the photo detector is given by the following equation:

$$I = RGP$$

where

P is the optical power received.

G is the gain of the preamplifier.

R is the responsivity of the photodetector.

The current produced by the photodetector is proportional to the optical power. The electric field generates noise that beats against the signal (signal-spontaneous beat noise) and noise that beats against itself (spontaneous-spontaneous beat noise).

The variance due to the different noise currents is given by the following equations:

$$\sigma^2_{thermal} = I_t^2 B_e$$
$$\sigma^2_{shot} = 2eR[GP + P_n(G-1)B_o]B_e$$
$$\sigma^2_{sig\text{-}spont} = 4R^2 GPP_n(G-1)B_e$$
$$\sigma^2_{spont\text{-}spont} = 2R^2[P_n(G-1)]^2(2\,B_o-B_e)\,B_e$$

If the amplifier gain is large, the thermal and shot noise values are very low. By filtering the noise before it reaches the pin photodiode, the optical bandwidth can be decreased. This reduces the spontaneous-spontaneous beat noise. This makes the signal-spontaneous beat noise the major noise component. The noise figure of the amplifier, which is the ratio of input signal-to-noise ratio (SNR_i) to output signal-to-noise ratio (SNR_o) is given by the following equations:

$$SNR_i = (RP)^2 \div 2R_e PB_e$$
$$SNR_o = (RGP)2 \div 4R^2 PG(G-1)n_{sp}hf_c B_e$$

The noise figure is given by the following equation:

$$Fn = SNR_i \div SNR_o = 2nsp$$

SUBCARRIER MODULATION

The center frequency of the optical signal is called the *optic carrier frequency*. The optical carrier is turned on and off by the OOK signal based on the bit that is transmitted. The data can first modulate an electric carrier signal in the microwave frequency range. The modulated microwave carrier then modulates the optical transmitter. The microwave carrier can be modulated in various ways, such as amplitude, phase, and frequency modulation. Digital and analog modulation schemes can be used in this process. The microwave carrier is called the subcarrier, and the optical carrier is the main carrier. This type of modulation is called *subcarrier modulation*.

Multiple data streams can be multiplexed to form a single optic signal. This is done using multiple microwave carriers at varying frequencies. At the receiving end, subcarriers are separated, and data is extracted from each carrier electronically. This process is called *subcarrier multiplexing*. Figure 5.8 depicts the subcarrier modulation circuit.

Figure 5.8
A subcarrier modulation circuit, in which the data signal first modulates a microwave carrier, which then modulates an optical carrier.

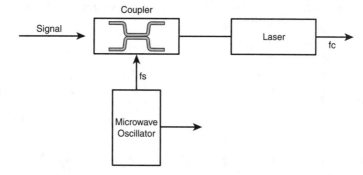

COHERENT DETECTION

A direct-detection receiver has disadvantages, such as thermal and noise currents. Using optical preamplifiers increases the sensitivity of such receivers. Coherent detection is a technique that improves the receiver's sensitivity. This type of detection increases signal gain by mixing it with a light signal from a local oscillator laser. The major noise component here is shot noise due to the local oscillator. Figure 5.9 depicts a coherent receiver.

Figure 5.9
Coherent detection to improve the receiver's sensitivity.

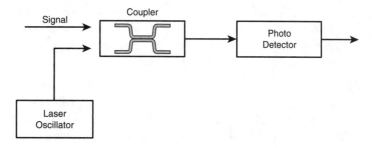

PART

I

CH

5

The incoming light signal is mixed with a local oscillator and is sent to the photodetector. Assuming that the phase and polarization of the two waves are the same, the power of the photodetector is given by the following equations:

$$P_r(t) = [\sqrt{(2aP)}\cos(2\pi f_c t) + \sqrt{(2P_{LO})}\cos(2\pi f_{LO} t)]^2$$

$$P_r(t) = aP + P_{LO} + 2\sqrt{(aP\,P_{LO})}(\cos[2\pi(f_c - f_{LO})t])$$

where

P is the power of the input signal.

P_{LO} is the power of the local oscillator.

f_c is the carrier frequency of the input signal.

f_{LO} is the frequency of local oscillator waves.

If the local oscillator power P_{LO} is made large, the shot noise component dominates the other noise components in the receiver.

Noise variance is given by the following equations:

$$\sigma_1^2 = 2eI_1B_e$$
$$\sigma_0^2 = 2eI_0B_e$$

You can neglect P when compared to P_{LO}, because it has a value less than −20dBm, and P_{LO} is 0dBm.

Therefore, the value of BER is given by the following equation:

$$BER = Q\sqrt{(RP \div 2eB_e)}$$

If $B_e = B \div 2$, $BER = Q\sqrt{M}$, where M is the number of photons per bit.

The sensitivity of a coherent receiver is better than that of a direct-detection receiver.

SUMMARY

Modulation is the process of converting signals from electrical form to optical form for transmission through fiber. Various techniques are used for modulation, such as on-off keying, PAM, PWM, QPAM, phase-shift keying, and frequency-shift keying. For transmission over short distances, direct modulation of the optical source is used. However, for long-distance transmissions, external modulation must be applied. Furthermore, to maintain the DC balance, line coding techniques are applied.

Demodulation involves the recovery of data at the receiving end. Receivers vary, depending on the parameter to which they are sensitive. In a direct-detection receiver, the energy received during the bit interval decides whether the bit is a 0 bit or a 1 bit. Thermal noise degrades the direct-detection receiver. The sensitivity can be improved using either an optical preamplifier or an APD. Coherent detection can also be used to increase sensitivity. This technique is not used, because the receiver structure is complicated and cannot overcome the impairments caused by polarization and phase differences.

The Evolution and Architecture of Optical Networks

CHAPTER

OPTICAL FIBER FABRICATION, POWER LAUNCHING, AND COUPLING

In this chapter

FIBER MATERIALS

The fabrication of fibers requires proper selection of the materials. The following are some of the selection criteria when you choose optical fibers:

- It must be possible to manufacture long, thin, supple fibers from the material.
- The material must be translucent to a specific wavelength so that it can guide the light efficiently.
- Materials that are physically compatible, having slightly different refractive indices for the core and the cladding, must be available.
- The material must be cheap and abundant.

The materials that satisfy these requirements are glasses and plastics. A variety of fibers are available for long- and short-distance transmissions. Glass fibers are widely used for long-haul transmissions due to their reduced attenuation. Plastic fibers are used for short transmission distances because they have significantly higher attenuation than glass fibers. Plastic fibers are mainly used in offensive environments where the mechanical strength of the plastic fibers offers an advantage over glass fibers.

GLASS FIBERS

Glass is manufactured by fusing a mixture of sulfides, metal oxides, and selenides. The resulting structure does not have a well-defined molecular pattern, as in the case of crystalline structures. Therefore, glass does not have a sharp or well-defined melting point. When glass is heated, it melts at a very high temperature and becomes a viscous liquid. The melting temperature, in this case, refers to the temperature at which the glass becomes liquid enough to free itself of the gas bubbles.

Note

Heating causes solid elements, compounds, and mixtures to melt. This melting occurs at a very well-defined temperature. This means that just a fraction of a degree below the melting temperature, the material is solid. In other words, it retains a well-defined shape. Just a fraction of a degree above the melting temperature, the material is liquid and can be poured. However, this is not the case with glass. Glass becomes softer or less viscous when it is heated to higher temperatures, and it has no easily defined melting temperature. It is in this sense that glass is a liquid that does not have a clearly defined freezing temperature when cooled down.

It is possible to define a *glass temperature* for such glassy materials. The definition is rather technical, but it indicates the temperature range around which the increase in viscosity on cooling is most rapid.

Note

Viscosity is a liquid's resistance to flowing smoothly due to forces holding the molecules together. Viscosity increases as the temperature decreases.

The most widely used optically transparent glasses for manufacturing optic fibers are the oxide glasses. The most common is silica (SiO_2), which has a refractive index of 1.458 at 850nm. Various dopants are added to produce two similar materials having slightly different indices of refraction for the core and the cladding. To increase the core's refractive index, dopants such as germanium oxide (GeO_2) and phosphorus pentoxide (P_2O_5) are added. To decrease the refractive index, dopants such as fluorine and boron oxide (B_2O_3) are added to silica. Table 4.1 summarizes the combinations of these materials.

TABLE 4.1   COMBINATIONS OF MATERIALS USED IN CORE AND CLADDING

Core	Cladding
GeO_2-SiO_2	SiO_2
P_2O_5-SiO_2	SiO_2
GeO_2-B_2O_3-SiO_2	B_2O_3-SiO_2
SiO_2	B_2O_3-SiO_2

The various advantages of glass are as follows:

- It has enough resistance to bend at temperatures as high as 1000°C.
- It has good chemical durability.
- It has high resistance to breakage due to thermal shocks. This is because of the low thermal expansion of glass.
- It has high transparency in the visible and infrared regions that is suitable for fiber-optic communication.

However, due to its high melting point, glass poses some problems, but these can be minimized by vapor deposition techniques. This technique is discussed in detail in the following sections.

HALIDE GLASS FIBERS

Due to the low transmission losses in the mid-infrared region (0.2μm to 8μm), fluoride glasses have been used for the manufacture of optical fibers in this region. Fluorides belong to the general halides group, which includes chlorine, fluorine, bromine, and iodine.

Silver halide fiber is intended for the transmission of light from 3 to 15μm. It is flexible and bends into a radius of a few centimeters. This fiber has a core of polycrystalline silver halide and is supplied in an opaque tube. Because of the material's high refractive index (n=2.2), total internal reflection takes place at the boundary with air. Unclad silver halide must be used when maximum power transmission is required, because it has slightly lower loss than clad silver halide and is less expensive.

Clad silver halide fiber is intended for the transmission of light from 3 to 15μm. It is flexible and bends into a radius of a few centimeters. This fiber has a core made of polycrystalline silver halide and a cladding layer made of silver halide with a low refractive index. Because the reflecting boundary is at the interface of these two layers and is not outside the fiber, the fiber's optical performance is unaffected by surface contamination. This type of "clad" silver halide is recommended for sensors.

CHALCOGENIDE OPTICAL FIBERS

Chalcogenide glass fibers were drawn into the first infrared (IR) fiber in the mid-1960s. Chalcogenide fibers fall into three categories: sulfide, selenide, and telluride. One or more chalcogen elements are mixed with one or more elements, such as As, Ge, P, Sb, Ga, Al, Si, and so on to form a two- component (or more) glass. These glasses have low softening temperatures more comparable to fluoride glass than to oxide glasses. They are very stable, durable, and insensitive to moisture. A distinctive difference between these glasses and the other IR fiber glasses is that they do not transmit well in the visible region, and their refractive indices are quite high.

Note

Chalcogenides are compounds of sulfur, selenium, and tellurium. The naturally occurring chalcogenides, such as orpiment and realgar, exist in the Earth's crust in great quantities. They are the best-known and most widely used material in integrated circuits. Chalcogenides such as germanium selenide and arsenic sulfide are semiconductors (poor conductors of electricity). Introducing specific elements through a process called *doping* alters their composition.

Among the various chalcogenide glasses, As_2S_3 (arsenic trisulphide) is the most widely used in making single-mode fibers, because the losses in these glasses typically are in the range of 1db/km.

PLASTIC OPTICAL FIBERS

Plastic optical fibers (POFs) are made from materials such as polymethyl methacrylate (PMMA) ($n = 1.49$), polystyrene ($n = 1.59$), polycarbonates ($n = 1.5$ to 1.57), fluorinated polymers, and so on. These fibers share the advantages of glass optical fibers in terms of insensitivity to electromagnetic interference, small size and weight, low cost, and the potential to carry information at high rates. The most important attribute of POFs is their large core diameters of about 1 mm, as compared to glass fibers, which have cores of 50 or 62.5mm. Such a large diameter results in easier alignment at joints. POFs are also more durable and flexible than glass fibers. In addition, they usually have a large NA, resulting in larger light-gathering power.

The performance of plastic optical fibers lies somewhere between conventional copper wires and glass optical fibers. Copper wires are expensive and suffer from electromagnetic interference. In comparison, plastic optical fibers are cheaper and free from interference. In addition, signals through copper wires can be tapped, but it is very difficult to tap signals from optical fibers in general. Compared to glass fibers, POFs are much easier to connect because of their large diameters. Coupling of light from a source is also very efficient due to large NA and large core diameter. Thus, although glass optical fibers dominate long-distance data communication, POFs are expected to provide low-cost solutions to short-distance applications such as local area networks (LANs) and high-speed Internet access. At gigabit rates of transmission, glass fibers are at least 30% more expensive than POFs, and the cost of copper increases dramatically.

Apart from short-distance communication applications, POFs are expected to find applications in many areas such as lighting for decorative signs and road signs, in museums where the property of fibers in non-UV transmission is very useful, in image transmission such as endoscopes, and in sensing applications.

Fluorescent or scintillating fiber is of interest in optical communication. It is ordinary plastic fiber doped with special elements. When light falls on a fluorescent fiber, it excites the dopant atoms in the fiber. When the atoms drop to a lower energy state, they emit light. Part of this light is collected within the fiber NA and is transmitted to both ends of the fiber. In scintillating fibers, light is generated when radiations such as alpha and beta particles, or gamma rays, are incident on the fiber. Many applications are being envisaged for fluorescent fibers, particularly due to their ability to capture light that falls anywhere along the length of the fiber. Applications include intrusion alarms and size determination. Scintillating optical fibers find applications in particle energy measurement, track detection, and so on.

FIBER FABRICATION

Basically, fiber manufacturers use two methods to fabricate multimode and single-mode glass fibers—vapor phase oxidation and direct melt.

In vapor phase oxidation, gaseous metal halide compounds, dopant material, and oxygen are oxidized (burned) to form a white silica powder (SiO_2). Manufacturers call SiO_2 soot.

Note

Silica and silicon dioxide are the same, but silica is the commonly used term.

Manufacturers deposit soot on the surface of a glass substrate or inside a hollow tube using one of the following four methods:

- Outside Vapor-Phase Oxidation (OVPO)
- Inside Vapor-Phase Oxidation (IVPO) or Modified Chemical Vapor Deposition (MCVD)
- Vapor-Phase Axial Deposition (VAD)
- Double-Crucible

This rod or tube is called preform. The fibers are drawn from the preform using the apparatus shown in Figure 6.1.

Figure 6.1
A schematic diagram of a fiber-drawing apparatus in which the fiber is drawn from a glass preform.

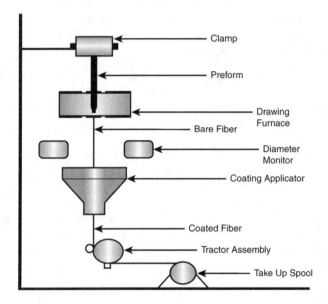

Clamp

Preform

Drawing Furnace

Bare Fiber

Diameter Monitor

Coating Applicator

Coated Fiber

Tractor Assembly

Take Up Spool

The finished glass preform is clamped and drawn into a continuous strand of glass fiber. First, the preform is lowered into the top of the draw furnace. The tip of the preform is heated until a piece of molten glass, called a gob, begins to fall from the preform like hot taffy. It pulls a thin strand of glass, thus making it into an optical fiber. The fiber goes through a precise online diameter monitor to ensure specified outside diameter. Next, coatings are applied and cured. At the bottom of the draw, the fiber is wound on spools. Each fiber is assigned a unique identification number that encodes all relevant manufacturing data, including raw materials and manufacturing equipment.

OUTSIDE VAPOR-PHASE OXIDATION

With the OVPO method, a layer of silica or the soot is first deposited from a burner onto a rotating rod or ceramic mandrel. The soot adheres to this glass rod, and a cylindrical glass preform is built up. By controlling the vapor stream, the composition and the dimension of the glass preform can be varied, thus creating the desired dimensions for the core and the cladding. This is called lateral OVPO.

After the deposition is complete, the preform is drawn into the fiber using the method just discussed. Figure 6.2 shows the manufacture of a glass preform using OVPO.

Figure 6.2
The OVPO process makes a glass preform by depositing the soot on a rod as desired.

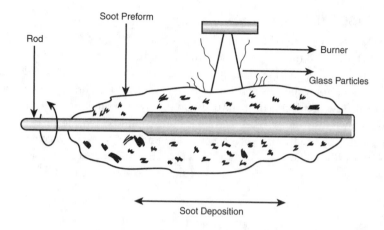

INSIDE VAPOR-PHASE OXIDATION

IVPO (or MCVD), shown in Figure 6.3, is a process that was developed at AT&T Bell Laboratories in the 1970s. In IVPO, the glass vapor particles arising from the reaction of the halide metal gases and oxygen flow through the inside of a revolving silica tube. An oxy-hydrogen torch travels back and forth past this tube to sinter the silica deposited into a clear glass layer. When the desired thickness of glass has been deposited, the vapor flow is discontinued, and the tube is heated strongly to collapse the solid preform. This preform is finally drawn into a fiber with the core having vapor-deposited material and the cladding with the original silica tube.

Figure 6.3
IVPO with the soot deposited on the inside of the silica tube.

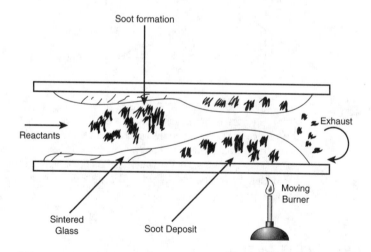

Note

Sintering is the process of forming a mass from a powder without melting it.

VAPOR-PHASE AXIAL DEPOSITION

VAD is another method of producing preforms (see Figure 6.4). This method is similar to OVPO. In VAD, the SiO_2 particles are formed in the same manner as in OVPO. The particles are deposited onto the end of a glass rod, which is in turn attached in the upright position to a motor. A porous preform is grown axially as a pulling machine rotates the rod upward. The preform is made into a solid rod by zone melting. The preform is then ready to be drawn into a fiber. This method is done completely inside a closed deposition chamber, so it has the advantage of a clean environment. However, no central hole is created, as is the case with OVDO. Finally, VAD has proven cost-effective, because the preform can be made in continuous lengths. Figure 6.4 shows the apparatus for VAD.

Figure 6.4
VAD, with the soot deposited in the inside of the tube.

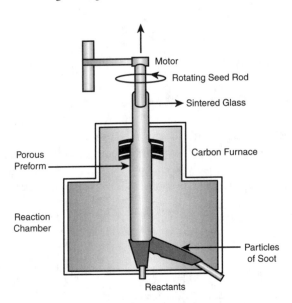

Note

Zone melting is a technique for purifying crystalline substances. A heating system, usually halogen lamps, passes slowly over a bar of the material to be refined, creating a molten region that carries impurities with it across the bar. Consequently, this process sweeps the impurities out of the sample and concentrates them at the end of the crystal, which is then cut off and discarded. This method is sometimes used to purify semiconductor crystals.

THE DOUBLE-CRUCIBLE METHOD

The double-crucible method, shown in Figure 6.5, is used to fabricate an optical waveguide by melting the core and clad glasses in the form of two suitably joined concentric crucibles and drawing a fiber from the combined melted glass.

Figure 6.5
The double-crucible method for fabricating silica and halide fibers.

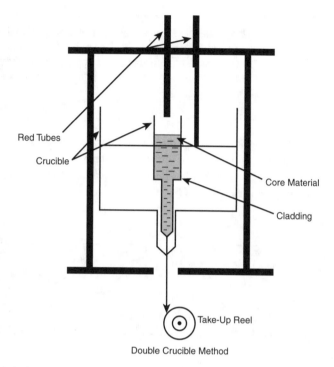

Red Tubes

Crucible

Core Material

Cladding

Take-Up Reel

Double Crucible Method

Silica and halide glass fibers are made using the double-crucible method. In this technique, one glass rod is made from silica powders for the core, and another is made for the cladding. These rods are then used as feed for each of the two concentric crucibles. The inner crucible contains the molten core, and the outer crucible contains the cladding. In a continuous process, the fiber is drawn from the molten state. The disadvantage of this method is the possibility of introducing contaminants during the melting process. These contaminants arise from the furnace environment and the crucible.

MECHANICAL PROPERTIES OF FIBERS

The mechanical properties of optical fibers play a very important role in determining the fibers' transmission capacity. The fibers must be able to withstand the stress induced during cabling and installation.

Glass is thought of as a brittle substance. In reality, however, the breaking stress of glass fibers is comparable to that of metal wires. The difference between glass and metal fibers is that under an applied stress, glass can be stretched elastically until it reaches its breaking point, whereas metals can be stretched well beyond their true elastic range. For example, copper wire can be elongated by more than 20% of its elastic range before it fractures, whereas glass can be elongated by only 1% before it breaks.

> **Note**
>
> Considering the elasticity factor, it may appear that fiber optics cannot be bent. However, it is possible to bend the optics along its bend radius, without causing harm to the signals or the fiber. The bend radius of an optic is typically in the range of 1-2 inches. A word of caution—it is not considered a good practice to bend the optics too much.

Due to the concentration of stress at the surface flaws, the strength of long glass fibers is limited. The size and dimension of the severest flaw determines the fracture strength of glass fibers. A hypothetical flaw model has been proposed, as shown in Figure 6.6. The crack shown in Figure 6.6 is called the Griffith microcrack.

Figure 6.6
A hypothetical model of the Griffith microcrack in an optical fiber.

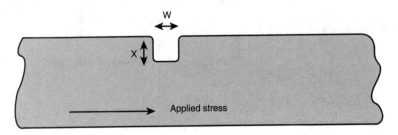

The strength of the crack for silica fibers is given by the following equation:

$$K = Y X^{1/2}\, \sigma \text{----------------------------------}(1)$$

where

K is the stress intensity factor.

X is the depth in millimeters.

Y is a dimensionless quantity that depends on the surface flaws. For most critical surface flaws, the value of $Y = \sqrt{\pi}$.

The maximum value of K depends on the composition of the glass.

Therefore, the maximum crack size allowable can be calculated from equation (1).

FIBER JOINTS

In any fiber-optic system, it is necessary to interconnect the fibers in such a way that losses are minimized. The interconnection might occur at the optical source, at the photodetector, and/or at intermediate points within the cable where the two fibers are connected. Two techniques are used to join the fibers, depending on whether the bond is permanent or temporary. A permanent bond is called a *splice*, and a demountable joint is called a *connector*.

Various parameters cause optical power loss at the joint:

- Input power distribution at the joint
- The length of the fiber between the source and the joint
- The geometric and waveguide characteristics of two fiber ends at the joint
- The fiber end-face quality

The optical power coupled depends on the number of modes that can propagate in each fiber. For example, if one fiber can propagate 400 modes and the other 300 modes, almost 80% of the power is coupled from the first fiber to the second.

Any two fibers joined have different radii, numerical apertures, and refractive-index profiles (α). Therefore, the fraction of the energy coupled is given by the following equation:

$$\alpha F = M_{comm}/M_E$$

where

M_{comm} is the common mode volume.

M_E is the number of modes in the emitting fiber.

The fiber-to-fiber coupling loss is given in terms of efficiency, as shown in the following equation:

$$L_f = -10 \log \eta F$$

An exact calculation of coupling loss between the different optical fibers is lengthy, because it involves nonuniform power distribution among the modes and the effects of propagation in the second fiber. The following sections discuss an estimate of the losses caused by mechanical misalignment and geometric mismatches. Variations in the waveguide properties between the two joined fibers can also cause losses.

→ To know more about the effect of waveguide properties on losses, **see** "Dispersion," **p. 37** (Chapter 2).

MECHANICAL MISALIGNMENT

The alignment of fiber cores is a very important parameter for the low-loss transmission of light through a connection. It affects the attenuation of the optical signal, especially for single-mode fibers, because of their small core size. Therefore, drastic measures must be taken to limit its effects.

Radiation losses occur from mechanical misalignments because the radiation cone of the sending fiber does not match that of the receiving fiber. The magnitude of loss depends on the degree of misalignment.

PART

II

CH

6

The misalignments present in fibers are as follows:

- Lateral displacement or axial misalignment occurs when the axes of the two fibers do not coincide and are separated by a distance d.

- Longitudinal misalignment occurs when the fibers have the same axis, but there is a gap s between the end faces.

- Angular misalignment occurs when the two end faces are not parallel and form an angle.

These types of misalignment between fibers are shown in Figure 6.7.

Figure 6.7
Losses in fiber due to three basic types of misalignment.

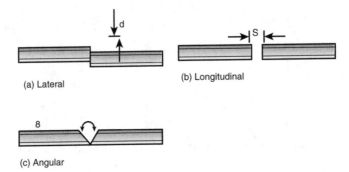

(a) Lateral

(b) Longitudinal

(c) Angular

The maximum loss is caused in the fiber axial misalignment.

GEOMETRIC MISMATCHES

In addition to these fiber misalignments, geometric properties affect the power coupling at the joints. These include variations in the core diameter, core area ellipticity, numerical aperture, refractive-index profile, and core-clad concentricity. These parameters vary because of the variety of fibers present. Therefore, the user has no control over them.

Loss due to different core diameters, assuming that the NA and the refractive-index profiles are equal, is given by the following equation:

$$L_f(a) = 10\log(a_R \div a_E)^2 \text{ for } a_R < a_E$$

$$0 \text{ for } a_R > a_E$$

If the diameter and the index profiles of the coupled fibers are equal, the loss due to the NA is given by the following equation:

$$L_f(NA) = -10\log[NA_R \div NA_E]^2 \text{ for } NA_R < NA_E$$

$$0 \text{ for } NA_R > NA_E$$

Finally, if the diameter and the NA of the two fibers are the same, the loss due to varying refractive-index profiles between the two fibers is given by the following equation:

$$L_f(\alpha) = -10\log\alpha_R(\alpha_E+2) \div$$
$$\alpha_E(\alpha_R+2) \text{ for } \alpha_R < \alpha_E$$
$$0 \text{ for } \alpha_R > \alpha_E$$

where

E and R are the emitting and receiving fibers.

a is the diameter of the core.

NA is the numerical aperture.

α is the refractive index.

L_f is the loss in the fiber.

The fiber end faces play a very important role when connecting or splicing a fiber. The end faces must be flat, perpendicular to the axes of the fiber, and smooth for efficient coupling of light. Various end preparation techniques are used, such as sawing, grinding, and polishing.

Conventional polishing techniques can produce smooth end faces perpendicular to the fiber's axis. However, this method is time-consuming and requires skilled operators.

With the controlled-fracture technique, illustrated in Figure 6.8, the fiber to be cleaved is scratched first to create a stress concentration at the surface. This technique easily produces very smooth surfaces. Fiber is then bent over a curved form while tension is applied. This causes uniform distribution of stress over the fiber. The maximum stress occurs at the scratch point so that a crack propagates through the fiber. This technique produces very smooth and perpendicular end faces.

Figure 6.8
The controlled-fracture technique, used for end-face preparation of the fiber.

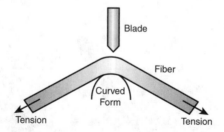

Physical contact reduces (or eliminates in some situations) the Fresnel reflections that are generated whenever the light passes the boundary between two media with different indices of refraction (in this case, glass and air). If a gap exists between the end faces of the fibers, multiple Fresnel reflections appear. Using epoxy that matches the refractive indices can reduce Fresnel reflections. Depending on the size of the gap, they can interfere constructively to create an important back reflection that affects the function of active components such as laser sources, amplifiers, and so on that exist in the optical link.

FIBER SPLICING

Splicing forms a permanent connection between fibers in the network. It is used to perform permanent repairs. It is usually used in optical links in which frequent connections and disconnections are not required. Various geometric properties and misalignment must be considered when splicing a fiber.

Various techniques are used for splicing. The two main methods are fusion splicing and mechanical splicing.

In fusion splicing, shown in Figure 6.9, the ends of the fibers are aligned either automatically by measuring the light transmitted or manually using micromanipulators and a microscope system for viewing the splice. The ends of the fibers are then melted together using a gas flame or, more commonly, an electric arc. Near-perfect splices can be obtained with losses as low as 0.02dB (best mechanical splice 0.2dB).

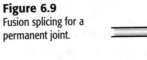

Figure 6.9
Fusion splicing for a permanent joint.

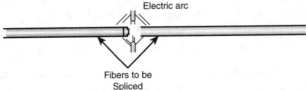

Electric arc

Fibers to be
Spliced

In mechanical splicing, shown in Figure 6.10, the two fiber ends are held together in a splice. This consists of a device, usually made of glass, that automatically brings the two fibers into alignment. The openings at each end of the device are usually fluted to allow the fibers to be guided into the capillary where the alignment takes place. The splice is first filled with epoxy gel whose refractive index is the same as that of the fiber's core or index-matching gel. After the fibers have been entered into the splice, they are adjusted to give the optimum transmission of light.

Figure 6.10.
Mechanical splicing
with temporary fiber
joints.

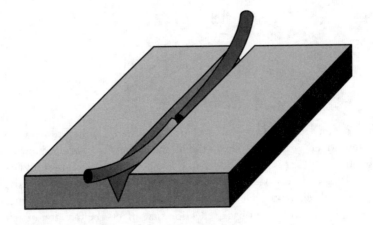

Mechanical splices are best used with multimode fiber. Some splices exist that are suitable for single-mode fiber, but they have a loss of 0.1dB. This is five times the loss of the best fusion splice.

It is necessary that you achieve near-perfect splicing to ensure that there is minimal loss of signals. In case of misalignments in splicing, the light from one fiber may not be able to pass through to the connecting fiber. In case of minor misalignments (possible in mechanical splicing), the splicing process should be able to ensure that the light can still pass through. However, the loss could be high.

Two important steps in the process of splicing that determine the effectiveness of the splicing process: *cleaving* and *polishing*. Cleaving is done to ensure that you get a flat perpendicular cleave at a proper distance from the end of the fiber connector. You would have to use polishing to ensure accuracy of the cleave.

Polishing the fiber ends removes most surface imperfections introduced by the fiber cleaving or cutting process. The most common technique is a multi-step manual polishing of the fibers after they are fixed in place in the connector. The first step is to give the surface of the fiber end a rough polish. The next step involves giving the surface of the fiber end a fine polish. Automatic polishers are a cost-effective way to reduce the labor involved.

Note

Several unsuccessful attempts have been made to replace the polishing with a one-step cleave technique. However, this process never really caught on.

FIBER CONNECTORS

Optical connectors are the means by which fiber-optic cable is usually connected to peripheral equipment and to other fibers. These connectors are similar to their electrical counterparts in function and outward appearance, but are actually high-precision devices. In operation, the connector centers the small fiber so that its light-gathering core lies directly over and in line with the light source (or other fiber).

These are the basic requirements for a good connector design:

- The connectors must have low coupling losses and must be able to maintain stringent alignment tolerances. The losses must not change after operation or after many connects and disconnects.

- Connectors of one type must be interchangeable from one manufacturer to another.

- A technician must be readily able to install the connector in the field environment, and the connector must not be sensitive to the skill of the technician.

- Environmental conditions such as temperature, dust, and moisture must cause small connector loss.

- Connectors must have reliable construction and must be inexpensive.

- The user must easily be able to connect and disconnect the connector by hand.

TYPES OF CONNECTORS

Connectors of different types are available, such as screw-on, bayonet, and push pull. The basic mechanism used in these connectors is either butt-joint or expanded beam.

In butt-joint connectors, a metal, ceramic, or plastic ferrule for each fiber is used. A precision sleeve is also present into which the ferrule fits. A precision hole is drilled into the ferrule, and the fiber is epoxied into it. Two butt-joint designs are used, mainly in both multimode and single-mode fibers—straight-sleeve and tapered-sleeve mechanisms.

With a straight-sleeve connector, the length of the sleeve and a guide ring on the ferrule are used to identify the end separation of the fibers. In a biconical connector, a tapered sleeve is used to accept and guide the ferrules. The guide ring and the sleeve length maintain the fiber separation.

Note

A *ferrule* is a kind of shaft or metal joint that is used for support or reinforcement.

Figures 6.11 and 6.12 show the types of butt-joint connectors.

Figure 6.11
A straight-sleeve butt-joint connector.

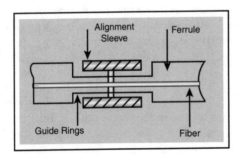

Figure 6.12
A tapered-sleeve butt-joint connector.

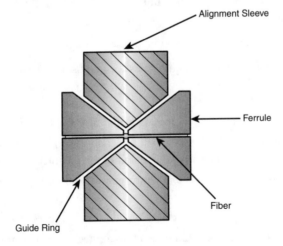

With an expanded-beam connector, shown in Figure 6.13, lenses are used on the ends of the fiber. The lenses either collimate light emitted by the transmitting fiber or focus the expanded beam on the core of the receiving fiber. As the light is collimated, the fiber end separation may take place within the connector. Therefore, there is less dependency on lateral alignment. Additional optical processing elements can easily be inserted into the expanded beam within the fiber ends.

Figure 6.13
An expanded-beam connector with a collimating/focusing lens.

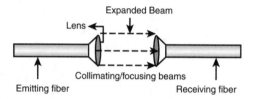

Expanded Beam
Lens
Collimating/focusing beams
Emitting fiber
Receiving fiber

Note

Collimation is the process of rendering parallel a ray of light in a certain direction or to bring it in the same line.

SUMMARY

Glasses and plastic satisfy the requirements of basic fiber materials. They are therefore widely used in the manufacture of optical fibers. The different types of fibers are halide glass fibers, chalcogenide glass fibers, and plastic optical fibers.

Plastic optical fibers are used for short-distance communications due to their high attenuation along the path. Glass fibers are best-suited for long-distance communications, because they have less attenuation.

The three basic methods of fiber preform fabrication are outside vapor-phase oxidation, inside vapor-phase oxidation, and vapor-phase axial deposition. The preform manufactured is then drawn into the fiber. In the double-crucible method, an optical waveguide is fabricated by melting the core and clad glasses in two suitably joined concentric crucibles and then drawing a fiber from the combined melted glass.

The mechanical properties of the fiber determine the amount of stress it can withstand. This is an important factor to consider when designing the fiber.

Fiber-to-fiber joints are of two types—splice or connector. Various misalignments are present because of the different refractive-index profiles, radii, and NA of the two fibers. Improper fiber end faces also cause loss of optical energy. This can be reduced by polishing the fiber's end faces. The controlled-fracture technique is a more economical method of making the end faces smooth.

PART
II

CH
6

Fiber splicing can be either fusion or mechanical. Fusion splicing is used for permanent or semipermanent joints, whereas in mechanical splicing, the fibers are only held together by an assembly.

Connectors are used for temporary connections. A good connector design must satisfy the basic requirements. The basic mechanisms used in most connectors are the butt-joint and the expanded-beam class.

CHAPTER **7**

SYSTEM PARAMETERS AND DESIGN CONSIDERATIONS

In this chapter

A TYPICAL OPTICAL SYSTEM MODEL

Second-generation optical networks marked the beginning of very high-speed communication, because Wavelength-Division Multiplexing (WDM) enabled the capacity of optical networks to increase tremendously by reusing light wavelengths. A typical WDM system is discussed here.

Figure 7.1 shows the different components of a WDM link. The transmitter consists of Distributed Feedback (DFB) lasers, one for each wavelength. An optical multiplexer is used to combine the signals at different wavelengths onto a single fiber. Optical power amplifiers are used in the path to increase transmission power. Line amplifiers are used to amplify the signal along the path. Compensation for dispersion might also be present at each amplifier stage. Before the signal is received by a separate photodetector, it is amplified by an optical preamplifier and is passed through a demultiplexer.

Figure 7.1
The components of a basic WDM link.

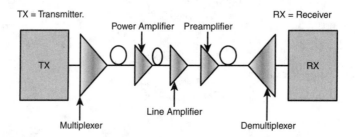

→ To learn more about distributed feedback lasers, **see** "Distributed Feedback Lasers," **p.75** (Chapter 4)

A network's physical layer is responsible for reliable transmission of bits. The Bit Error Rate (BER) and the additional system margin give the measure of quality for the digital signal in the system. The BER must be of the order 10^{-9} to 10^{-15}. It is typically 10^{-12}. Here, only digital signals are considered, although analog signals can be transmitted reliably through the fiber. The physical layer is also responsible for initializing the link. It is necessary for protection against harmful laser radiation.

> **Note**
>
> The physical layer is the lowermost layer of the OSI/ISO model. It is responsible for transmitting the data in bits.

PENALTIES OF THE SYSTEM COMPONENTS

The physical layer must take into account the various impairments in the system that result in power penalty. When there is impairment, more signal power is required at the receiver to maintain the BER constant. The system's power penalty is defined as the reduction in the signal-to-noise ratio caused by a certain impairment.

Let P_1 be the power received during the on state or when the 1 bit is transmitted, and let P_0 be the power received during the off state or when the 0 bit is transmitted. The corresponding current is given by the following equations:

$$I_1 = RP_1$$
$$I_0 = RP_0$$

where R is the responsiveness of the photodetector.

The BER of a system having no impairments with equal possibility of 1s and 0s is given by the following equation:

$$BER = Q(R(P_1 - P_0)) \div \sigma_1 + \sigma_0$$

where σ_1 and σ_0 are the standard noise deviations during the 1 and 0 bit period, assuming that the noise is Gaussian.

Let P_{11}, P_{00}, σ_{11}, and σ_{00} denote the received powers and the standard noise deviations, respectively, in the presence of impairments. The power penalty is then given as follows:

$$PP = -10\log\,[(R(P_{11} - P_{00})) \div \sigma_{11} + \sigma_{00}] \div [(R(P_1 - P_0)) \div \sigma_1 + \sigma_0]$$

The power penalty in the different types of receivers is mainly because of the various noise components present, such as thermal noise, shot noise, and amplifier beat noise. In pin receivers, the major noise component is thermal noise. Therefore, $\sigma_1 = \sigma_0 = \sigma_{th}$. The power penalty for such a system is given by the following equation:

$$PP = -10\log\,[R(P_{11} - P_{00})] \div [(P_1 - P_0)]$$

➔ To learn more about thermal noise in receivers, **see** "Sources of Noise in Optical Systems," **p.310** (Appendix B)

In Avalanche Photodiode (APD) receivers, the main noise component is the shot noise that is caused by photodetector gain. In other amplified systems, the dominant noise component is the beat noise caused by the amplifier. For both cases, the noise variance is proportional to the signal power. If the power during the 0 bit is assumed to be very small compared to the power during the 1 bit, the noise variance during the 1 bit is high. Therefore, a receiver that is optimized sets its threshold level at a near-0 level, and a normal receiver sets the threshold to the average power received. The normal receiver, therefore, has a higher BER.

➔ To learn more about avalanche photodiodes and pin receivers, **see** "Receivers," **p.78** (Chapter 4)

The power penalty, however, is almost the same for both pin and APD receivers. It is given as follows:

$$PP = -5\log(P_{11} \div P_1)$$

Polarization plays a very important role in signal impairments, because the signals interfere with each other. When the interfering signals have the same state of polarization, the signal damage is heavy. Therefore, the system must be designed to handle the worst cases of signal interference to reduce the power penalty.

PART

II

CH

7

Note   *Polarization* is the alignment of the lightwaves in a particular direction.

TRANSMITTER DESIGN PARAMETERS

The main parameters of a transmitter are output power, extinction ratio, the type of modulation, rise/fall time, and wavelength stability and accuracy.

Depending on the type of transmitter, the output power varies. Direct feedback lasers give an output power of about 1mW to 10mW. An optical power amplifier is used to boost the output power.

Extinction ratio is defined as the ratio of power (P_1) transmitted during the 1 bit period to the power (P_0) transmitted during the 0 bit period.

Let the limited transmitted power be P. For good transmission, you must ensure that $P_1=2P$ and $P_0=0$. Therefore, ideally, the extinction ratio becomes infinity. However, a practical system has an extinction ratio between 10 and 20.

The input and output power with an extinction ratio of r are given by the following equations:

$$P_0=2P \div r+1$$
$$P_1=2rP \div r+1$$

The power penalty due to extinction ratio in a practical system is given by the following equation:

$$PP=-10\log[r-1\div r+1]$$

The upper limit for the power transmitted is dictated by the safety considerations for the system. Therefore, the actual formula depends on the limiting factor for that particular system.

The type of modulation used might be direct, or separate, external modulation. Although direct modulation is cheaper, it causes pulse broadening. This increases the system's power penalty.

RECEIVER DESIGN PARAMETERS

The main parameters that need to be considered in designing a receiver are its sensitivity and the load. Sensitivity is defined as the average output power required for obtaining a particular BER at a certain bit rate. The overload parameter defines the maximum power input that a receiver can accept. APD receivers are highly sensitive and are mostly used in high-bit-rate systems that usually operate at 2.5Gbps. Pin receivers along with optical preamplifiers can produce sensitivity comparable to APD receivers.

→ To learn more about avalanche photodiodes and pin receivers, **see** "Receivers," **p.78** (Chapter 4)

OPTICAL AMPLIFIER TYPES AND DESIGN

Optical amplifiers are widely used for long-distance applications. They have become an essential component to compensate for system losses. The most widely used amplifiers are Erbium-Doped Fiber Amplifiers (EDFAs). All optical amplifiers increase the power level of the incident light by a *stimulated emission* process. The mechanism of *population inversion* used in laser diodes is applied.

→ To learn more about stimulated emission and population inversion, **see** "Basic Laser Principles," **p.72** (Chapter 4)

The basic types of optical amplifiers and their applications are described in the following sections.

INLINE OR LINE OPTICAL AMPLIFIERS

When single-mode fibers are used for transmission, the effect of fiber dispersion is minimal, because only a single mode is propagating within the fiber, and there is no overlapping of signals. Therefore, the signal being transmitted does not require complete regeneration. A simple amplifier is sufficient to compensate for signal losses. This is shown in Figure 7.2.

Figure 7.2
Line amplifiers for simple regeneration of signals.

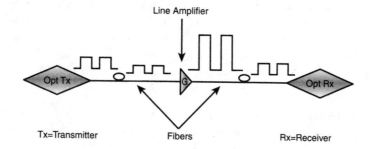

PREAMPLIFIERS

Optical preamplifiers provide larger gain and higher bandwidth than APDs. They are used as front-end amplifiers for optical receivers. They increase the strength of the optical signal at the receiver end. They suppress the noise produced due to receiver electronics. An optical link with a preamplifier is shown in Figure 7.3.

Figure 7.3
A preamplifier, used to improve receiver sensitivity.

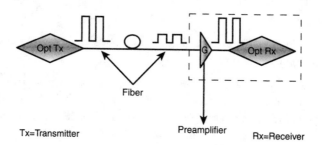

POWER AMPLIFIERS

These devices are placed immediately after the transmitters to boost the signal power, as shown in Figure 7.4. This causes an increase in the signal transmission distance, depending on the gain of the power amplifier and the losses in the fiber. The amplifier is designed to provide maximum output power.

Figure 7.4
A power amplifier boosts the signal power.

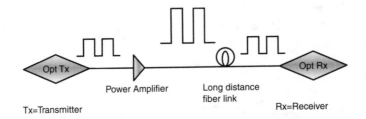

Power Amplifier

Long distance fiber link

Tx=Transmitter

Rx=Receiver

The amplifier is not a perfect device, so certain deviations from the ideal behavior need to be considered. First, noise is generated in the amplifier. Second, the amplifier gain depends on the power input. When the input power is high, the amplifier saturates and the gain starts decreasing. This might cause undesirable power variations in the network. In EDFAs, the gain is not constant over the passband. This might also result in problems in the network when many amplifiers are cascaded. This is because the signal degrades along the chain of fiber as the number of cascaded stages increases. The power transients present in the amplifier stages might cause the gain to increase, thus reducing the input power to the amplifier. Automatic Gain Control (AGC) is employed to keep the output power of each amplifier stage constant, regardless of the input power.

The output power of an optical amplifier depends on the pump power and the amplifier design. The amplifier's saturated gain is therefore given by the following equation:

$$G = 1 + P_{sat} \div P_{in} \ln G_{max} \div G$$

where

G_{max} is the unsaturated gain.

G is the saturated gain.

P_{sat} is the saturation input power.

P_{in} is the input power.

Figure 7.5 shows the plot of amplifier gain versus input signal power. The amplifier gain decreases as the input power increases.

When cascaded amplifiers are used, amplifier gain becomes a critical issue. This is because the amplifier gain is not the same at each wavelength. Therefore, small variations in the gain at the input cause large variations in the power difference of the channels at the output. Therefore, you must design amplifiers with a flat passband.

Figure 7.5
Dependence of amplifier gain on input power.

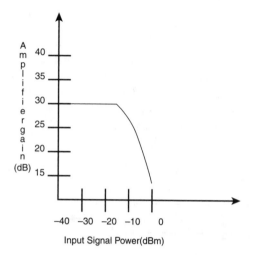

Few approaches have been proposed to overcome the lack of gain flatness. One of these approaches is *pre-emphasis*. In this case, the low-gain signals are amplified or transmitted with higher powers. The main objective of a pre-emphasis circuit is that the receivers must receive the signals with the same signal-to-noise ratio, and it must be within the receiver's dynamic range. However, the amount of equalization that can be performed is limited, so additional techniques might be needed.

Another method is to provide equalization at each stage of the amplifier. Here, after every stage, the channel powers are equalized. This is done by demultiplexing the channels, attenuating the signals, and then multiplexing them back together. This increases the hardware in the path and therefore adds penalties. Another method uses an Acousto-Optic Tunable Filter (AOTF), in which each channel is attenuated differently by applying RF signals at varying frequencies. Each RF signal controls the attenuation of a particular wavelength. By controlling the signal's RF powers, equalization is achieved. This method has limitations, such as requiring much RF power. Additional losses in both cases are also present due to crosstalk. The best solution is to use an optical filter within the amplifier having a carefully designed passband to compensate for the amplifier's gain spectrum. This ensures a flat spectrum at the amplifier's output.

→ To learn more about AOTF, **see** "Acousto-Optic Tunable Filter," **p.59** (Chapter 3)

TYPES OF CROSSTALK

Crosstalk is the undesired interference of signals on the desired signal. Most of the components of a WDM system, such as filters, wavelength multiplexers and demultiplexers, switches, optical amplifiers, and the fiber itself, induce crosstalk. There are two types of crosstalk in signals—*interchannel* and *intrachannel*. Crosstalk causes a power penalty.

PART

II

CH

7

INTRACHANNEL CROSSTALK

Intrachannel crosstalk arises if the interfering signal is at a wavelength that is within the receiver's electrical bandwidth. This causes the interfering signal to leak into the desired signal's receiver. One source of this type of crosstalk is when the wavelength demultiplexer is cascaded with a wavelength multiplexer, as shown in Figure 7.6. Ideally, a demultiplexer separates incoming wavelengths onto different output fibers. However, owing to the nonideal suppression of the signal at the demultiplexer, a portion of the signal at wavelength λ_i leaks into the adjacent channel having a wavelength of λ_{i+1}.

Figure 7.6
Intrachannel crosstalk caused by signals interfering at wavelengths within the receiver's electrical bandwidth.

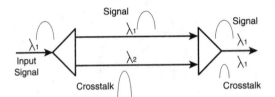

Another reason for crosstalk is the nonideal isolation of the ports in a switch from one another. Maximum crosstalk is introduced when the polarization state of the crosstalk signal is the same as that of the interfering signal. The crosstalk is also at a maximum when the interfering signal and the input desired signal are exactly out of phase. Therefore, the system must be designed considering these factors.

INTERCHANNEL CROSSTALK

Interchannel crosstalk occurs when the interfering signal is at a wavelength that is very different from the desired signal, such that their difference is greater than the receiver's electrical bandwidth. There are various causes of interchannel crosstalk. For example, a demultiplexer is meant to select one channel and reject the others. However, this is not the case with practical systems, because the demultiplexer might not be accurately tuned to the channel's specific wavelength. An optical switch might also cause crosstalk if the isolation between the switch's ports is imperfect. Figure 7.7 shows interchannel crosstalk caused by an optical switch.

Figure 7.7
Interchannel crosstalk in an optical switch.

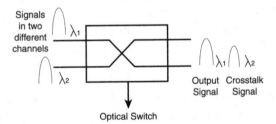

CROSSTALK IN NETWORKS

Crosstalk is an important factor that must be considered in networks. Because the signal travels through many nodes in the network, it accumulates crosstalk from the components at each node.

CROSSTALK IN BIDIRECTIONAL SYSTEMS

In bidirectional systems, transmission of data occurs in both directions over one fiber (see Figure 7.8). Although ideally it is not wrong to transmit data at the same wavelength in both directions, it is usually not preferred because of reflections. It might happen that the back reflection that is close to the transmitter at one end—say, end X—will cause a lot of power to the receiver of X, causing crosstalk. The reflected power might be larger than the power received at the other end—say, end Y. The reflections at the end equipment can be controlled, but it is difficult to limit them within the fiber. Therefore, such systems use different wavelengths in different directions. Optical circulators and WDM mux/demux might be used to separate the two directions at the end.

Figure 7.8
A bidirectional transmission system, where data transmission occurs in both directions.

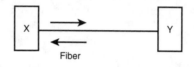

In a circulator, crosstalk arises due to imperfect isolation. If WDM mux/demux is used, crosstalk arises because the signal being transmitted might get reflected within the multiplexer to a port that is used to receive the signal. Figure 7.9 shows a bidirectional network using mux/demux.

Figure 7.9
Separating the directions in a bidirectional system using WDM mux/demux. This method introduces crosstalk.

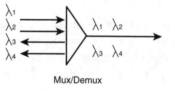

CROSSTALK REDUCTION TECHNIQUES

You can efficiently reduce crosstalk if the suppression is done at the device level. The network designer calculates the crosstalk suppression required at each of the devices cascaded. Crosstalk is minimized using the approaches discussed in this section.

One approach is spatial dilation, in which a 2×2 optical switch having crosstalk E is used. To minimize crosstalk, the switch is dilated by adding unused ports to it, reducing the crosstalk to E^2, as shown in Figure 7.10. In this case, the number of switches becomes large, so dilation is difficult to achieve.

Another approach to reduce crosstalk is to use wavelength dilation. This is useful if a single switch must handle multiple wavelengths.

Figure 7.10
The spatial dilation technique reduces crosstalk.

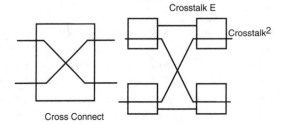

In a network, many mux/demux and filters are cascaded. When cascading is done, the overall passband is much smaller than the passband of the individual filters. Therefore, as the number of cascaded stages increases, the required wavelength stability and accuracy also goes up. The narrowing of the passband when cascaded stages increase is shown in Figure 7.11.

Figure 7.11
Narrowing of the bandwidth as the number of filter stages increases.

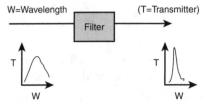

DISPERSION PENALTY

Dispersion occurs when the different components of the signal being transmitted travel with different velocities in the fiber and arrive at the receiver at different times. The signal at the receiving end arrives smeared because of dispersion. This causes the signals to interfere with each other, leading to power penalties. The length of the fiber decides the amount of dispersion induced.

The various types of dispersion present in optical communication systems are modal, polarization, and chromatic. Modal dispersion occurs only in multimode fibers because of the different modes traveling with different velocities. Polarization mode dispersion (PMD) arises because of imperfections in the fiber core. Chromatic dispersion occurs when a pulse's different frequency components travel with different group velocities within the fiber and reach the other end at different times. Chromatic dispersion is measured in terms of ps/nm-km, in which ps (picoseconds) is the time spread of the pulse, nm is the spectral width of the pulse, and km is the link length.

PENALTY FOR CHROMATIC DISPERSION

The exact derivation of the penalty for chromatic dispersion is quite complicated. The limitation for chromatic dispersion is given by the following equation:

$$D \ LB(\delta\lambda) < E$$

where

D is the chromatic dispersion of the fiber at the operating wavelength.

B is the bit rate.

L is the link length.

$\delta\lambda$ is the spectral width of the transmitted signal.

E is the fraction of the bit period.

The spectral width depends on the type of source, which can be modulated either directly or externally. However, the spectral width increases due to *chirp*.

> **Note**
> When a laser input signal oscillating in a single longitudinal mode is directly modulated, there is a dynamic broadening of the pulse known as *frequency chirp*.

Decreasing the extinction ratio can reduce chirp. The spectral width of the signal also increases because of back reflections from the various components, such as connectors, splices, and so on.

Dispersion management is an important issue in WDM networks. There are several ways to reduce chromatic dispersion:

- Modulate externally in combination with direct feedback lasers.
- Use fiber that has a small amount of dispersion.
- Provide dispersion compensation.

External modulation is used for high-speed systems. They reduce the nonlinearities that are induced, such as chirp and dispersion. An external modulator modifies the output power emitted by the laser. A variety of external modulators are available, either as an independent device or as an integrated package with the lasers.

The other two methods are discussed in the following sections.

SINGLE-MODE FIBER TYPES AND THEIR APPLICATIONS

Three types of single-mode fibers are used. They have differing chromatic dispersion, depending on how they are manufactured.

Standard single-mode fiber is the most commonly deployed fiber in the United States and Europe. It was designed to provide zero-chromatic dispersion at a wavelength of 1310nm for long-distance transmission. The maximum chromatic dispersion of such fibers is about 20ps/nm-km at 1550nm and is typically 17ps/nm-km.

Dispersion-Shifted Fiber (DSF) was developed because of the need for low-loss and zero-chromatic dispersion at 1550nm. DSF has a chromatic dispersion maximum of 3.3ps/nm-km and typically 0 at 1550nm. This kind of fiber is widely deployed in Japan.

Nonzero Dispersion Fiber (NDF) came into existence because DSF was unsuitable for WDM networks because of the high penalty caused by four-wave mixing and fiber nonlinearities.

NDF has a chromatic dispersion in the 1 to 6ps/nm-kmin 1550nm range. This reduces the penalty caused by fiber nonlinearities and also maintains the advantages of DSF.

Dispersion-Compensated Fiber (DCF) reduces the effect of FWM by inserting into the link a loop of fiber having characteristics that negate the effect of the accumulated dispersion on the transmitting fiber. This process is called *dispersion compensation*. If the transmitting fiber has low positive dispersion, the DCF has negative dispersion. Therefore, the total accumulated dispersion after some distance is zero. However, the absolute dispersion at all points on the fiber is nonzero, which causes phase mismatch between wavelength channels. This eliminates the possibility of effective FWM production.

POLARIZATION-MODE DISPERSION

Owing to the ellipticity of the fiber core, different polarization travels with different velocities in the fiber, causing Polarization-Mode Dispersion (PMD). The signal energy distributed over the different state of polarization changes slowly with time. This might occur because of variations in the ambient temperature, which also increases PMD. The individual components of the network add to PMD as well. Many polarization-dependent effects influence system performance. One of these is Polarization-Dependent Loss (PDL)—the loss of a component that depends on the State of Polarization (SOP). SOP also fluctuates with the Signal-to-Noise Ratio (SNR), so careful attention must be paid to keep the PDL within limits.

NONLINEAR EFFECTS IN A FIBER

The fiber can be considered a linear medium as long as the optical power in the fiber is small. However, when the power level is large, the nonlinear effects need to be considered. These effects play an important role in high-speed and WDM systems.

Two effects cause nonlinearities. The first one is because of the scattering effects caused by the interaction of lightwaves or phonons in the silica medium.

The two main scattering effects observed are Stimulated Raman Scattering (SRS) and Stimulated Brillouin Scattering (SBS). The second set occurs because of the dependence of the refractive index on the optical power. It includes FWM, SPM, and XPM.

→ To learn more about the limitations of nonlinearities on optical communication systems, **see** "Nonlinear Effects," **p.39** (Chapter 2)

SRS is caused when two or more signals at different wavelengths are injected into the fiber and power is transferred from lower- to higher-wavelength channels. SRS is not a big problem in systems that have a small number of channels, due to the signal's high threshold power, but it might cause severe effects when the number of wavelengths is large. Adopting certain measures reduces the effects of SRS:

- Keep closely spaced channels.
- Reduce the distance between the amplifiers to bring the power level below the threshold.

SBS occurs when the lightwaves involved are acoustic phonons. In this case, the interaction occurs at a very narrow line width of about 20Mhz. SBS occurs if the line width is 20Mhz or greater. It can create significant distortion in a single channel. SBS produces gain in the direction opposite the direction of transmission that depletes the transmitted signal and requires an isolator to shield the signal at the transmitter end.

The SBS penalty can be reduced as follows:

- Keep the power below the SBS threshold.
- Increase the source's line width.
- Use phase modulation rather than amplitude modulation, because it reduces the power present in the optical carrier, thereby reducing the power penalty.

Four-wave mixing depends on the phase of the interfering signals. When the interfering signals travel with the same group velocity—that is, no dispersion—the effect of FWM is greater. However, when the interfering signals travel with different group velocities, the waves overlap in and out of phase, and the net effect reduces the mixing efficiency.

Doing the following can reduce the penalty due to FWM:

- Choose the channel spacing carefully so that there is proper overlapping of the signal.
- Increase the channel spacing, because this increases the mismatch of the group velocities. However, this increases the system's overall bandwidth and the penalty due to SRS.
- Reduce the transmitter power and amplifier spacing.
- Introduce different delays in the transmission path to randomize the phase relationship between the various wavelengths. This is achieved by multiplexing/demultiplexing wavelengths in the middle of the transmission path.

WAVELENGTH STABILIZATION

In WDM systems, the wavelength drift due to temperature variations is negligible. Typically, mux/demux made up of silica has a temperature coefficient of 0.01nm/°C. DFB has a temperature coefficient of 0.1nm/°C.

The DFB laser must be kept wavelength-stabilized. If the laser temperature is maintained within +/–0.1°C, it is possible to stabilize the laser to +/–0.01nm/°C. The laser comes with a thermistor and a cooler. The variations in the thermistor's resistance are used to monitor the temperature. The laser's wavelength also changes due to the laser's aging. Sometimes an external feedback loop is used, where a portion of the output is returned to a frequency discriminator at the input. This stabilizes the laser output. Changes in the wavelength at the output due to temperature can be monitored.

Depending on the temperature range, wavelength stabilization might also become necessary for mux/demux. For example, if the multiplexer and demultiplexer are aligned at an ambient temperature of 25°C, the ends of the link might differ by 50°. If a temperature coefficient of 0.01nm/°C is assumed, there is a difference of 0.5nm between the center wavelengths of the multiplexer and demultiplexer. This difference is very high.

The laser wavelength also depends on the *drive power*. Therefore, the drive power must be constant so that there is no wavelength shift because of current changes. As the laser ages, the need for the drive current to produce the same output increases. The output power also decreases with time. With tighter channel spacings, the laser is operated at constant output power, tolerating the penalty due to reduced power output.

DESIGN CONSIDERATIONS IN A SYSTEM

You have seen the different system parameters and their interactions that need to be considered while designing an optical network. The type of fibers that are used for optical systems vary with the data rate, the distance of transmission, and the fiber's limitations.

DIFFERENT TYPES OF FIBER

The choice of fiber to be used depends on which type of system is deployed:

- For single-channel systems, DSF is an ideal choice, because these systems operate at very high bit rates over long transmission distances. However, DSF is unsuitable for WDM networks because of FWM.

- If there is no limitation on chromatic dispersion, SMF is the best choice, because it is least affected by the fiber's nonlinearities.

- As bit rates and the distance increase, chromatic dispersion becomes limited and dispersion compensation needs to be applied. DCF is used in such cases.

- For WDM systems over long distances and high bit rates, NDF is a good alternative.

SPACING BETWEEN AMPLIFIERS AND THE POWER TRANSMITTED

The power transmitted per channel is limited by the saturation power of the optical amplifier, nonlinear effects, and safety factors. The distance between amplifier stages is maximized to reduce the number of amplifiers, thus reducing the cost. The power transmitted per channel, link length, amplifier noise figure, and receiver sensitivity determines the maximum distance between the amplifier stages. The penalty due to nonlinearities might also decrease the amplifier spacing.

CHANNEL SPACING

The wavelength spacing must be as large as possible to make it easier to multiplex and demultiplex the channels. This also reduces the penalty due to FWM and allows future upgrades for higher bit rates.

However, if the channel spacing is tight, you can accommodate more channels in the limited amplifier bandwidth. It is also easier to flatten the gain of an amplifier over a smaller bandwidth. The penalty due to SRS also decreases if the bandwidth is small.

WAVELENGTHS

The number of wavelengths that can be used in a system is decided by the total amplifier output power. The limited output power needs to be shared among the different channels in the system. So as the number of wavelengths increases, the power per channel decreases; thus, the total system span also decreases. The wavelength stability and selectivity of mux/demux also limits the number of wavelengths.

ALL-OPTICAL NETWORKS

In an All-Optical Network (AON), the switching and routing functions are performed without any electronic regeneration. The design of a network is more difficult than a point-to point link for the following reasons:

- The network is susceptible to crosstalk.
- The problem of mux/demux misalignment is more pronounced in a network than in a point-to-point link.
- Wavelength stability and accuracy requirements are tighter because of bandwidth narrowing in cascaded mux/demux.
- Equalization of power is required, because the lightwaves travel through different paths and have different path lengths.
- Loss, nonlinearities, and dispersion are greater, because they accumulate at each node.

TRANSPARENCY TO VARIOUS FORMATS

WDM systems are advantageous because they are transparent to bit rate, protocol, and the modulation format. A WDM system can be designed to operate at a maximum bit rate, and it supports all bit rates below that maximum. The maximum bit rate affects amplifier spacing, bandwidths, and dispersion. Therefore, the system must be designed to support a maximum bit rate.

SUMMARY

This chapter covered the effect of impairments, considering the typical example of a WDM system. Problems caused by power penalty, amplifier cascades, dispersion, nonlinearities, and crosstalk play a significant role in the new generation of optical networks. The two types of crosstalk in the system are intrachannel and interchannel. Point-to-point links do not suffer much because of these impairments. Different types of fibers are also used, depending on the application and the system's limitations. These include Dispersion-Shifted Fiber (DSF), Dispersion-Compensated Fiber (DCF), and Nonzero Dispersion Fiber (NDF). Transmission system design requires careful consideration of each of these impairments. The system must be designed considering the various penalties caused by the components, and the overall cost of the system must be minimized.

PART

II

CH

7

CHAPTER 8

GENERATIONS OF OPTICAL NETWORKS

In this chapter

FIRST-GENERATION OPTICAL NETWORKS

Optical networks might be classified into first-generation and second-generation networks based on the evolution of networks. First-generation optical networks use optical fiber as the transmission medium. However, all the switching, processing, and routing functions are performed using electronic equipment. First-generation optical networks include synchronous optical networks (SONET), synchronous digital hierarchy (SDH) networks, and asynchronous transfer mode (ATM) networks. These form the heart of the telecommunications infrastructure in North America, Europe, and Japan, respectively. First-generation networks also include a variety of enterprise networks, such as enterprise system connection (ESCON), high-performance parallel interface (HIPPI) networks, and fiber channel networks, which are used for computer interconnections with other computers and peripheral systems. First-generation optical networks also include fiber distributed data interface (FDDI) networks, widely deployed in local area networks (LANs), and metropolitan area networks (MANs). The following sections explore these networks in detail.

SYNCHRONOUS DIGITAL HIERARCHY NETWORKS

Earlier networks that were based on plesiochronous transmission were unable to meet the demands of services such as videoconferencing, remote database access, and multimedia file transfer, because these required more bandwidth.

PLESIOCHRONOUS DIGITAL HIERARCHY

To understand the factors that led to the standardization of SDH, this section discusses how multiplexing was done in networks prior to SDH. In the early 1970s, digital transmission systems began to make their presence known by utilizing a method known as pulse code modulation (PCM), proposed by Northern Telecom Company in North America in 1937. PCM defined a method by which analog waves could be represented in binary forms. Using this method, it was possible to represent a standard 4KHz analog signal as a 64Kbps digital bit stream. Therefore, this capability was believed to produce less-expensive transmission systems by combining several PCM channels and transmitting them along the same copper wire, which previously had been occupied by a single analog signal.

The European countries had adopted a standard time-division multiplexing (TDM) scheme in which 30 64Kbps channels were combined to produce a single channel with an approximate bit rate of 2Mbps. As the demand for telephonic applications increased, the levels of traffic in the network increased. Consequently, the 2Mbps bit stream rate was insufficient to cope with the excess traffic occurring in the network. To avoid using a large number of 2Mbps links, it was decided to use another level of multiplexing. Europe implemented this standard by combining four 2Mbps channels to produce a single 8Mbps channel. This type of multiplexing differed from the previous one in that the incoming signals were combined 1 bit at a time instead of 1 byte at a time. This method of combining 1 bit at a time is known as *bit interleaving*, and combining 1 byte at a time is known as *byte interleaving*.

Further levels of multiplexing were introduced to the existing standards as traffic increased. This resulted in bit rates, such as 34Mbps, 140Mbps, and 565Mbps, that provided a hierarchy of bit rates. However, this multiplexing hierarchy had some drawbacks. When a number of 2Mbps channels were multiplexed, these channels might differ slightly from one another in their bit rates because each channel is generated by different pieces of equipment with slightly different bit rates. Therefore, before the two channels are bit-interleaved, they must be brought up to the same bit rate through the addition of dummy bits called *justification bits*. This process of adding dummy bits is called *bit stuffing*. These dummy bits must be discarded during the demultiplexing of signals to get back the original signal. This process is called a *plesiochronous operation*, which means "almost synchronous" in Greek. The problem of slightly differing bit rates between channels that are to be combined existed in all the levels of the multiplexing hierarchy. Therefore, the use of plesiochronous operation throughout the multiplexing levels led to the adoption of a standard called plesiochronous digital hierarchy (PDH).

PDH has the following limitations:

- PDH is inflexible. It cannot extend itself by linking to other high-speed systems.

- The process of multiplexing and demultiplexing is very tedious, because the task of identifying the exact location of the justification bit and extracting it is time-consuming.

- Managing the huge amount of multiplexing equipment in the network poses a great problem.

- The PDH has very little provision for performance monitoring and network management.

ORIGIN AND MULTIPLEXING TECHNIQUES OF SDH

PDH had reached a point where it could not withstand the increasing demand for bandwidth. In addition, the process of extracting the individual signal bits from high- capacity systems by demultiplexing the whole system and multiplexing it back became very tedious. As a result, synchronous transmission systems took over from PDH. Synchronous transmission systems came into existence based on many needs, such as network management capability, standard interfaces between equipment from different vendors, and the need for similar standards in the United States and Europe. The work performed to fulfill these needs resulted in the development of synchronous digital hierarchy (SDH) by the Consultative Committee for International Telegraph and Telephone (CCITT). In North America, the American National Standards Institute (ANSI) published its SONET standards, which are actually thought of as a subset of worldwide SDH standards. The CCITT standardized a number of basic transmission rates within the SDH. The first of these is 155Mbps, normally referred to as STM-1, where STM stands for synchronous transfer mode. Higher transmission rates such as STM-4 (equivalent to 622Mbps) and STM-16 (equivalent to 2.4Gbps) were also defined. The SDH recommendation by CCITT also defined a multiplexing structure in which an STM-1 signal can carry a number of lower-rate signals as payload, thereby allowing the PDH signals to be carried over a synchronous network. As a result, the transition from PDH to SDH became very smooth, and the network still used the existing PDH equipment. PDH signals in the range of 1.5Mbps and 140Mbps can be packaged into an STM-1 frame.

The SDH multiplexing hierarchy is shown in Figure 8.1. SDH defines a number of containers, each of which corresponds to a specific plesiochronous rate. The plesiochronous signal is mapped to an appropriate container. Each container has some control information known as *path overhead*. The path overhead contains data on error rates, which in turn helps in the management of networks. The container and the path overhead together form a virtual container (VC).

Figure 8.1
The SDH hierarchy showing the different mapping of lower signals.

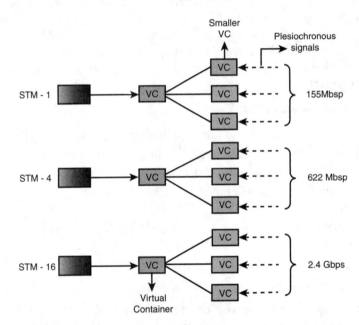

The process of loading containers and attaching overheads to it is repeated at all levels of the SDH system, resulting in the nesting or multiplexing of smaller VCs to larger ones.

In a synchronous network, all the equipment is synchronized to an overall network clock. Sometimes there might be a delay in the transmission link, and the location of VCs inside an STM-1 frame might also not be fixed. Therefore, each VC is tracked using a pointer that is added to the overload of the larger VC. The small VCs might in turn contain pointers to the smaller VCs within it. This multiplexing structure makes it easy to extract a low-speed stream from a high-speed stream, thereby overcoming the drawback faced by multiplexing in a PDH system. The process of multiplexing smaller VCs into larger ones is repeated until a single large VC is obtained. This large VC is loaded into the payload area of the STM-1 frame. The payload area of the STM-1 frame becomes full because of the nesting of large VCs and the addition of more information to the section overhead area of the STM-1 frame. The section overhead contains control information about the operation, administration, maintenance, and provision (often called OAM&P) facilities and stays with the payload for all multiplexing stages.

ADVANTAGES OF SDH

The SDH system has the following advantages:

- SDH has many techniques for network survivability. In case one of its links fails, the network's self-healing ring architecture automatically diverts the traffic until the link is repaired. Deployment of optical fibers throughout the network and use of control information during data transmission guarantees high performance and low rate of breakdowns.

- The network management functions incorporated in the SDH frame structure provide many functions, such as performance monitoring, configuration management, network security, and inventory management.

- The SDH network uses less equipment. This leads to lower cost in terms of maintenance and power consumption.

- The SDH standardizes the different transmission equipment, even to the smallest level, so that network operators can buy equipment from different vendors with relative ease.

- SDH offers a future-proof network that will not become obsolete in the near future, because SDH can upgrade the software and add extensions to the existing equipment.

SYNCHRONOUS OPTICAL NETWORKS

A synchronous optical network (SONET) is a standard for optical transmission formulated by Exchange Carriers Standards Association (ECSA) for ANSI, which sets industry standards in the United States for many industries, including the telecommunications industry. The SONET standard has also been recognized by the International Telecommunication Union (ITU), which sets standards for international telecommunications. SONET offers the following benefits, which earned it worldwide recognition:

- Compatibility of equipment from different vendors that manufacture according to standards

- Synchronous networking

- Enhanced OAM&P facilities

- A more efficient way of multiplexing using add/drop multiplexing

- Standards-based self-healing survivable rings in the network to prevent network breakdowns

- Compatibility to transport other services, such as ATM

The multiplexing techniques of SONET are very similar to SDH, except that some of the terms in the SONET architecture are different.

→ To learn more about SONET and its applications, **see** Chapter 9, "Synchronous Optical Networks," **p. 167**

ASYNCHRONOUS TRANSFER MODE NETWORKS

In this information age, there is constant demand for various new services, such as High-Definition TV (HDTV), videoconferencing, high-speed data transfer, video telephony, and home education through distance learning. This big demand introduced the need for a flexible network that would provide all these services in the same way. However, today's telecommunication networks are specially designed to provide only one specific service and are incapable of transporting any other service. They suffer from the following drawbacks:

- Each network supports only one specific service.
- New services in the future might have unknown requirements. A service-specific network is incapable of providing these new service requirements.
- Sharing resources between networks is impossible.

Therefore, the need arose for a single flexible network that could do the following:

- Support all types of services
- Customize itself to the new needs of future services
- Use its resources efficiently and share them with other networks
- Use new technologies, such as optical and semiconductor technologies

This led to the evolution of the ATM network.

ATM is defined as a high-performance network that uses packet switching and multiplexing techniques to transfer data through fixed-length cells of 53 bytes, each capable of carrying different types of traffic. ATM is a switch technology, which makes it different from the traditional LAN architecture. Specifically, ATM is a CCITT standard for cell switching that operates at ANSI speeds ranging from 1.544Mbps to 10Gbps. Large packet switches can be built rather inexpensively with the use of fixed cell size.

> **Note**
>
> With *packet switching*, messages are divided into packets, which contain the destination address, before they are sent. Each packet is then transmitted individually through the same or different routes to its destination. After all the packets forming a message arrive at the destination, they are recompiled into the original message.

→ To learn more about switches and their applications, **see** "Switches," **p. 83** (Chapter 4)

ATM TECHNOLOGY

The use of variable-length packets resulted in unpredictable delays, which in turn made a network unsuitable for carrying voice and video data. However, all information is transmitted in the form of fixed-length packets in ATM. These packet cells consist of 48 bytes of user information plus 5 bytes for the header, as shown in Figure 8.2. ATM is suitable for carrying real-time information because the cell size is fixed and network delay and retrieval time can be predicted.

Note

ATM cells are standardized at 53 bytes because of an international compromise. During the standardization process there was a conflict within the International Telegraph and Telephone Consultative Committee (CCITT) regarding the payload size of an ATM cell. The United States wanted 64 byte payloads because it was optimal for U.S. networks. European countries and Japan wanted 32 byte payloads because it was optimal for their networks. In the end, a 48 byte payload was selected as a compromise. This 48 byte payload plus the five byte header equals 53 bytes for the ATM cell.

Figure 8.2
The frame structure of the ATM cell.

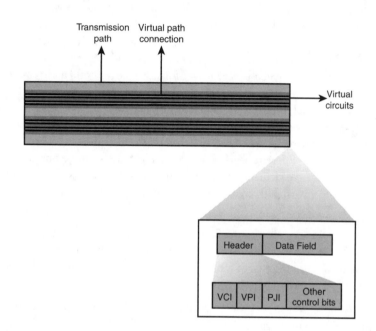

INFORMATION TRANSFER IN ATM   Two factors play an important part in the process of information transfer in ATM: *error-free transmission* and *transmission on time*.

Error-free transmission determines a network's capability to transfer error-free information. Errors are introduced as a result of imperfections such as noise caused by the telecommunication system, blocking of traffic due to limited equipment, and system errors. Bit error rate (BER) is the parameter used to measure imperfections. It is defined as the ratio between erroneous bits and transmitted bits.

Time transparency determines a network's capability to transport information from the source to the destination in minimal time. It can also be defined as the absence of delays. Delays play an important role in real-time services, such as video and voice. These services can be disrupted by very large delays.

An ATM cell structure has a data field and a header, as shown in Figure 8.2. The header is used to identify the cells of a virtual channel through an identifier. An identifier is assigned when a call is set up to transfer information through the proper routing of packets. To learn more about virtual channels, you will now see how information is transferred in an ATM network.

Information is transferred between users in a network through connections. ATM is connection-oriented. Because of this, a logical/virtual connection is set up before information flows from the terminal to the network. The two types of connections in an ATM are *virtual path connections* and *virtual channel connections*.

A virtual channel (VC) connection, otherwise known as a *virtual circuit*, is the basic unit used in information transfer. It carries a steady stream of cells, in a certain order, between users. A collection of virtual circuits can be nested in a virtual path connection. A *virtual path* is a connection that is set up end-to-end across a network. The ATM network does not transfer individual cells that belong to a particular virtual circuit. All cells within a virtual path are routed the same way, which is very useful for fast recovery of data in case of system breakdown. With an ATM network, a user can directly connect to another user by establishing a virtual circuit, which can transfer data over the network without any additional overhead. An ATM also uses virtual paths internally for the purpose of nesting virtual circuits between switches in the network. Two ATM switches might have different virtual channel connections belonging to different users. These virtual channels can be bundled by the two ATM switches into a single virtual path connection. Therefore, this virtual path connection can be handled by the virtual path cross-connects, between the two switches, as a single channel.

Virtual circuits can be permanently established, thereby giving users steady access, or they can be set up dynamically for the duration of the call. Setting up the VC dynamically allows the network service to adjust itself to the demand by allocating more bandwidth to a particular virtual circuit during peak traffic. This establishment includes the allocation of ATM cell identifiers and resources.

The different ATM cell identifiers are Virtual Path Identifier (VPI), Virtual Channel Identifier (VCI), and Payload Type Identifier (PTI). VPI and VCI are unique for cells that belong to the same virtual path and virtual circuits within that path. Within a virtual circuit, the cells are assigned a unique PTI, depending on the type of information they carry. The information might be user information or special information about network management and control.

ATM handles the needs of both voice and data, thereby rejoining the communication that was disjointed by computers and telephones. ATM has strong support from manufacturers, telephone companies, and users, both domestically and internationally. ATM offers the following four service rates:

- **Constant Bit Rate (CBR)**—Specifies a fixed bit rate so that data is sent in a steady stream. This is similar to a leased line.

- **Variable Bit Rate (VBR)**—Provides a specified data transfer rate. However, data is not sent evenly. This is ideal for voice and videoconferencing data.

- **Unspecified Bit Rate (UBR)**—Does not guarantee any data transfer levels. This is used for applications that can tolerate delays, such as file transfer.

- **Available Bit Rate (ABR)**—Provides a guaranteed minimum capacity. It allows data to be transmitted in bursts at higher capacities when the network is free.

ENTERPRISE SERIAL CONNECTION NETWORKS

To meet the information and processing needs of the future, today's enterprise networks need to transfer data at a very fast rate. Today's data centers (where data is stored) must do the following:

- Move data over a longer distance so that processors, cables, and control units can be located and interconnected beyond boundaries
- Share the available resources as the network grows, and manage them dynamically
- Interconnect to local and wide area networks

IBM's Enterprise Systems Connection (ESCON) meets all these requirements. ESCON is a marketing name for a set of IBM and vendor products. ESCON interconnects mainframe computers with one another, with the attached storage area or data center, with locally attached workstations, and with other devices using fiber-optic technology and dynamically modifiable switches called *ESCON directors*. In IBM mainframes, the local interconnection of hardware units is known as channel connection or local connection. ESCON's fiber-optic cabling can extend the local networks connected to the mainframe network up to 60 kilometers with a chain of director switches. The data rate on the link itself is up to 200Mbps. Vendors might provide additional distance and higher amounts of throughput.

IBM's ESCON provides the following features:

- **Fiber-optic links**—An ESCON fiber-optic link consists of optical fiber technology, the ESCON I/O (input/output) interface, and ESCON products.
- **Dynamic connectivity**—In an enterprise network, vital data traffic becomes heavy due to high traffic demand. Therefore, the network must have a backup facility that is immediately triggered in case of severe system breakdown. The backup can be in the form of hardware equipment and network elements. Therefore, the network needs to be flexible and should connect to other channels, which act as control units to manage the network. The connections must have less equipment, and new control units must be added without disturbing the existing setup. One setup's channels and control units must not be affected by the failure of other channels, even though they coexist. All these needs are addressed by the concept of *dynamic connectivity*. Dynamic connectivity is achieved by constructing a physical layout of the ESCON network using *switched point-to-point topology*. In this topology, multiple channels can share the same path by switching between channels and control units. Therefore, the process of adding channels or control units is easy. You connect these channels to the nearby switching point, which provides a path across the entire network. In addition, the number of physical interfaces drastically decreases, as shown in Figure 8.3.

Figure 8.3
A switched point-to-point topology in ESCON.

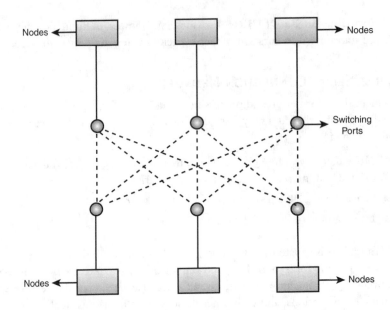

Interconnectivity is the ability to operate across systems with different communication protocols. An ESCON environment extends the network's ability to exchange data with resources inside or outside the enterprise network. Large amounts of data can be sent to remote processors, and these processors can act as backup servers in case of disaster and also for data warehousing.

To support the use of fiber-optic links and to provide dynamic connectivity to these links, ESCON provides a new I/O interface and tools for managing connectivity. In addition, ESCON provides certain provisions to ensure that the existing enterprise networks can coexist and that its resources do not become obsolete. Therefore, enterprise networks can upgrade their networks and start using the ESCON environment.

FIBER DISTRIBUTED DATA INTERFACE

Fiber Distributed Data Interface (FDDI) is the standard for data transmission on fiber-optic cables. FDDI is a LAN-type network with a transmission rate of about 100Mbps. It can support thousands of users. Although it uses optical fiber as the transmission medium, copper wires are used for short distances, mainly to connect end systems.

> **Note**
>
> Another LAN type network, Ethernet—an IEEE standard—enables two or more systems to share a common cabling system. Although originally developed to work over coaxial cables, current Ethernet specification enables it to work over optical fibers also, with speeds of up to 1000Mbps.

The FDDI protocol is based on the token ring protocol. A *token ring* network is a LAN in which all computers are connected in a ring or star topology, as shown in Figure 8.4. A token-passing scheme, binary digit, is used to prevent the collision of data between two computers that want to send messages at the same time. The token ring protocol is the second most widely used protocol on a LAN. The IBM Token Ring protocol led to the development of a standard version, specified as IEEE 802.5. The IEEE 802.5 token ring technology provides for data transfer rates of either 4Mbps or 16Mbps.

Figure 8.4
A token ring network.

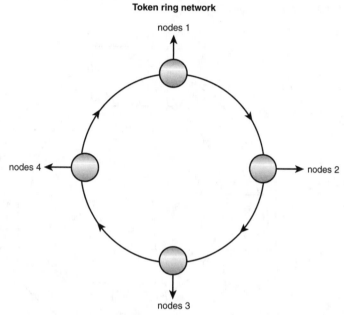

Token ring network

nodes 1

nodes 4

nodes 2

nodes 3

This is how a token ring protocol works:

1. Empty information frames are continuously circulated in the ring network.

2. When a computer has a message to send, it inserts a token into an empty frame. To perform this insertion, 0 is changed to 1 in the token bit part of the frame, and a message and a destination identifier are inserted into the frame.

3. The frame is then examined by each successive workstation in a cyclic fashion. If the workstation finds the message's destination, it copies the message from the frame and changes the token back to 0.

4. When the frame gets back to the original source from where it was sent, the source sees that the token has been changed to 0 and that the message has been copied and received. It then removes the message from the frame.

5. A new frame is constructed to circulate as an empty frame, ready to be taken by a workstation when it has a message to send.

The IEEE sets the standard for the token ring protocol. You will now look at the technology behind the working of FDDI.

FDDI uses a *dual-ring topology*, which contains two token rings rotating in opposite directions (see Figure 8.5). A ring is set up for possible backup in case the primary ring fails. If the secondary ring is not needed for backup, it can also carry data, extending the capacity of data transmission. A *dual-attached station* on the network is attached to both these rings. A dual-attached station on the ring has at least two ports: port 1, where the primary ring comes in and the secondary ring goes out, and port 2, where the secondary ring comes in and the primary ring goes out.

Figure 8.5
A dual-ring topology shown in a FDDI network.

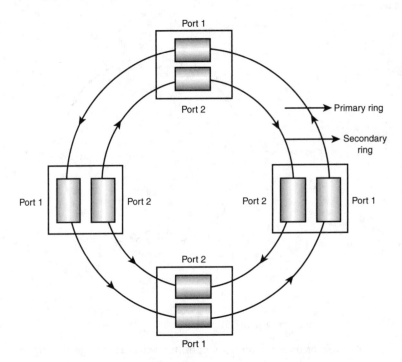

FDDI uses light pulses to transmit data from one station to the next. The FDDI uses a bit as the smallest form of information. A bit can have a 0 or a 1 as its value. FDDI generates this value as the result of a change in the state of the light coming from the other station. A station reads the light, approximately in the interval of 8 nanoseconds, to get a sample of light coming from the other station. The bit values are generated depending on whether the state of light is off or on.

You will now look at how the information is put on the network by the stations. A station gains the right to transmit information when it finds a token being passed on the network. The token is a control signal comprised of a unique sequence of bits that circulates on the medium following each information transmission. When a station has something to send, it captures the token, sends the information in well-formatted FDDI frames, and then releases the token. A FDDI frame consists of many bytes. A collection of bytes corresponds to specific information, such as frame control information, destination address, source address, and information field. After completing the information transfer, the station passes the token to the network. A station on the ring network, which has the same address as the destination address, extracts the data and retransmits the frame to the next station on the ring. When the frame returns to the originating station, a new token, which is devoid of destination address, is issued by the originating station, thereby permitting the other stations to transmit data. In this manner, the token-access control scheme allows all stations to share the network bandwidth in an orderly and efficient manner. FDDI networks also have the capability to support early token release, which can increase the overall speed of the FDDI network to around 140MBps.

Note

In the early token release mechanism, the originating station issues a free token immediately after transmitting the frame, instead of waiting for the token to comeback to the originating station.

FDDI-II is a new version of FDDI that adds the capability to add circuit-switched service to the network so that voice signals can also be handled. Work is underway to connect FDDI networks to the developing SONET.

FIBER CHANNEL

In recent years, the need for faster data transfer has become the order of the day. In addition, high-performance computers have gained focus in the data communication industry. Data-intensive network applications, which require very high speeds of data transfer, are unable to cope with the existing network interconnects between computers. Therefore, fiber channel has become a necessity. Fiber channel combines the best of channel and network technology. The main purpose of fiber channel is to develop a practical and inexpensive means of transferring data between desktop computers, workstations, mainframes, super-computers, and other storage devices. *Fiber channel* is a set of standards defined by ANSI.

There are two basic types of data communication: channels and networks. A *channel* is a closed, direct, hardware-intensive connection that connects external peripheral devices to the workstation. A *network* is an aggregation of connected nodes, such as workstations or file servers, that has its own protocol for managing the interaction between the nodes. A network is unstructured and unpredictable and can easily adapt to a changing environment.

A fiber channel has three topologies: *point-to-point*, *arbitrary loop*, and *fabric*. Let's explore them in detail.

The point-to-point topology consists of two directly connected fiber channel devices, as shown in Figure 8.6. One fiber connects the port of the transmitting device to the port of the receiving device, and the other connects in the reverse direction. There is no sharing of resources. A link must be established between the devices before communication can start.

Figure 8.6
A point-to-point topology in a fiber channel network, where the devices are connected directly.

Transmit fiber

Computer Node — Port

Port — Computer Node

Receive fiber

An arbitrary-loop topology is the most complex and dominant topology in a fiber channel network. It connects to 127 ports. Figure 8.7 shows an arbitrary loop with four ports. An arbitrary loop functions in a manner similar to a token-passing scheme. When a node on the loop wants to transmit data, it must first gain control of the loop. It does this by transmitting an Arbitrary Primitive signal (ARBx), in which x denotes the node's Arbitrary Loop Physical Address (ALPA). The ARBx passes around the loop. After the node that originated the ARBx receives its own ARBx, it gains control of the loop to transmit data and can communicate with other nodes of the network by transmitting an Open Primitive Signal (OPN) to the destination node. After this happens, there is a point-to-point connection between the two nodes. If more than one node wants to communicate at the same time, control of the loop is given to the one that has the lowest bit value in terms of destination node addresses. There is no limit to how long a node might retain control of the arbitrary loop. This demonstrates the fiber channel's channel aspect. Figure 8.7 shows how a connection is established.

Figure 8.7
An arbitrary loop in a fiber channel network.

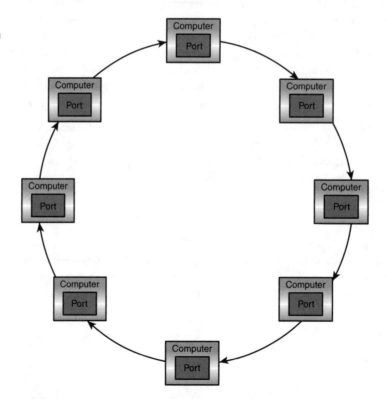

A fabric topology is used to connect devices in a cross- point switched configuration, as shown in Figure 8.8. The benefit of this topology is that many devices can communicate at the same time. The topology also requires a switch to connect to the devices. The switch connecting these devices is known as a *fabric*. The fabric connects the N_Port of the node station with the F_Port of the fabric switch. When many ports are connected to the fabric, it assigns a Native Address Identifier (S_ID) to the ports for use in data communication.

Figure 8.8
A fabric topology implemented in a fiber channel network.

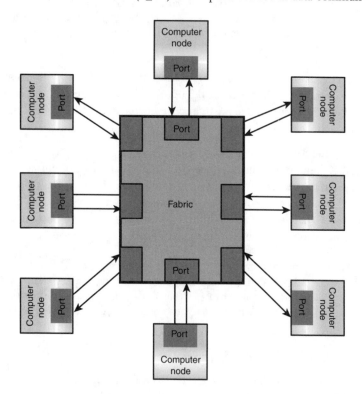

A fiber channel provides three classes of service for efficient transmission of different types of data. Users select these classes depending on the characteristics of their application, such as packet length and transmission duration.

Class 1 is a service by which two nodes can communicate using a dedicated connection, which is equivalent to a physical connection between the nodes. After the service is established, it guarantees full bandwidth of the connection, which leads to high-throughput transactions. In class 1, frames are delivered in the same order in which they are transmitted.

Note

A frame is the basic unit of communication between two N_Ports. Frames are composed of a starting delimiter, a header, the payload, and an ending delimiter. The starting and ending delimiters contain information about where the frame begins and ends. The header contains information about the frame, the routing direction, and the type of data carried by the frame. The payload contains the actual data to be transmitted.

Class 2 is a connectionless service that allows the sharing of bandwidth by multiplexing frames from multiple sources onto the same channel or channels. This service also guarantees the delivery of frames. However, the frames might not be delivered in the same sequence as they are transmitted.

Note

> Both class 1 and class 2 services transmit information about the delivery of frames. The acknowledgment frame is sent from the destination node even if the frames are not delivered due to heavy traffic in the form of acknowledgments.

Class 3 service is very similar to class 2, except that the delivery of frames is not guaranteed. This type of transfer is fast because the network is not congested with acknowledgment frames. This kind of service plays an important role in broadcast systems, where the emphasis is on timely delivery of frames.

A fiber channel has many benefits. A fiber channel is approximately three times faster than the Small Computer System Interface (SCSI). It is expected to replace SCSI as the transmission interface between servers and clustered storage devices. It is also more flexible in terms of distance, because devices placed even 10 kilometers apart can easily communicate. Long distances between devices require optical fibers as the physical medium. However, fiber channel also works using copper cables for shorter distances.

Note

> SCSI is a set of standard electronic interfaces proposed by ANSI. It enables personal computers to communicate with peripheral hardware such as disk drives, tape drives, CD-ROM drives, printers, and scanners quickly and more flexibly than any previous interface.

HIGH-PERFORMANCE PARALLEL INTERFACE

High-Performance Parallel Interface (HIPPI) is a high-speed transfer protocol designed by ANSI. HIPPI was designed based on the following guidelines:

- The data transfer rate must have a speed equivalent to 800Mbps.
- The process of data transfer must be simple so that performance can be maximized and complexity can be minimized.

Here are the salient features of HIPPI:

- It transfers data at the rate of about 800Mbps or 1600Mbps.
- It uses a 50- or 100-pair connection of copper wires.
- It transmits up to 25 meters of cable.

The components of the HIPPI protocol are the HIPPI physical layer (HIPPI-PH), the HIPPI framing protocol (HIPPI-FP), and the HIPPI switch control (HIPPI-SC).

The HIPPI-PH standard at the physical layer defines the signaling of the HIPPI protocol. HIPPI is a one-way protocol, so it is a simplex protocol. Connecting one HIPPI protocol to a HIPPI protocol in the opposite direction sets up a duplex HIPPI protocol.

HIPPI-SC is responsible for setting up the connections for data transmission in a network. The HIPPI network consists of a number of HIPPI switches connected to each other and to the nodes, as shown in Figure 8.9. The transmission in the HIPPI network is basically performed by the source requesting a connection. HIPPI switches use relevant information from the request of the source and try to set up a connection. The process of data transfer is explained in detail next.

Figure 8.9
Data transmission in a network using the HIPPI protocol.

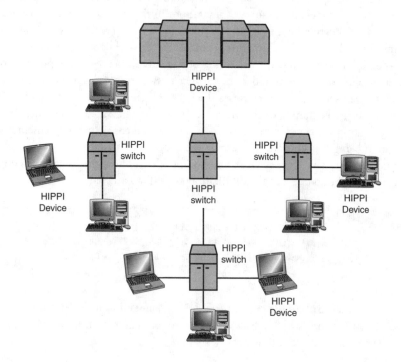

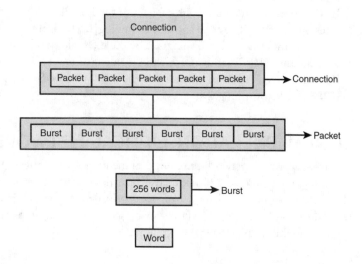

HIPPI transmits data through signals. The basic elements of data transmission are the connection, the packet, the burst, and the word. Each connection is a collection of any number of packets. Each packet consists of a number of bursts. Each burst consists of 1 to 256 words of data. Each data word is 32 bits long. The HIPPI protocol works by transmitting data through communication lines, where each line is dedicated to performing its own function.

First, the source raises a request line to set up a connection. The destination raises a connect line if it accepts the source's invitation. In this way, as soon as a connection is established, the destination sends a ready pulse and a *credit* back to the source. The ready pulse is important because the destination controls the flow of data by sending the ready pulse only when it knows that it can handle data of so many frames. A ready pulse is so fast that it travels parallel to the bursts and gives advance notice to the source as to how much data the source can send. The source raises the packet line for packet transmission. The burst line is raised at the beginning of the burst transmission. The 32 data bus lines carry the data during the transmission burst. The packet, burst, and data bus lines remain high as long as the data is being transmitted. The clock line is provided by the source. It contains the timing information. The interconnect line is a set of two lines, one in each direction. It communicates that the source and the destination are still connected.

Note

Credit refers to the number of frames the destination can handle. It is sent to the source beforehand. This is very handy in controlling the flow in a situation where the destination receives more frames than it can handle.

You can now explore the current trends and happenings in HIPPI. The restriction imposed on HIPPI in terms of the distance between nodes and the number of connections led to experiments that are still underway.

Serial HIPPI is an attempt to overcome the 25-meter distance handicap through the use of HIPPI modems. These modems connect to the HIPPI-PH layer through the use of copper cables on one side. They use another technology to transmit data over long distances by converting the data to the format used by the technology. This converted data is transmitted to another HIPPI modem, which in turn converts it back for transmission in another HIPPI-PH layer. A HIPPI extender device uses SONET STS-12 frames to transport HIPPI packets over long distances.

SECOND-GENERATION OPTICAL NETWORKS

In first-generation networks, the physical medium is the optical fiber link. In second-generation networks, the physical layer provides certain mechanisms through which bandwidth can be provided on a variable basis, depending on demand. In addition, the introduction of the optical layer has made second-generation networks such as wavelength division multiplexing (WDM) more useful.

OPTICAL LAYER

The ITU has defined a new layer called the *optical layer* that provides lightpaths to the higher layers. A *lightpath* is an end-to-end connection established across an optical network. An optical layer must be able to define a transport system by using an optical layer system. The traditional transport system design includes terminals, amplifiers, and other network elements, all of which are designed to work together as a closed system. An optical layer is divided into three sublayers, as shown in Figure 8.10.

Figure 8.10
Sublayers of an optical layer.

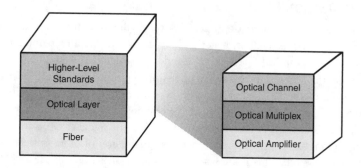

The top layer is the optical channel layer. It transmits the lightpaths. The middle layer is the optical multiplex layer, which represents a link in the route of a lightpath. The lightpath transmits through several links, which in turn carry multiplexed waves. A single optical multiplex layer consists of many link segments that belong to the optical amplifier section. This section is the bottom layer of an optical layer. The important components used in an optical layer are optical add/drop multiplexer, optical cross-connects, and optical switches, as shown in Figure 8.11.

Figure 8.11
An optical WDM system using the components of an optical layer.

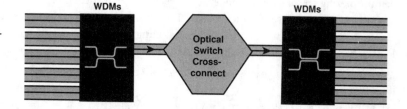

→ To learn more about add/drop multiplexers and their applications, **see** "Implementation in an Add/Drop Multiplexer," **p. 55** (Chapter 3)

→ To learn more about optical switches and their applications, **see** "Switches," **p. 83** (Chapter 4)

The important features of an optical layer are as follows:

- **Transparency**—Because lightpaths defined in a network provide end-to-end connectivity, they can be used to send data in a random format and bit rate.

- **Wavelength reusability**—A network can reuse a wavelength many times, because the number of lightpaths used is much greater than the number of wavelengths. Therefore, the waves have nonoverlapping paths.

- **Reliability**—Providing an alternative nonoverlapping lightpath for the one currently being used can prevent a failure in the network connection. This lightpath acts as a backup path and provides continuous service.

- **Virtual topology**—This consists of a set of lightpaths connecting various nodes regardless of which physical route they follow. Therefore, it simplifies the network for communication with higher layers.

WAVELENGTH DIVISION MULTIPLEXING NETWORKS

There has been a sharp increase in network traffic due to many Internet-related applications that demand high-speed data transfer and large bandwidths. Fiber-optic networks provide a promising future. Optical fibers as waveguides provide reliable and low-cost communication. The light sources used in present-day fiber-optic communication are laser diodes (LDs) and light emitting diodes (LEDs). Their spectral width ranges from a few nanometers to tens of nanometers. Therefore, a single source of fiber-optic transmission utilizes only a fraction of the available bandwidth of about 800nm. Several light signals can be accommodated in this wavelength range. Therefore, simultaneous transmission of more optical signals over the same fiber is possible. This is known as wavelength-division multiplexing (WDM). WDM has attracted much attention because it can be used to design high-capacity optical networks. In addition, it can be used to upgrade existing systems. A wide variety of signals, such as audio, video, and data, can be transmitted through the same fiber by expanding the system without modifying the existing fiber-optic cables. This promises a future-safe network.

THE ARCHITECTURE OF WDM NETWORKS

A WDM system uses multiplexing to combine the optical channels at the transmitting end through a *multiplexer*. In most applications, multiplexers are direction couplers. WDM uses demultiplexing to split the channels at the receiving end through a *demultiplexer*. Spectral filters that separate different optical channels are usually demultiplexers. They can be constructed using a combination of devices, including wavelength selective couplers, gratings, Fabry-Perot interferometer, Mach-Zehnder interferometer, and acousto-optical filters.

→ To learn more about multiplexers and demultiplexers, **see** "Multiplexers and Demultiplexers," **p. 60** (Chapter 3)

WDM systems have two configurations—one-way and two-way, as shown in Figure 8.12. Whereas the one-way system requires one transmitter and one receiver for each channel, the two-way system requires both a transmitter and receiver for each end of every channel.

There are two kinds of WDM—simple WDM or dense WDM. The only difference between them is the spacing between the multiplexed channels in the fiber, as shown in Figure 8.13.

The transmission in a WDM system is affected by various factors. You need to consider these factors while designing the WDM system.

Figure 8.12
The two configurations of WDM systems—one-way and two-way.

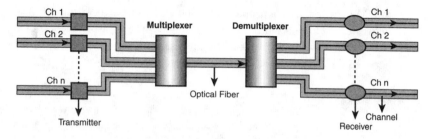

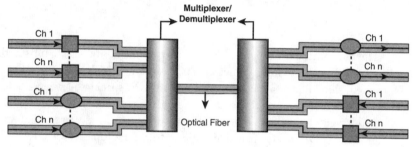

Figure 8.13
A WDM system with dense WDM and simple WDM.

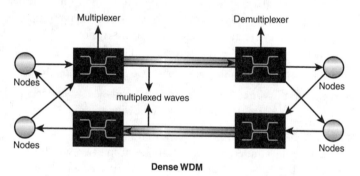

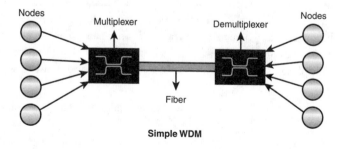

WDM networks have a problem of dispersion associated with multiplexing and the spacing between the multiplexed channels in a single fiber. To avoid this problem, the light channels of different wavelengths emitted by the laser must be such that they allow sufficient spacing between the lightwaves so that the wavelengths do not overlap.

> **Note**
>
> *Dispersion* is the degradation of the electromagnetic waves that are propagating in the physical medium by the signals traveling in the same medium with different propagating velocities.

The phenomena of stimulated Raman scattering and four-wave mixing of waves expose the optical channels to interference effects, resulting in high cross talk. Therefore, the WDM system should be designed in such a way that the spacing between channels should be sufficient and uneven to minimize dispersion and cross talk. Two more developments also led to the efficient design of WDM systems in real networks: the use of Erbium-doped fiber amplifier (EDFA) and the use of static add/drop multiplexers. EDFAs, which are placed at 80km to 120km intervals, enable the direct amplification of the optical signal without the need for a regenerator. In addition, the use of static add/drop multiplexers allows a small number of adjacent wavelengths, usually the bottom two or four, to be added and dropped without the need to demultiplex the entire group.

→ To learn more about four-wave mixing, **see** "Four-Wave Mixing," **p. 89** (Chapter 4)

The two types of WDM networks are broadcast-and-select networks and wavelength-routed networks. They are described in the following sections.

BROADCAST-AND-SELECT NETWORKS   A local broadcast-and-select WDM optical network can be constructed by connecting network nodes using two-way fibers to a passive star coupler, as shown in Figure 8.14. A node transmits a signal of a particular wavelength to the star coupler. The signals from multiple nodes are optically combined by the star coupler and are forwarded to all the nodes. A node's receiver is tuned to only one of the wavelengths, so it can receive the information signal only by using an optical filter. Communication between sources and receivers can follow one of two methods—single-hop or multihop. In single-hop communication, the signals do not go through the intermediate nodes on the way to the destination node, as explained earlier. This is shown by a dotted line in Figure 8.14. Multihop communication is the opposite of single-hop communication. In a multihop network, when a source transmits on a particular wavelength λ_1, more than one receiver can be tuned to this wavelength and might pick up the required wavelength from the multiplexed signal stream. Therefore, the multihop network supports *multicast* services.

→ To learn more about passive star couplers, **see** "Wavelength Characteristic of Couplers," **p. 46** (Chapter 3)

The advantage of these networks is their simple design and multicasting capability. However, these networks cannot reuse wavelengths or support more nodes. Therefore, they are not scalable above a limit. Another disadvantage of these networks is that they cannot cover long distances, because the signal suffers attenuation due to splitting across all ports.

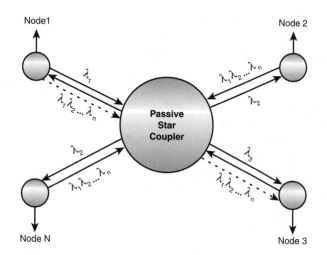

Figure 8.14
A WDM broadcast-and-select network using a passive star coupler.

WAVELENGTH-ROUTED NETWORKS   Wavelength-routed networks are the simplest form of WDM networks. The network consists of a *photonic switching fabric* comprised of active switches connected by fiber links to form an arbitrary physical topology, as shown in Figure 8.15. Each node is connected to an active switch through a fiber link. The device at the user end and its corresponding switch are called a network node. The basic technique of communication occurs through the process of wavelength switching. There are two types of switching processes. The first type dynamically switches signals from one link to another by changing the WDM routing in the network. The other type of switching involves wavelength conversion, in which the information present in the signal is transferred from one wavelength to another. A wavelength-routed network operates through a lightpath. A lightpath, as mentioned earlier, is an optical communication channel between two nodes in the network, and it consists of more than one fiber link. The lightpath is routed through the network using the active switches of the nodes in its path.

A fundamental requirement in a wavelength-routed optical network is that two or more lightpaths traversing the same fiber link must always be on channels with different wavelengths so that they do not interfere with one another. However, there can be a situation in which two lightpaths might have the same wavelength in their path. For example, in Figure 8.15, nodes 1 and 3 are connected through switches 1, 2, 3, 4, and 5 using the wavelength λ_1, and nodes 4 and 5 are connected through switches 3 and 4 using the wavelength λ_2. The lightpaths have the same wavelength in the link between switches 3 and 4. However, if a wavelength conversion function is used, the two light paths can use the same wavelength λ_2 for transmission in that stretch and therefore enable the wavelength to be reused.

OPTICAL TIME-DIVISION MULTIPLEXING NETWORKS

Due to the increasing demand for more bandwidth, networks started applying a number of techniques, including wavelength division multiplexing (WDM) and time-division multiplexing (TDM). Optical time-division multiplexing networks (OTDM) arise from the application of TDM in optical networks. To increase the transmission speed of optical digital signals, TDM technology multiplexes several low-speed pulse streams so as to not overlap them in time with each other. By using the optical multiplexer and demultiplexer, OTDM multiplexes and demultiplexes optical pulse signals without converting them to electrical signals. One form of OTDM is similar to a broadcast-and-select network. In this form, the different nodes share the same transmission medium, and each node gets different time slots to transmit data in round-robin manner. Another form of OTDM network is the optical packet-switched network. This network uses a high-speed optical packet switch instead of an electronic packet switch. A node takes a packet transmitted from the source, reads the packet's header, and switches it to the appropriate node. In situations where two packets from two different nodes are to be switched to the same node, one of the packets is buffered or is sent through another node to the output node.

Figure 8.15
A simple WDM wavelength-routed network.

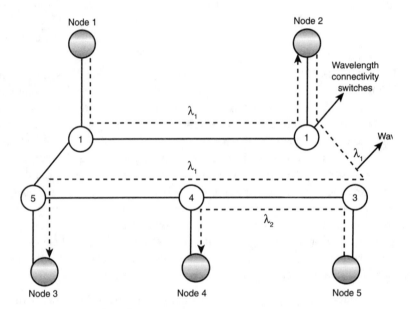

CODE-DIVISION MULTIPLE ACCESS NETWORKS

Unlike WDM and TDM, code division multiplexing is used mainly in broadcast environments because they provide multiple access. The concept of multiple access means that many users can access the network simultaneously. Code-division multiple access (CDMA) does not assign a specific frequency to each user. However, users have access to the entire bandwidth of the communication channel simultaneously to enable multiple access. In CDMA, unique digital codes are assigned to each user's transmission. These codes are called *pseudo-random digital sequences*. A receiver is programmed to this code so that it can retrieve the correct code from the transmission channel. This led to the coining of the term CDMA.

CDMA is based on the spread-spectrum technology, which means that it spreads the data signal over a much greater bandwidth than the signal bandwidth. Spreading the signal over the frequency spectrum or time domain results in spread spectrum. The two most popular spread-spectrum techniques are *frequency hopping (FH)* and *direct-sequence spread spectrum (DSSS)*.

Frequency hopping, as the name implies, takes the data signal and modulates it with a carrier signal that hops in a random fashion. However, data signals hop in a known sequence from frequency to frequency over a wide band of frequencies because the bandwidth is divided into *n* frequency channels for a given period of time. The frequency-hopping technique reduces interference, because an interfering signal from a narrow-band system affects the spread-spectrum signal only if both are transmitting at the same frequency at the same time. The transmission frequencies are determined by a spreading or hopping code. The receiver must be set to the same hopping code and must listen to the incoming signal at the right time and at the correct frequency to properly receive the signal.

Direct-sequence spread spectrum combines a data signal at the sending station with a higher data rate bit sequence known as a *chipping code* (also called *processing gain*), which spreads user data according to a spreading ratio. Processing gain is also defined as the difference in the signal-to-noise ratio (SNR) before and after spreading. The chipping code is a redundant bit pattern for each bit that is transmitted. It increases the signal's resistance to interference. If one or more bits in the pattern are damaged during transmission, the original data can be recovered due to the transmission's redundancy. The receiver must be set to the same chipping code to receive the signal.

Note

SNR is the ratio of the amplitude of the desired signal to the amplitude of the noise signals at a given point in time. It is measured in decibels (dB).

The benefits of CDMA are as follows:

- No limit to the number of users who can access the network. However, this approach might degrade the network's quality.

- The users have privacy and security, because only receivers that have a correct code can access a given message.

- A dramatic improvement in the voice quality in a cellular system using CDMA.

- CDMA reduces interference with other electronic devices.

SUMMARY

First-generation optical networks include synchronous optical networks, synchronous digital hierarchy networks, and asynchronous transfer mode networks. These form the heart of the telecommunications infrastructure in North America, Europe, and Japan. First-generation networks also include a variety of enterprise networks, such as enterprise serial connection, high-performance parallel interface, and fiber channel. These are used for interconnections with other computers and peripheral systems. In addition, first-generation optical networks include fiber distributed data interface, widely deployed in LANs and MANs. Second-generation networks include wavelength-division multiplexing networks, optical time-division multiplexing networks, and code-division multiple access networks.

CHAPTER **9**

SYNCHRONOUS OPTICAL NETWORKS

In this chapter

THE NEED FOR SYNCHRONIZATION

Due to the different digital hierarchies of the signal, encoding techniques, and multiplexing strategies, communication between localized systems has become costly.

The various signal formats that are used for communication are as follows:

- *DS-1* uses the AMI encoding scheme. It robs a bit from an 8-bit byte for signaling. A DS-1 signal consists of 24 voice signals and 1 framing bit per frame. It has a rate of 1.544Mbps.

- In the *B8ZS* bipolar encoding scheme, every bit is used for transmission. Therefore, it has a rate of 64Kbps per channel.

- The *CEPT-1* signal consists of 30 voice signals and two channels for framing and signaling, so it has a rate of 2.048Mbps. CEPT-1 uses the HDB3 coding technique.

Multiplexing procedures can also differ between signals. They can be byte interleaving or bit interleaving. Therefore, communication between different networks requires complex multiplexing/demultiplexing and coding/decoding processes for converting signals from one format to another. This increases the system's overall cost.

Asynchronous systems have traditionally been used with each terminal clocked at a different rate. However, synchronization is important in digital transmission systems. Synchronization means providing a clock or a set of repetitive pulses to keep the data bit rate constant. Asynchronous transmission causes variations in the bit rate, and the signals are free-running and unsynchronized.

Multiple stages are used in asynchronous transmission, and additional bits are added for synchronization. Signals such as asynchronous DS-1 are multiplexed, and extra bits are added to account for variations in signal rates. This is called *bit stuffing*. Then, framing bits are added to form the DS-2 stream. The higher rates are multiplexed in the same way.

SONET standardizes the rates and formats of the various signals to be multiplexed, thereby solving the problems involved in asynchronous transmission and the different digital hierarchies. In a synchronous system such as SONET, the average clock rate is the same or nearly the same—that is, plesiochronous.

SONET is designed to be a transport mechanism that maps existing asynchronous circuit-based traffic to a synchronous payload envelope, thereby greatly simplifying the process of demultiplexing traffic at the other end of the connection. Legacy multiplexing equipment that switched asynchronous traffic requires bit stuffing to accommodate jitter as well as extraction of payload at each switching point in the network. SONET eliminates the need to fully extract the payload by providing pointers to the start of the payload and a common clock referenced to a stable reference point. Figure 9.1 shows a typical SONET network.

Figure 9.1
SONET network multiplexing, in which different input data formats are multiplexed onto a single fiber-optic cable.

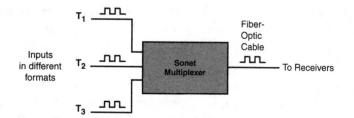

→ To learn more about plesiochronous multiplexing, **see** "Plesiochronous Multiplexing," **p. 213** (Chapter 11)

SONET FRAME STRUCTURES

The basic building block of a SONET optical interface is a Synchronous Transport Signal (STS-1) with a basic rate of 51.84Mbps. Higher-level signals are integer multiples of the base rate. For example, STS-3 is three times the rate of STS-1, as shown in the following equation:

$$3 \times 51.84 = 155.52\text{Mbps}$$

An STS-12 rate is given by the following equation:

$$12 \times 51.84 = 622.08\text{Mbps}$$

Figure 9.2 shows the basic frame structure of a SONET. The derivation of the line rate is explained in detail next.

Figure 9.2
The STS-1 frame format with the synchronous payload envelope and the transport overhead.

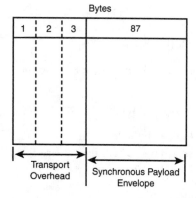

The STS-1 consists of two parts:

- The STS payload, Synchronous Payload Envelope (SPE), which carries information
- The STS transport overhead, which carries signaling and protocol information

The STS payload and the STS transport overhead enable communication between intelligent nodes on the network, permitting administration, surveillance, provisioning, and control of a network from a central location. SONET also defines several sub-STS-1 signaling rates. These are known as virtual tributaries. They are designed to carry lower-speed signals such as DS-1s and DS-2s through a SONET network. Virtual tributaries are discussed in detail in the following sections.

The STS-1 frame structure consists of 9 rows and 90 columns, as shown in Figure 9.3. The first three columns are used for transport overhead. Therefore, the STS-1 payload envelope consists of 87 columns and 9 rows, for a total of 783 bytes. The first column is the path overhead (POH), occupying 9 bytes. Two more columns are designated as fixed stuff that is not used in the actual transmission (columns 30 and 59). Therefore, the actual number of bytes used for the transmission of useful data is 756 bytes, which is designated as the payload capacity.

Figure 9.3
The STS-1 payload envelope and its capacity for carrying data.

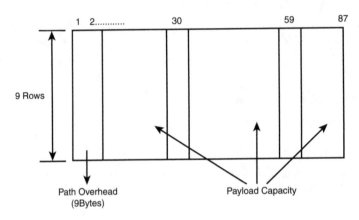

STS-1 SPE

The basic line rate of an STS-1 signal is derived as follows:

Actual line rate: 90 columns × 9 rows × 8 bits/byte × 8000 frames/sec = 51.84Mbps

Columns 4 to 90 are the SPE.

Actual data rate: 87 columns × 9 rows × 8 bits/byte × 8000 frames/sec = 50.112Mbps

Higher line rates are obtained by multiplexing the lower line rates. The STS-1 or Optical Channel (OC-1) signal can be repeated n times, where the values of n are 1, 3, 12, 48, and 192. Therefore, the OC-192 has the line rate given in the following equation:

51.84Mbps × 192 = 9953.28Mbps

STS-1 SPE can begin anywhere in the envelope capacity. It usually begins in one frame and ends in another. The STS payload pointer in the transport header holds the location of the byte where the STS-1 SPE begins. Each payload is associated with a POH and is used to communicate information regarding how the payload is mapped in the STS-1 SPE and where it must be delivered. Figure 9.4 shows the STS-1 frame structure.

Figure 9.4
The STS-1 frame structure, showing payload mapping.

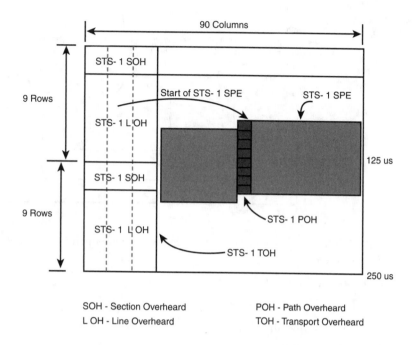

PART

II

CH

9

SOH - Section Overheard
L OH - Line Overheard

POH - Path Overheard
TOH - Transport Overheard

The STS-*n* frame structure uses many such STS-1 modules. The transport overheads for the individual modules need to be frame-aligned, but this is not required for the corresponding STS-1 SPE, because the payload pointer is present to indicate the location of the SPE.

Super-rate services such as broadband ISDN have a rate higher than that of STS-1. Therefore, STS-1s are concatenated to form an STS-*nc* signal that is multiplexed, switched, and transported through the network as a single entity. The STS-*nc* SPE consists of $n \times 87$ columns and 9 rows of bytes. Only one set of STS-1 path overhead is needed in the STS-*nc* SPE. Here, *n* represents the number of STS-1s that are concatenated.

Note

The *STS-n* signal is formed by byte interleaving n STS-1 signals. Whereas, the *STS-nc* signal is formed by concatenating n STS-1 signals.

SONET OVERHEAD

SONET carries a substantial amount of overhead information to enable easier multiplexing and greatly expanded operations, administration, maintenance, and provision (OAM&P).

A typical SONET end-to-end connection is shown in Figure 9.5.

Figure 9.5
The SONET system hierarchy showing the various components of the SONET network.

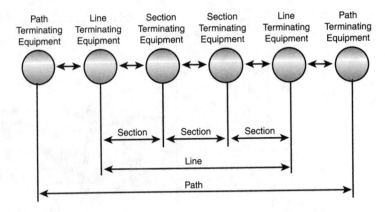

A typical SONET system consists of the following components, which are discussed in the following sections:

- Path-terminating equipment
- Line-terminating equipment
- Section-terminating equipment
- Section overhead
- Line overhead
- Path overhead

PATH-TERMINATING EQUIPMENT

For multiplexing and demultiplexing STS payload, STS *path-terminating equipment (PTE)* is used. It performs the functions of originating, modifying, accessing, and terminating the path overhead. It can also perform any combination of these actions.

LINE-TERMINATING EQUIPMENT

Line-terminating equipment (LTE) originates and/or terminates the line signal. It can originate, access, modify, or terminate the line overhead, or it can perform a combination of these actions.

SECTION-TERMINATING EQUIPMENT

Two adjacent SONET network elements form a section. *Section-terminating equipment (STE)* can be a terminating network element or a regenerator. It can originate, access, modify, or terminate the section overhead. It can also perform a combination of these actions.

SECTION OVERHEAD

The *section overhead* contains 9 bytes of the transport overhead accessed, generated, and processed by section-terminating equipment. This overhead supports the following functions:

- Performance monitoring (STS-*n* signal)

- Local orderwire

- Data communication channels to carry information for OAM&P

- Framing

The section overhead is found in the first three rows of columns 1–9, as shown in Figure 9.6.

Figure 9.6
Section overhead:
Rows 1–3 of the
transport overhead.

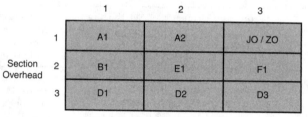

Section Overhead

Transport Overhead

Table 9.1 shows section overhead byte by byte.

TABLE 9.1   SECTION OVERHEAD BYTES AND THEIR FUNCTIONS

Byte	Byte Type	Description
A1 and A2	Framing bytes	Indicates the beginning of an STS-1 frame. When four consecutive framing patterns are received with errors, an OOF (Out Of Frame) condition is declared. When two consecutive error-free framing patterns are received, an in-frame condition is declared.
J0	Section trace (J0)/ section growth (Z0)	One binary byte C1 was earlier assigned to each STS-1 signal of an STS-*n* frame in the order in which they appear. This has been refined either as the section trace byte (in the first STS-1 of STS-*n*) or as a section growth byte (in the second through *n*th STS-1s). This byte is assigned prior to inter leaving, and it remains until deinterleaving.
B1	Section bit-interleaved parity code (BIP-8)	Allocated to the first STS-1 signal for section error monitoring. Even parity is used to check for the regenerators used in the STE. Each piece of section equipment calculates the B1 byte of the current STS-*n* frame and compares it with the B1 byte received from the first STS-1 of the next STS-*n* frame. If the B1 bytes match, there is no error. If the B1 bytes do not match and the thresh old is reached, the alarm indicator is set. The B1 bytes of the rest of the STS-*n* frame are undefined.

TABLE 9.1   CONTINUED

Byte	Byte Type	Description
E1	Section orderwire byte	Allocated for use as a local orderwire channel in voice communication between regenerators, hubs, and remote terminal locations. A SONET frame is 125usec or 64Kbps, which is the same as voice channel and therefore is defined. This byte is defined for the first STS-1 signal of an STS-n frame, and the rest are undefined.
F1	Section user channel byte	Set aside for the users' purposes. It terminates at all section-terminating equipment within a line. It can be read from and written to at each section-terminating equipment in that line.
D1, D2, and D3	Section data communications channel (DCC) bytes	Forms a 192Kbps message channel providing a message-based channel for OAM&P between pieces of section-terminating equipment. The channel is used from a central location for alarms, control, monitoring, administration, and other communication needs. It is available for internally generated, externally generated, or manufacturer-specific messages. This byte is defined for the first STS-1 signal of an STS-n frame, and the rest are undefined.

LINE OVERHEAD

Line overhead contains 18 bytes of overhead accessed, generated, and processed by line-terminating equipment. This overhead supports the following functions:

- Locating the SPE in the frame
- Multiplexing or concatenating signals
- Performance monitoring
- Automatic protection switching
- Line maintenance

Line overhead is found in rows 4–9 of columns 1–9, as shown in Figure 9.7.

Table 9.2 shows line overhead byte by byte.

Figure 9.7
Line overhead bytes:
Rows 4–9 of the
transport overhead.

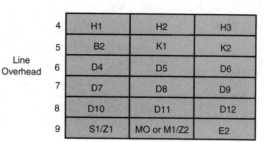

Line
Overhead

Transport
Overhead

TABLE 9.2 LINE OVERHEAD BYTES AND THEIR FUNCTIONS

Byte	Byte Type	Description
H1 and H2	STS payload pointer	Two bytes are allocated to a pointer that indicates the offset in bytes between the pointer and the first byte of the STS SPE. The pointer bytes are used in all STS-1s within an STS-n to align the STS-1 transport overhead in the STS-n and to perform frequency justification. These bytes are also used to indicate concatenation and to detect STS path alarm indication signals (AIS-P). In the case of STS-nc signals, only one pointer is needed. The first pointer bytes contain the actual pointer to the SPE, and subsequent pointer bytes contain a concatenation indicator—10010011 11111111.
H3	Pointer action byte	Is present in all the STS-1 signals within the STS-n frame. It is used for frequency justification. This is the extra SPE byte in the event of a negative pointer adjustment. The value contained in this byte, when it is not used to carry the SPE byte, is undefined.
B2	Line bit-interleaved parity code (BIP-8)	Determines whether there is an error on the transmission line. It uses even parity and is calculated over all bits of the line overhead and STS-1 SPE of the previous STS-1 frame. The value is then placed in the B2 byte of the line overhead before scrambling. This byte is provided in all STS-1 signals in an STS-n signal.
K1 and K2	Automatic protection switching (APS channel) bytes	Used for protection signaling between line-terminating entities for bidirectional automatic protection switching and to detect alarm indication signals (AIS-L) and remote defect indication (RDI) signals. These bytes are defined only for STS-1 number 1 signal in an STS-n frame.

TABLE 9.2	CONTINUED	
Byte	**Byte Type**	**Description**
D4 to D12	Line data communications channel (DCC) bytes	Nine bytes of the first STS-1 of an STS-n frame form a 576Kbps message channel from a central location for OAM&P information (alarms, control, maintenance, remote provisioning, monitoring, administration, and other communication needs) between line entities. They are available for internally generated, externally generated, and manufacturer-specific messages. A protocol analyzer is required to access the line-DCC information. The D4 to D12 bytes of the rest of the STS-n frame are undefined.
S1	Synchronization status (S1)	Located in the first STS-1 of an STS-n. Bits 5 through 8 of that byte are allocated to convey the synchronization status of the network element.
Z1	Growth (Z1)	Located in the second through nth STS-1s of an STS-n, where $3 <= n <= 48$. This byte is allocated for future growth. Note that an OC-1 or STS-1 electrical signal does not contain a Z1 byte.
M0	STS-1 REI-L (M0)	Is defined only for STS-1 in an OC-1 or STS-1 electrical signal. Bits 5 through 8 are allocated for a line remote error indication function (REI-L, formerly called line FEBE), which conveys the error count detected by an LTE.
M1	STS-n REI-L (M1)	Located in the third STS-1 (in the order of appearance in the byte-interleaved STS-n electrical or OC-n signal) in an STS-n ($n >= 3$). It is used for an REI-L function.
Z2	Growth (Z2)	Located in the first and second STS-1s of an STS-3 signal. It is located in the first, second, and fourth STS-1s of an STS-n ($12 <= n <= 48$). This byte is allocated for future growth.
E2	Orderwire byte	Provides a 64Kbps channel between line entities for an express orderwire. It is a voice channel for use by technicians and is ignored as it passes through the regenerators.

PATH OVERHEAD

STS *Path Overhead (POH)* contains 9 evenly distributed POH bytes per 125 microseconds, starting at the first byte of the STS-SPE. STS POH provides for communication between an STS SPE's point of creation and its point of disassembly. This overhead supports the following functions:

- Performance monitoring of the STS-SPE
- Signal label (the content of the STS-SPE, including the status of mapped payloads)
- Path status
- Path trace

The POH is found in rows 1–9 of the first column of the STS-1 SPE, as shown in Figure 9.8.

Figure 9.8
Path overhead bytes
carrying information
about the mapping of
payloads present in
rows 1–9 and column
1 of the STS-1 SPE.

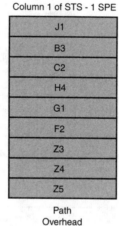

Column 1 of STS - 1 SPE

| J1 |
| B3 |
| C2 |
| H4 |
| G1 |
| F2 |
| Z3 |
| Z4 |
| Z5 |

Rows 1 to 9

Path
Overhead

Table 9.3 describes POH byte by byte.

TABLE 9.3   POH BYTES AND THE FUNCTIONS THEY PERFORM

Byte	Byte Type	Description
J1	STS path trace byte	User-programmable byte repetitively transmits a 64-byte (16-byte) E.164 format string. This allows the receiving terminal in a path to verify its continued connection to the intended transmitting terminal.
B3	STS path bit-interleaved parity code (path BIP-8) byte	Parity code (even) used to determine if a transmission error has occurred over a path. Its value is calculated over all the bits of the previous SPE before scrambling.
C2	STS path signal label byte	Used to indicate the content of the STS-SPE, including the status of the mapped payloads.
		The following hex values of the C2 byte are defined:
		0×00—Unequipped signal (no path originate equipment)
		0×01—Equipped signal (standard payload)
		0×02—Floating VT mode

TABLE 9.3	CONTINUED	
Byte	**Byte Type**	**Description**
		0×03—Locked VT mode
		0×04—Asynchronous mapping for DS-3
		0×12—Asynchronous mapping for 139.264Mbps
		0×13—Mapping for ATM
		0×14—Mapping for Distributed Queue Dual Bus (DQDB)
		0×15—Asynchronous mapping for FDDI
H4	VT multiframe indicator byte	Provides a generalized multiframe indicator for payload containers. At present, it is used only for tributary unit structured payloads.
G1	Path status byte	Used to convey the path-terminating status and performance back to the originating path-terminating equipment. Therefore, the duplex path in its entirety can be monitored from either end or from any point along the path.
F2	Path user channel byte	Used for user communication between path elements. For example, in a DQDB application, the F2 byte is used to carry DQDB layer management information.
Z3,Z4,Z5	Growth	Reserved for future functions.

Note

The POH portion of the SPE remains with the payload until it is demultiplexed.

Although SONET provides a synchronous frame structure, it does not constrain the user payload to occur at specific positions in the SONET frame. Instead, it enables the user payload to "float" within and across SONET frame boundaries by using fields in the overhead bytes of the SONET frame to point to the beginning of the user payload. From a user perspective, SONET provides a byte-synchronous physical layer medium.

To compensate for frequency and phase variations, SONET uses the concept of *pointers*. They enable the transport of synchronous payload envelopes over networks having separate network clocks, but almost the same timing (plesiochronous). The delays and data loss associated with the networks are highly minimized using pointers due to the presence of buffers for synchronization. Pointers provide a flexible and dynamic phase alignment of these STS payloads, thereby making inserting, dropping, and cross-connecting these payloads over the network easy. Signal wander and jitter can also be readily minimized.

POINTERS AND POINTER ADJUSTMENTS

The payload pointer gives the location of the beginning of the payload within the SONET structure. Differences in phase and frequency between two SONET network elements (NEs) can be handled through the use of payload pointers.

If the sending SONET NE is faster than the receiving SONET NE, the receiving SONET NE introduces a negative pointer adjustment and shifts the payload ahead by 1 byte (8 bits). In this manner, the receiving SONET NE can keep up with the sending SONET NE without loss of information. This is called negative byte stuffing or negative pointer justification, and it is illustrated in Figure 9.9.

Figure 9.9
Negative pointer justification slips a byte ahead to synchronize between the sending and receiving network elements.

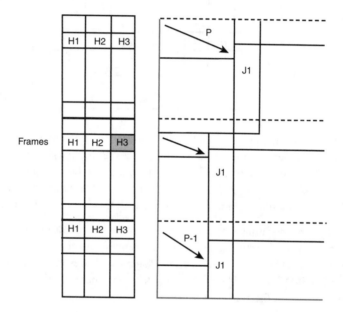

Similarly, if the sending SONET NE is slower than the receiving SONET NE, a positive pointer adjustment of 1 byte is introduced. This is called positive byte stuffing or positive pointer justification, as shown in Figure 9.10.

PAYLOAD MAPPING

DS-3 signals are mapped to SONET using stuffing bits to account for variations in timing between DS-3 and the SONET system. DS-1 signals can be mapped using one of these methods:

- Asynchronous mapping
- Floating-byte synchronous mapping
- Locked-byte synchronous mapping
- Bit-synchronous mapping

Figure 9.10
Positive pointer justification slips back a byte to synchronize between the sending and receiving network elements.

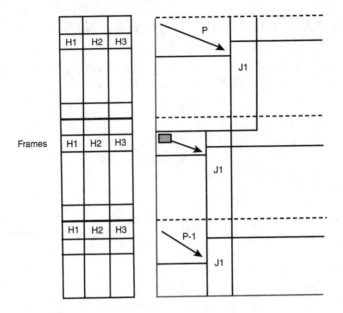

In asynchronous mapping, the DS-1 or E-1 signal is mapped to VT1.5 asynchronously using stuff bits to accommodate timing differences. Pointers are used to indicate the beginning of the VT frame. With asynchronous mapping, the DS-1 signal is transported without slips and without retiming the signal. However, it is subject to pointer adjustments that occur due to any frequency differences between SONET NE in the transmission path.

Floating-byte synchronous mapping differs from asynchronous mapping in that it does not include stuff bits to accommodate timing differences between the payload and SONET NE. This mapping enables direct access to DS-0 signals. However, it requires the DS-1 to be locked to the SONET NE. Any frequency difference between the incoming payload and the first SONET NE in the transport causes slips.

Locked-byte synchronous mapping does not allow for any stuff bits or pointers in the mapping process. Therefore, the DS-1 must be locked to the SONET NE. A slip buffer must be provided to accommodate timing differences throughout the transport.

Note

Slip buffers are used to hold information about where the next payload is mapped, because locked byte mapping does not have pointers to indicate this.

Bit-synchronous mapping is the same as locked-byte synchronous mapping, except that it does not assume that the DS-1 structure is organized into DS-0s. The DS-1 is passed as a single bit stream with or without DS-0 or DS-1 frames. Most networks use asynchronous mapping to transport DS-1 signals.

MULTIPLEXING METHODS IN SONET

SONET multiplexing occurs at the line layer of the SONET's four-layered architecture, where *n* STS-1 signals are multiplexed to create the STS-*n* electrical signal. This is shown in Figure 9.11.

Figure 9.11
Forming the STS-n signal from the STS-1 signal.

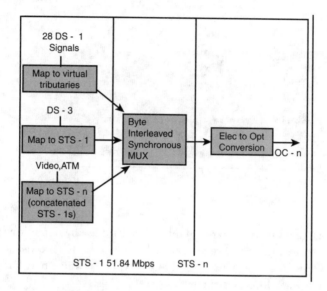

Before the basic STS-1 SPE is formed, a virtual tributary (VT) structure is formed. VTs are used to take sub-STS-1 asynchronous inputs such as DS-1s and output a synchronous tributary. Bit stuffing is definitely needed to form the VT, because the VT rate is made to have a faster line rate than the input signal to account for clock variations in the asynchronous signals. Table 9.4 summarizes the three different types of VTs.

TABLE 9.4   VIRTUAL TRIBUTARIES AND THEIR DATA RATES

Type	Transport for (Typically)	VT Rate
VT-1.5	DS-1 1.544Mbps	1.728Mbps
VT-2	CETP 2.048Mbps	2.304Mbps
VT-6	DS-2 6.312Mbps	6.912Mbps

VT payloads and VT path overhead comprise the virtual tributary's synchronous payload envelope and are similar to the STS's payload. Within an STS-1 frame, each VT occupies a number of columns, and within STS-1, many VT groups can be mixed to form an STS-1 payload. To accommodate different mixes of VTs in an efficient manner, the STS-1 SPE is divided into seven groups. A VT group may contain one VT-6, three VT-2s, or four VT-1.5s. A VT group must contain only one size of VTs, but different types of VT groups may be mixed into one STS-1 SPE.

After all functions associated with VT mappings are completed, an STS-1 SPE is formed. As shown in Figure 9.12, this STS-1 SPE is multiplexed with others to form a higher line rate STS signal, such as STS-3.

Figure 9.12
Multiplexing three
STS-1 signals to form
an STS-n frame.

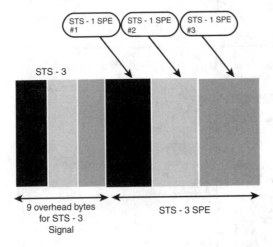

All mappings and multiplexing in the SONET standard use byte interleaving methods. Essentially, bytes are interleaved such that the low-speed signals are visible in the high-speed signals. This is one big advantage of SONET. It is possible to extract low-speed signals without fully demultiplexing the higher-level signals.

COMPONENTS OF THE SONET NETWORK

The SONET is comprised of several network elements that are responsible for its efficient operation:

- Terminal multiplexers
- Regenerators
- Add/drop multiplexers
- Digital cross-connects

TERMINAL MULTIPLEXERS

Terminal multiplexers concentrate several signals onto an STS-1 signal, STS-3 signal, or OC-*n* backbone. They are also called path-terminating equipment. Simply put, a terminal multiplexer is a point-to-point transmission device. Its two output paths terminate at the same SONET multiplexer, but run over two separate cables. Figure 9.13 shows the simplest implementation of a SONET link.

Figure 9.13
Terminal multiplexers enable the multiplexing of various channels.

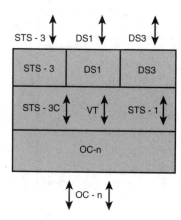

REGENERATORS

Regenerators are elements that are required when the multiplexers are situated far from each other. This causes the signal level to drop very low, causing loss of data. The regenerator clocks off and replaces the section overhead bytes before the signal is retransmitted. The line overhead, path overhead, and payload are unaltered. Figure 9.14 shows a regenerator.

Figure 9.14
A regenerator increases the strength of the optical signal without affecting the other parameters.

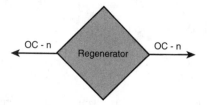

ADD/DROP MULTIPLEXERS

One of the features of SONET technology that makes it unique is add/drop multiplexing (ADM). In the asynchronous world, every time a signal is accessed, the entire signal must be multiplexed or demultiplexed. With SONET, signals can be added and dropped anywhere along the ring. This reduces the number of back-to-back multiplexers that are required. This, in turn, lowers capital costs and increases network efficiency. Figure 9.15 shows an add/drop multiplexer.

Figure 9.15 illustrates how a typical ADM looks: An OC-3 passes through the ADM as it would in a ring or linear configuration. ADMs take STS-1s and concatenate them into specific types of SONET OC circuits, set up in ring fashion to ensure that each circuit will be automatically backed up in case of fiber break or equipment failure.

In rural applications, an ADM can be deployed at a terminal site or any intermediate location to consolidate traffic from widely separated locations. Several ADMs can be configured as a survivable ring.

Figure 9.15
Add/drop multiplex-
ers can add and/or
drop signals any-
where in the trans-
mission's path.

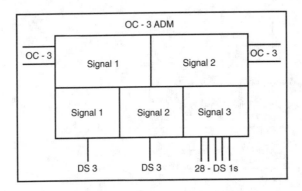

> **Note**
>
> A network is *survivable* if it has good fault tolerance and a good fault-detection mecha-
> nism. Such networks must be able to autonomously detect a faulty node and take the
> necessary action. Such networks can be reconfigured to reroute the traffic.

SONET enables drop and repeat, also known as drop and continue, a feature used in both telephony and cable TV applications. With drop and repeat, a signal terminates at one node, is duplicated/repeated, and is then sent to the next and subsequent nodes.

In ring survivability applications, drop and repeat provides alternative routing for traffic passing through interconnecting rings in a matched-nodes configuration. If the connection cannot be made through one of the nodes, the signal is repeated and is passed along an alternative route to the destination node.

In multinode distribution applications, one transport channel can efficiently carry traffic between multiple distribution nodes. When transporting video, for example, each program-ming channel is delivered (dropped) at the node and is repeated for delivery to the next and subsequent nodes. Not all bandwidth (program channels) needs to be terminated at all nodes. Channels not terminating at a node can be passed through without physical interven-tion to other nodes.

The add/drop multiplexer provides interfaces between the different network signals and SONET signals.

DIGITAL CROSS-CONNECTS

Digital cross-connects (DCS) are the perfect vehicle to migrate from asynchronous trans-mission to SONET. Telephone companies and carriers use DCS. A DCS supports asynchro-nous interfaces and a SONET-compatible matrix to perform cross-connects. A cross-connect can accommodate many network devices, and it can pass SONET network management information to them. Network provisioning, maintenance, monitoring, and testing are natural functions for digital cross-connects.

DCSs come in several sizes and shapes. Some must be modified to accommodate SONET. A DCS 1/0 takes in a DS-1 signal and cross-connects at the DS-0 level, operating independently of SONET. A 3/3 DCS receives DS-3 signals and connects at the same level. If it has enough bandwidth to handle the 51.854Mbps STS-1 signal, a 3/3 can easily be upgraded to SONET. The 3/1 cross-connect might have the most problems fitting into the SONET world. A 3/1 DCS cross-connects at the DS-1 level using time-division switching. A matrix designed for a DS-1 structure cannot process a VT1.5 signal, and there might be problems processing STS-1 signals that consist of multiple VTs concatenated into higher-rate signals.

SONET can use two types of digital cross-connects—wideband (WDCS) and broadband (BDCS). A WDCS cross-connects signals at the DS-1 level and terminates SONET and DS-3 signals. It can cross-connect floating VT1.5s between OC-n terminations and clear-channel DS-1s. It also transparently connects DS-1 interfaces to DS-3 and OC-n terminations. Figure 9.16 shows switching using WDCS.

PART

II

CH

9

Figure 9.16
Wideband digital cross-connects connecting signals at various levels.

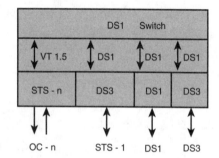

Broadband digital cross-connects perform two-way cross-connects at DS-3 and STS-1 and concatenate signals at STS-n levels. Cross-connects are transparent at the DS-3 levels and between DS-3s and OC-ns. Any DS-3 that is framed synchronously or asynchronously can be cross-connected if it is running at the nominal DS-3 rate. Figure 9.17 illustrates BDCS.

Figure 9.17
BDCS with two-way cross-connects at DS-3, STS-1, and STS-n levels.

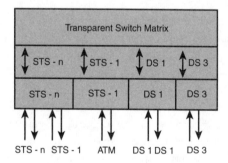

As an interface between the central office switch and transmission signals, the SONET-compatible cross-connect simplifies terminating and switching signals at central offices. Under SONET, optical signals are groomed with a cross-connect or on a digital switch.

CONFIGURATIONS IN A SONET NETWORK

The four basic SONET network configurations are point-to-point, point-to-multipoint, hub, and ring.

The point-to-point network in its simplest form can consist of two SONET (terminal) multiplexers linked by fiber. The multiplexers act as concentrators of DS-1s and other tributaries. Figure 9.18 shows a point-to-point network.

Figure 9.18
The point-to-point network topology, in which each node is connected to the other by a fiber.

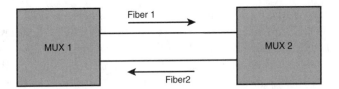

A point-to-multipoint network expands on the point-to-point architecture by inserting add/drop multiplexers along the fiber link connecting the terminal multiplexers. The ADMs can pick up or drop off network traffic to other points along the fiber path between the terminal multiplexers. Figure 9.19 shows a point-to-multipoint network.

Figure 9.19
Point-to-multipoint topology with ADMs to add or drop signals as required along the path.

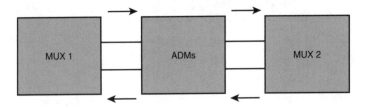

In a hub network, shown in Figure 9.20, a cross-connect switch serves as a central point (or hub) to interconnect multiple point-to-point or point-to-multipoint networks. These are two typical implementations of a hub network:

■ Using two or more ADMs and a wideband cross-connect switch to support cross-connecting the tributary services at the tributary level

■ Using a broadband digital cross-connect switch to enable cross-connecting at either the SONET level or the tributary level or both

In the ring architecture, shown in Figure 9.21, multiple ADMs are put into a ring configuration, typically with two fiber rings connecting them. Traffic generally flows in a clockwise direction over one ring and counterclockwise over the other ring so that if one fiber is cut or one fiber ring is disabled, traffic is rerouted over the other ring. The relatively simple designs of SONET networks also make them easy to manage and maintain, easing the burden on network administrators.

Figure 9.20
A hub topology with
digital cross-connects
as the central point.

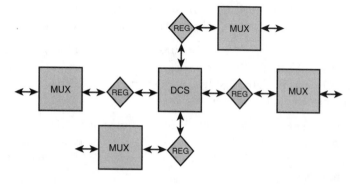

Figure 9.21
ADMs in a ring con-
figuration.

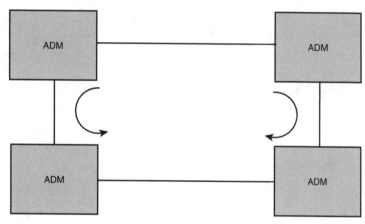

SUMMARY

Synchronization between different signals is essential because of the many different signal hierarchies and encoding techniques. Synchronization is achieved by adding extra bits to the signals; this process is called bit stuffing.

SONET provides a standard for the rates and formats of the various signals to be multiplexed.

The basic building block of a SONET optical interface is an STS with a basic rate of 51.84Mbps. The STS consists of two parts—the payload and the transport overhead.

SONET's frame structure consists of 9 rows and 90 columns, with a frame rate of 125usec. The first three columns are used for transport overhead, accounting for 27 bytes, so the actual data rate is 50.112Mbps.

The basic STS signal is called STS-1. Many such STS-1 signals are concatenated to form an STS-n frame.

The STS payload pointer in the transport header holds the location of the byte where the STS-1 SPE begins. STS-1s are concatenated to form an STS-nc signal, which is multiplexed, switched, and transported through the network as a signal entity.

SONET carries a substantial amount of overhead information to enable easier multiplexing and greatly expanded operations, administration, maintenance, and provisions.

Section overhead consists of 9 bytes of transport overhead. Line overhead contains 18 bytes of transport overhead. STS POH contains 9 evenly distributed POH bytes per 125 microseconds, starting at the first byte of the STS-SPE. SONET uses pointers to compensate for frequency and phase variations.

DS-3 signals are mapped into SONET using stuffing bits to account for variations in timing between the DS-3 and the SONET systems. DS-1 signals can be mapped using asynchronous mapping, floating-byte synchronous mapping, locked-byte synchronous mapping, or bit-synchronous mapping.

SONET multiplexing occurs at the line layer of SONET's four-layered architecture. n STS-1 signals are multiplexed to create an STS-n electrical signal.

SONET also defines several sub-STS-1 signaling rates called virtual tributaries. They are designed to carry lower-speed signals, such as DS-1s and DS-2s, through a SONET network. SONET makes it possible to extract low-speed signals without fully demultiplexing higher-level signals.

Networking elements for efficient operation of SONET are terminal multiplexers, regenerators, add/drop multiplexers, and digital cross-connects. Digital cross-connects can be wideband (WDCS) or broadband (BDCS).

The four basic SONET network configurations are point-to-point, point-to-multipoint, hub, and ring.

SONET provides substantial overhead information to enable quicker troubleshooting and detection of failures before they degrade to serious levels. SONET provides more powerful networking capabilities than the existing asynchronous systems.

CHAPTER 10

SECOND-GENERATION OPTICAL NETWORKS

In this chapter

WAVELENGTH DIVISION MULTIPLEXING

With advancements in lasers and optoelectronic device technology, it is possible to transmit more than one wavelength over a single fiber. This is known as Wavelength Division Multiplexing (WDM). Adding wavelengths to a fiber increases the fiber's bandwidth capacity and eliminates the need for additional fibers. As a result, one wavelength can be used to transport different channels. For example, one wavelength is used to transmit OC-3 traffic and the other to transmit OC-12 traffic. WDM can also be used to transport heterogeneous traffic such as SONET over one network and ATM over another. As optical technology moves forward, it will be possible to have many wavelengths over one fiber. The high density of wavelengths over the same fiber has led to the coining of the term Dense Wavelength Division Multiplexing (DWDM).

WDM offers an attractive solution to increasing LAN bandwidth without disturbing the existing embedded fiber that populates most buildings and campuses. It continues to be the cable of choice. By multiplexing several relatively coarsely spaced wavelengths over a single installed multimode network, the aggregate bandwidth can be increased.

Multichannel optical systems were relatively unknown in 1980, but more technological progress has been made since then. The applications can include a multiplexed high-bandwidth library resource system, simultaneous information sharing, supercomputer data and processor interaction, myriad multimedia services, video applications, and other undreamed-of services. As demands for network bandwidth increase, the need for multiuser optical networks with issues such as functionality, compatibility, and cost will determine which systems will eventually be implemented.

THE BASIC WDM SYSTEM

In a basic WDM system, shown in Figure 10.1, an optical source must emit light at different wavelengths. These wavelengths are then multiplexed onto a single fiber and are transmitted through a high-bandwidth optical fiber. At the receiving end, the different wavelengths are recovered using receivers tuned to the specific wavelength. Each laser modulates the signal at a particular speed. The fiber's total information-carrying capacity is the sum total of the bit rates of the individual lasers.

Figure 10.1
A basic WDM system with different wavelengths on one fiber.

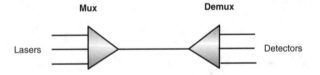

For example, if 10 2.5Gbps signals are transmitted on a single fiber, the system capacity becomes 25Gbps. This wavelength parallelism circumvents the problem of typical optoelectronic devices, which do not have bandwidths exceeding a few gigahertz unless they are exotic and expensive. The speed requirements for individual optoelectronic components are therefore relaxed, although a significant amount of total fiber bandwidth is still being utilized.

A different requirement exists for the demultiplexer, because photodetectors are usually sensitive over a broad range of wavelengths. This can include WDM channels. To prevent unwanted, spurious signals from entering the receiving channel, a demultiplexer must exhibit good channel isolation or a narrow spectral width. Very stable filters with sharp wavelength cutoffs must also be used.

> **Note**
>
> The *spectral width* is the wavelength interval over which the magnitude of all spectral components is equal to or greater than a specified fraction of the magnitude of the component having the maximum value.
>
> In optical communications applications, the usual method of specifying spectral width is the full width at the half-maximum of the signal level. This method might be difficult to apply when the spectrum has a complex shape.

DIFFERENT ARCHITECTURES OF A WDM SYSTEM

Two common network topologies used in WDM are the star network and the ring network.

STAR NETWORK

In a star network, shown in Figure 10.2, all computers connect to a central point called a hub. The central hub can be active or passive. The data is first sent to the hub and then is forwarded to the appropriate destination. If the star is a multiaccess star, hosts must synchronize their sending. If the star is a switch/router with multiple point-to-point links, hosts do not need to synchronize. Failure of the central hub causes the entire network to collapse.

Figure 10.2
A star topology with a central hub and hosts connected to it.

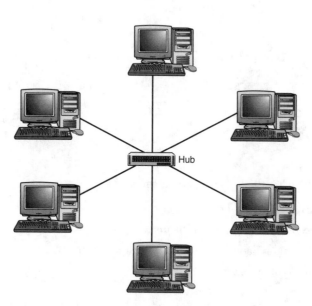

The advantages of the star topology are as follows:

- Easy to manage
- Easy to locate node and cable problems
- Well-suited for expansion into high-speed networking
- Has more equipment options

The star topology also has the following disadvantages:

- Susceptible to a single point of failure
- Requires more network cable at the start

RING TOPOLOGY

WDM networks can also be of the *ring* variety, as shown in Figure 10.3. Rings are popular because they are easy to implement for any geographical configuration. In a ring topology, each node in the unidirectional ring can transmit on a specific signature wavelength, and each node can recover any other node's wavelength signal by means of a wavelength-tunable receiver. Originally, data was passed in only one direction. Now, high-speed ring technologies consist of two loops for redundant data transmission in opposite directions.

Figure 10.3
Peripheral devices connected in a ring fashion.

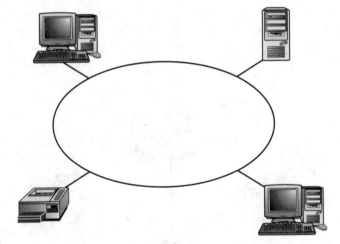

The ring topology has the following advantages:

- Easy to manage the network
- Easy to locate node and cable problems
- Has efficient and reliable transmission over long distances
- Handles high-volume traffic well

The ring topology has the following disadvantages:

■ Requires more network cable and equipment at the start
■ It does not have as many equipment options as for a bus

In conventional communications networks, the router can replace the node. The router is better suited for data networks. In WDM applications, a router that performs DS-*n* and OC-*n* network connections, optical multiplexing, and switching and that provides real-time quality of service (QoS) starts to behave like a traditional node. Therefore, although conceptually nodes and routers are different, in this case the router can be treated as a node.

SINGLE-HOP NETWORKS

With both the star and the ring networks, each node has a specific wavelength, and any two nodes can communicate with each other by transmitting on that wavelength. This implies that we require *n* wavelengths to connect *n* nodes. The advantage is that data transfer occurs over an uninterrupted optical path between the origin and the destination. This is known as a *single-hop network*. The data transferred over the optical network starts at the originating node and reaches the destination node without stopping at any other intermediate node.

However, the disadvantage of a single-hop WDM network is that the network and all its components must accommodate *n* wavelengths. This might be difficult or even impossible to achieve in a large network. The transmission capability cannot accommodate 1,000 distinct wavelengths for a 1,000-user network.

Four possibilities exist for transmission over the fiber-optic medium, depending on the type of components at the source and the destination: Fixed-Wavelength Transmitter, Fixed Receiver (FT-FR); Fixed-Wavelength Transmitter, Tunable Receiver (FT-TR); Tunable-Wavelength Transmitter, Fixed Receiver (TT-FR); and Tunable-Wavelength Transmitter, Tunable Receiver (TT-TR). The characteristics of these four combinations of components are discussed in the following sections.

FIXED-WAVELENGTH TRANSMITTER, FIXED RECEIVER (FT-FR)   FT-FR has the following characteristics:

■ There are no tuning delays.
■ All nodes can broadcast with their own unique wavelength.
■ The number of channels that can be implemented is limited due to the fixed number of wavelengths.
■ The network is expensive.

FIXED-WAVELENGTH TRANSMITTER, TUNABLE RECEIVER (FT-TR)   FT-TR has the following characteristics:

■ The receiver must be notified either by scanning or through control channel.
■ The cost is high, and delay is greater due to tuning at the receiver.
■ It leads to collision of data packets at the receiver.

TUNABLE-WAVELENGTH TRANSMITTER, FIXED RECEIVER (TT-FR)   TT-FR has the following characteristic:

■ If no control is used, collision occurs.

TUNABLE-WAVELENGTH TRANSMITTER, TUNABLE RECEIVER (TT-TR)   TT-TR has the following characteristics:

■ It's the most flexible.
■ It has an unlimited number of nodes.
■ It's expensive because of device and signaling cost.
■ It has high propagation delay due to tuning.

MULTIHOP NETWORKS

An alternative to requiring *n* wavelengths to accommodate *n* nodes is to have a multihop network. Such a network has two nodes that can communicate with each other by sending the signal through a third node with many intermediate hops. Figure 10.4 shows a dual-bus, multihop, eight-node WDM network. Each node can transmit on two wavelengths and receive on two other wavelengths.

Figure 10.4
A multihop network with two nodes talking to each other through a third node.

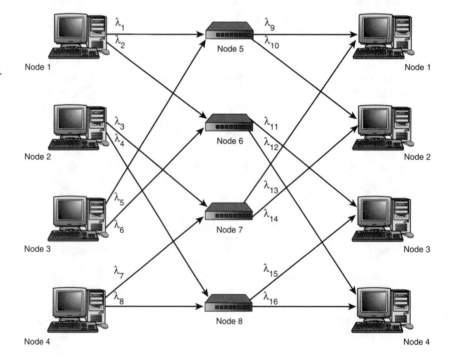

The end nodes can be computers communicating with each other through routers. For example, if node 1 wants to communicate with node 5, it transmits on wavelength λ_1, and only a single hop is required. However, if node 1 wants to communicate with node 2, it must first transmit to node 5, which then transmits to node 2, incurring two hops. Any extra hops are harmful for the following reasons:

- An increase in the transmission time between two communicating nodes, because a hop typically requires some form of detection and retransmission.

- A decrease in throughput, because a relaying node can transmit its own data while it is in the process of relaying another node's data.

However, multihop networks do reduce the required number of wavelengths and the components' wavelength tunability range.

Single-hop and multihop networks have the features listed in Table 10.1.

TABLE 10.1 FEATURES OF SINGLE-HOP AND MULTIHOP NETWORKS

Single-Hop Networks	Multihop Networks
The hop distance is minimal	The hop distance is greater
Inherent transparency	Transparency through intermediate devices
Low processing requirements at the node	Processing requirements are high at the intermediate nodes
High channel utilization	Channel utilization is good

DENSE WAVELENGTH DIVISION MULTIPLEXING ARCHITECTURE

Dense Wavelength Division Multiplexing (DWDM) is a fiber-optic transmission technique that involves multiplexing many different wavelength signals onto a single fiber. Therefore, each fiber has a set of parallel optical channels using slightly different wavelengths. It employs light wavelengths to transmit data through parallel or serial communication. DWDM is a crucial component of optical networks that enables the transmission of data, voice, video-IP, ATM, and SONET/SDH over the optical layer. Systems with 4 to 40 channels, with up to 10Gbps per channel, are commercially available from several vendors, and the technology is advancing rapidly. Systems with 80 or more channels will soon be available.

A DWDM signal can be carried at different rates (OC 3/12/24) and in different formats. Although the data transfer formats IP, ATM, and SONET/SDH provide unique bandwidth management capabilities, all three are transported over the optical layer using DWDM. This capability enables the service provider to respond to customer demands over one network. Future DWDM terminals will carry up to 80 wavelengths of OC–48—a total of 200Gbps or up to 40 wavelengths of OC–192—a total of 400Gbps. By using ultrawideband optical-fiber amplifiers, lightwave signals can be boosted to carry over 100 channels (or wavelengths) of light.

Note
Lucent's latest DWDM system provides up to 400Gbps capacity over a single strand of fiber, which is equivalent to carrying the per-second traffic of the entire worldwide Internet over one fiber.

The most important components of any DWDM system are transmitters, receivers, Erbium-doped fiber amplifiers, DWDM multiplexers, and DWDM demultiplexers. Figure 10.5 shows the structure of a typical DWDM system.

Figure 10.5
The structure of a DWDM system.

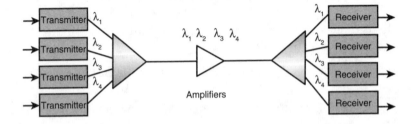

DWDM LASERS

DWDM systems use high-resolution or narrowband lasers transmitting in the 1550nm wavelength band. Operation in the 1550nm range provides the following two benefits:

- Minimizing optical power loss as the signal propagates along the fiber, allowing much greater transmission distances with better signal integrity.

- Permitting the use of optical amplifiers to boost signal strength for extended distances. Optical amplifiers cost less than electrical amplifiers, because they do not have to regenerate the individual optical signals.

Lasers transmitting in a narrow band are used because they enable close channel spacing and minimize the effects of other signal impairments, such as chromatic dispersion. They otherwise limit the distance allowed before the signal is regenerated electronically.

OPTICAL MULTIPLEXER

The optical multiplexer combines the transmitted signals at different wavelengths onto a single optical fiber, and the demultiplexer separates the combined signal into its component wavelengths at the receiver. Several technologies are currently used for optical multiplexing and demultiplexing, including thin-film dielectric filters and various types of optical gratings. Some multiplexers are constructed as completely passive devices (they require no electrical input). Passive optical multiplexers behave much like very high-precision prisms to combine and separate individual colors of the WDM signal. Similar to prisms, most passive optical devices are reciprocal devices, meaning that they function in the same way when the direction of the light is reversed.

Typically, a WDM multiplexer/demultiplexer provides multiplexing and demultiplexing functions. Some multiplexers can transmit and receive on a single fiber. This capability is known as *bidirectional transmission*.

OPTICAL RECEIVER

The optical receiver is responsible for detecting the incoming lightwave signal and converting it to an appropriate electronic signal. The receiving device processes this signal. Optical receivers are very often wideband devices. In other words, they can detect light over a relatively wide range of wavelengths, from about 1280nm to 1580nm. For instance, it is not a problem to directly connect two compatible network interfaces with different transmitter wavelengths, although one end is transmitting at 1310nm and the other at 1550nm.

OPTICAL AMPLIFIER

An amplifier is sometimes used to boost an optical signal to compensate for power loss, or attenuation, caused by propagation over long distances. Before the development of optical amplifiers, the only way to boost an optical signal was to regenerate it electronically. In other words, you had to convert the optical signal to an electrical signal, amplify it, convert it back to an optical signal, and then retransmit it. Electronic regeneration of a WDM signal requires a separate regenerator for each wavelength on the fiber. Alternatively, a single optical amplifier can simultaneously amplify all the wavelengths on one fiber. This allows the cost of signal amplification to be spread over several users or applications.

An additional benefit of the optical amplifier is that as a strictly optical device, it is protocol- and bit-rate-independent. In other words, an optical amplifier operates the same way regardless of the framing or bit rate of the optical signal. This allows a great deal of flexibility in that an optically amplified link can support any combination of protocols, such as ATM, SONET, Gigabit Ethernet, or PPP, at any bit rate up to the maximum design limit.

OPTICAL LAYERS

The term *optical layer* denotes the functionality of second-generation optical networks, such as WDM networks, that provide lightpaths to their users. This layer resides under existing layers such as SONET.

Note

A *lightpath* is a connection between two nodes in the network. You set it up by assigning a dedicated wavelength to it on each link in its path.

The optical layer has three sublayers.

The first layer is the lightpath layer, also called the Optical Channel (OC) layer. This layer is responsible for end-to-end routing of lightpaths. Each lightpath traverses a number of links in the network, and each of these links carries multiple wavelengths.

The Optical Multiplex Section (OMS) layer is used to represent a point-to-point link along the lightpath's route. Each OMS in turn consists of several link segments in which each segment is a link between the two optical amplifier stages.

Each link segment belongs to the Optical Amplifier Section (OAS) layer.

Therefore, in principle, after the interfaces between the different layers are defined, it is possible for vendors to provide standardized equipment ranging from just optical amplifiers for WDM links to entire WDM networks.

SUMMARY

Wavelength Division Multiplexing (WDM) involves transmitting more than one wavelength over one fiber. This effectively utilizes the fiber's entire bandwidth, thereby eliminating the need for additional fibers.

Dense Wavelength Division Multiplexing (DWDM) is an optical technology used to increase bandwidth over existing fiber-optic backbones.

DWDM works by combining and transmitting multiple signals simultaneously at different wavelengths on the same fiber. In effect, one fiber is transformed into multiple virtual fibers.

Two common network topologies that are used in WDM are the star network and the ring network.

In both star and ring networks, data transfer can occur with an uninterrupted optical path between the origin and the destination. This is called a single-hop network.

A multihop network is one in which two nodes can communicate with each other by sending data through a third node, with many intermediate hops possible.

The term optical layer denotes the functionality of second-generation optical WDM networks. The optical layer has the following three sublayers: the Optical Channel (OC), the Optical Multiplex Section (OMS), and the Optical Amplifier Section (OAS).

CHAPTER 11

BROADCAST AND SELECT TOPOLOGIES

In this chapter

BROADCAST STAR TOPOLOGY

The star topology is the most complex topology, but it has a few advantages over other configurations. A central node that directs signal traffic controls the activities in a star architecture. Each node is connected point-to-point with the central node, which is either active or passive. A variation of the star configuration allows you to connect individual nodes with each other directly as well as through a central node. This is an expensive but powerful variation that can handle enormous traffic. The disadvantage is that failure of the central node causes the entire network to collapse.

In broadcast network architecture, the network sends the signal received from each node to all the other nodes. Two topologies that are widely used for broadcast networks are bus and star.

The star network uses optical couplers. The optical coupler can be built using 2×2 couplers, or it can be a single integrated optical device. Figure 11.1 shows an 8×8 optical coupler built using 2×2 star couplers.

Figure 11.1
A broadcast star topology in which the signal received is sent to all the nodes.

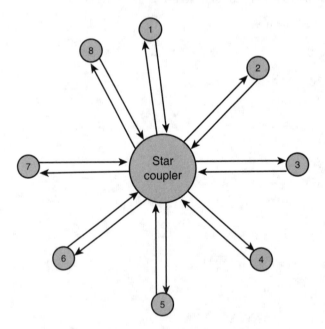

In many cases, it is not possible to have a single broadcast star for the entire network. This is because of the large number of nodes that increase the splitting losses or because the nodes are not geographically close. In this case, a large number of broadcast stars can be connected in the fashion required by the application. In an interconnected star network, the broadcast stars are connected to a wavelength router. In Figure 11.2, four stars are interconnected using four wavelengths. Each star uses a unique wavelength to transmit to another star and a uses unique wavelength to receive from another star. An Arrayed Waveguide

Grating (AWG) router can be used as the wavelength router. Each broadcast star uses the same set of wavelengths for communication within that star.

Figure 11.2
Interconnected stars with each star coupler transmitting at a unique wavelength.

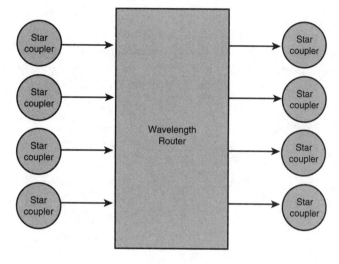

Interconnected Stars

LOGICAL TOPOLOGY DESIGN AND ROUTING IN OPTICAL NETWORKS

A second-generation optical network offers different services to the layer or network above it. One such service is the lightpath service, in which the network provides a dedicated optical path between two nodes. This is quite similar to a circuit-switched network, in which a dedicated path is provided for the connection. The topology design problem now involves the design of two topologies—the physical or fiber topology of the wavelength-routing network, and the logical or lightpath topology that is seen by a network that lies above the wavelength-routing network. While designing topologies, you must consider the problems of routing lightpaths through the physical topology and routing data traffic over the lightpath topology.

Several government and industry-funded prototyping and development activities in WDM optical networks are being conducted at various research and development centers. Optical networks can be deployed on top of an existing physical fiber plant that provides a transparent all-optical signal path to its upper layer, thereby providing broadband services. For instance, an all-optical layer between the physical and ATM layers in a broadband ISDN network will significantly improve both the efficiency and flexibility of broadband services. One attractive feature of optical networks is the ease of logical reconfigurability. In other words, any desired logical network topology can be embedded on top of any given physical fiber plant, subject to the limitations on the number of available wavelengths and transceivers.

Over the past few years, several regular logical topologies have been proposed for optical networks. This chapter briefly describes logical network topologies and explains their various performance metrics, such as average hop distance, routing, fault tolerance, and scalability.

By properly configuring the network elements on a given physical fiber plant, you can embed different logical topologies by employing multiple parallel WDM channels. For example, you can embed a logical ring topology on a physical broadcast passive star network by properly tuning the transceivers at the nodes as shown in Figure 11.3.

Figure 11.3
Broadcast and select optical networks with logical topology embedded over the physical topology.

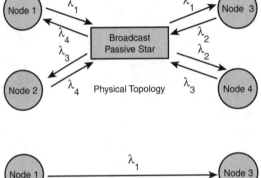

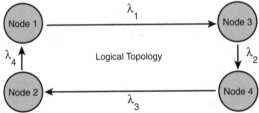

If the network topology is expected to be static, fixed-wavelength transceivers are used instead of tunable ones. For example, Node-1's transmitter can be tuned to wavelength λ_1 and Node-1's receiver to wavelength λ_4.

A wavelength-routed network has routers that use different switching configurations to incorporate different logical topologies. In a wavelength-routed network, the major advantage is wavelength reuse, in which fewer wavelengths are required to support the same topology. For example, one wavelength, λ_1, is required to transmit data in a wavelength-routed network, whereas four wavelengths are required in a broadcast network. This is shown in Figure 11.4.

OPTICAL NETWORK TOPOLOGIES

An optical network topology can be of the single-hop or multihop type.

In a single-hop topology, signals are carried from the source node to the destination node without any optoelectronic conversion. The information is routed through multiple optical devices such as passive star couplers, all-optical multiplexers, and all-optical routers. However, no electronic processing takes place in these devices.

Figure 11.4
A wavelength routed network in which routers are employed to reduce the number of wavelengths used for transmission.

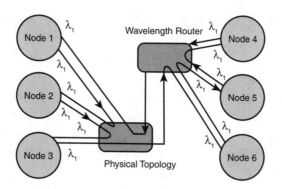

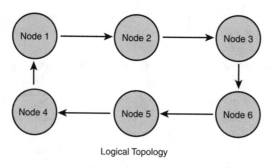

Logical Topology

Note

A *hop* is defined as a logical connection between two nodes without any optoelectronic processing at intermediate devices.

In multihop topology, the information passes through intermediate nodes, where optoelectronic conversion and processing take place. The information is then transmitted over another link on a different wavelength.

A single-hop topology suffers from two major drawbacks:

- The need for sensitive transceivers
- The need for coordination between the end equipment before transmission

In contrast, a multihop network does not require very sensitive wavelength receivers or pre-transmission coordination. A multihop network has two topologies—*regular* and *arbitrary*.

In a regular topology, the nodal connectivity patterns are systematic and well-defined. In an arbitrary multihop topology, the nodes do not have any predefined connectivity pattern. You can add new nodes to the existing nodes provided that hardware resources such as transceivers are available. The Internet is a good example of an arbitrary multihop topology.

The design of a multihop logical optical network architecture must meet the following requirements:

- The average distance between the two nodes must be small and must be inversely proportional to the network utilization.

- A very small number of transceivers must be used to make the network economically attractive. The number of transceivers required at a node must not depend on the network population.

- Only a small set of distinct wavelengths must be used for physical embedding of the logical network topology.

- It must be possible to add nodes to or remove nodes from the network one at a time, with minimal impact on network configuration and performance.

- Routing procedures must be simple, because each forwarding node might be required to electronically process thousands of messages per second. At the end of each hop, the message is converted from optical to electronic form, and a routing decision is made based on the destination address contained in the message. Regular multihop networks are often preferred to irregular or arbitrary ones, because they usually provide simple routing schemes due to their well-defined connectivity patterns. In an arbitrary network, routing decisions are based on routing tables that are updated periodically.

- A logical topology must be able to tolerate maximum node and link failures. In general, a logical topology is more fault-tolerant if there are more alternative paths between its node pairs. In the event of link and/or node failure, the affected traffic must be routed through alternative path(s) with sufficient spare capacity.

The three common regular topologies used widely are bus, star, and ring.

In a logical bus topology, each node is equipped with two fixed-tuned transmitters and two fixed-tuned receivers. A transmitter of node i is connected to a receiver of node i+1. The other transmitter of node i is connected to the receiver of node i–1. Only one pair of transceivers is used for the first node and the last node. Access to an optical data bus is achieved using a coupling element that can be either active or passive. An active element performs optoelectric conversion before any data processing. However, a passive coupler does not process the data; it is used only to passively tap power from the optical bus. Figure 11.5 shows the optical bus topology.

→ To learn more about star and ring topologies, **see** "Different Architectures of a WDM System," **p. 191** (Chapter 10)

Various other topologies have been suggested for multihop networks, including Shuffle Net, de Bruijn graph, and toroidal Manhattan street network. Shuffle Net is discussed here.

Figure 11.5
A bus topology with active or passive coupling elements.

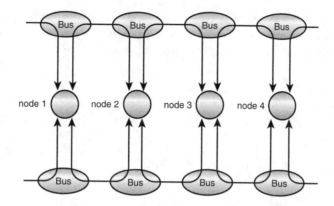

SHUFFLE NET TOPOLOGY

In 1971, H. S. Stone proposed the Shuffle Net topology for parallel processing. A scheme called perfect shuffle is widely used to interconnect patterns in multiprocessors. For optical networks, the extension of this consists of a cylindrical arrangement of k columns, each having p^k nodes, where p is the number of fixed transceiver pairs per node. The total number of nodes N is therefore as follows:

$$N = k \times p^k$$

where

$$k = 1, 2, 3 \ldots$$
$$p = 1, 2, 3 \ldots$$

Figure 11.6 is a generalization of the perfect shuffle with p=2, k=2. In general, in a (p,k) Shuffle Net, node (r,c) (that is, row r, column c) is connected to nodes (p.r mod p^k, (c + 1) mod k), (p.r mod p^k + 1, (c + 1) mod k), and (p.r mod p^k + p, (c + 1) mod k).

Figure 11.6
p=2, k=2 Shuffle Net.

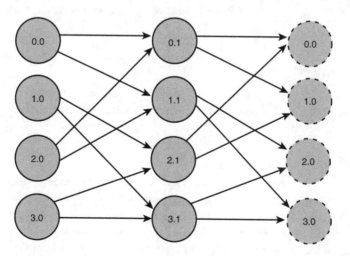

Shuffle Net is a symmetric and homogeneous topology. In other words, the network looks the same from any node. Due to Shuffle Net's cylindrical connectivity pattern, routing is reliable and fault-tolerant. Shuffle Net's various parameters are discussed in the following section.

DIAMETER AND AVERAGE HOP DISTANCE

The average hop distance, h, between two arbitrary nodes in a (p,k) Shuffle Net is given by the following equation:

$$h=[kp^k(p-1)(3k-1)-2k(p^k-1)]\div[2(p-1)(kp^k-1)]$$

Its diameter is $2k-1$.

LINK UTILIZATION

Due to multihopping, only a fraction of the link capacity is actually utilized for carrying direct traffic between the two specific nodes connected by a link. The remaining link capacity is used to forward multihop traffic. Let n_h be the number of nodes that are h hops away from the source node. The network has $Np=k.p^k$ $p=kp^{k+1}$ links, so the total network capacity is given by the following equation:

$$C=kp^{k+1}\div h$$

The network capacity is approximately 40% for large networks. The per-user throughput is given by the following equation:

$$C\div N=p\div h$$

The throughput can be increased by selecting fewer columns (k) and more transceiver pairs per node (p).

Note   *Throughput* is defined as the fraction of the network capacity that carries useful data.

LINK CONGESTION

Due to shortest-path routing and uniform traffic demands, some of the links are more congested than others. This results in degraded network performance. To reduce link congestion, different routing and fault-tolerance strategies are suggested.

ROUTING

The routing algorithm is distributed. In other words, the routing decision is made independently at each node. Some variations of *shortest-path routing* are also proposed. In one scheme, when a packet is more than k hops away from the destination, multiple shortest paths to the destination exist, and the packet gets routed on an outgoing link with the least number of queued packets. If more than one such link exists, one of them is selected randomly. In some cases, packets take longer paths, but they still reach their destinations faster.

In *deflection routing*, another variation on the shortest-path routing scheme, some packets are intentionally misrouted to prevent congestion. In this case, if two or more packets contend for the same outgoing link at a node, one of the packets is routed through that link. Instead of the remaining packets getting stored for their preferred route, they are immediately deflected to possibly longer routes through other available outgoing links at the node.

Note that if a packet at an intermediate node is more than k hops away from its destination, multiple shortest paths exist between the intermediate node and the destination node. The intermediate node in such a case can act as a "don't care" node, and the packet can be routed through any of the p outgoing links. This reduces congestion, especially in large networks. Because this routing is probabilistic, the aggregate capacity is less than the capacity provided by the shortest-path *store-and-forward* scheme.

FAULT TOLERANCE

In the case of multiple node failures, network connectivity is lost. For example, in degree-2 Shuffle Net, the removal of two nodes or links can disconnect the network. Because of Shuffle Net's cylindrical connectivity pattern, alternative routing is possible as long as the network is connected. For example, if node (1,1) in Figure 11.6 fails, a packet from node (0,0) to node (3,0) can be routed through node (0,1) to (1,0) to (3,1) to (3,0). However, this alternative path causes the packet to take two more hops than in the shortest-path route. In some instances, the alternative routing does not even increase the path length. For example, the path length from node (1,0) to node (0,1) is the same as the path length between nodes (2,1), (0,0) or nodes (3,1), (2,0).

BROADCASTING AND SCALABILITY

Shuffle Net has poor scalability because the number of nodes must be in the form kp^k. Therefore, with two transceivers at each node, an eight-node Shuffle Net (that is, p=2, k=2) can be scaled only up to a 24-node Shuffle Net (that is, p=2, k=3).

GEMNet, Hypercube, and TreeNet are other topologies that are widely used for optical routing to improve the network's overall performance.

MEDIUM ACCESS PROTOCOLS

In a broadcast-and-select network, any signal transmitted by the node is broadcast to other nodes and, depending on the address information present in the signal, the specific node selects and accepts the data packet. If two nodes transmit simultaneously on the same wavelength, due to the nodes' broadcast nature, the signals collide, causing loss of information. If two nodes transmit simultaneously on different wavelengths to the same receiver, there could be data loss because the receiver is tuned only to a single wavelength. The receiver would pick the signal from the node that is transmitting on the same wavelength and lose the signal from the other node. Therefore, to avoid contention and collisions, coordination is required between the different nodes in the network. The mechanism that provides coordination is called the Medium Access Control (MAC) protocol.

MAC protocols are designed according to the needs of the application, hardware requirements, and the level of performance required. Some applications require dedicated lines utilizing the entire wavelength, and others might use shared wavelengths. The hardware requirements can be a single transmitter and receiver tuned to either a fixed wavelength or a range of wavelengths. The level of performance is measured in terms of throughput and network delay. Data in a broadcast network might get lost due to contention or collisions. This reduces throughput, because useful data is lost.

Protocols that are widely used for media access control include Slotted Aloha/Slotted Aloha (SA/SA) and Dynamic Time-Wavelength-Division Multiple Access (DT-WDMA).

SLOTTED ALOHA/SLOTTED ALOHA PROTOCOLS

To control which computers are allowed to transmit at any given time, a protocol is required. The simplest protocol is known as Aloha taken from a Hawaiian word, meaning hello. Aloha enables any computer to transmit at any time, but each computer must add a checksum at the end of its transmission to allow the receivers to identify whether the frame was correctly received.

Aloha does not guarantee that the frame of data will actually reach the recipient without corruption. It therefore relies on ARQ (Automatic Request) protocols to retransmit any corrupted data. An Aloha network only works well when the medium has a low utilization, because it leads to a low probability of the transmission colliding with that of another computer. Therefore, the chances of data getting corrupted are less.

> **Note**
>
> Carrier Sense Multiple Access (CSMA), the backbone of Ethernet networks, also uses a highly refined model of Aloha. CSMA is highly suited for networks with high medium utilization.

Aloha and Slotted Aloha is a family of protocols that are designed assuming that the number of wavelengths used, W, is less than the number of nodes. Also, a control wavelength is present for slot synchronization, which is the (W+1)st control wavelength. This protocol also requires a fixed transmitter and receiver tuned to the control wavelength and a tunable transmitter and receiver for data transmission. In Aloha protocol, for a single-channel network, the node transmits the packet of data as soon as it receives it.

In the Slotted Aloha protocol, the time is divided into slots, depending on the data packet's maximum size. The data packet is transmitted immediately after the slot. If there is no simultaneous transmission from any other node in the same slot, the packet is received successfully. If not, there is a collision, and the nodes retransmit the packet after a random time interval.

In a multichannel network, the data as well as the control channels are divided into time slots. However, the size of the data slot is considered an integral multiple of the control slot.

In other words, the size of the data slot is L times the control slot. This assumption is made because the control packets are usually smaller than the data packets.

The basic operation of a Slotted Aloha is as follows: Whenever a node, n, has a packet of data to send, it sends a control packet in the control slot and the data packet in the data slot. The protocol used on the control wavelength is the Slotted Aloha protocol. Therefore, it is known as Slotted Aloha/Slotted Aloha (SA/SA) protocol.

The control packet is sent in the wavelength (W+1), and the data packets are sent on one of the data wavelengths ranging from 1 to W. The control packet has the receiving node's address—say, node q—for the corresponding data packet, and also the wavelength on which the data packet will be transmitted. Thus, provided that the data packets don't collide, the packet transmitted by node n in the time slot on the intended wavelength is received by node q, tuned to the same wavelength, and the packet is successfully received. Figure 11.7 shows the slots in an SA/SA protocol.

Figure 11.7
Slotted Aloha/Slotted
Aloha protocol.

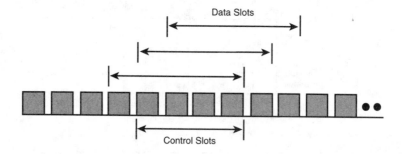

As soon as the packet is available for transmission at the node, it simply informs other nodes about the packet in the control slot and transmits it in the next data slot. This feature is called *tell and go*. A protocol has the tell and go feature if it has a low access delay. Figure 11.8 shows the basic operation of the Slotted Aloha/Slotted Aloha protocol.

> **Note**
>
> *Access delay* is defined as the delay between the time when a packet is available for transmission at the node and the time when it is first transmitted.

A network's access delay must be low. For a successful transmission, both the data and the control slot must be free from collision. Another protocol that is widely used for multiwavelength optical networks is Dynamic Time-Wavelength-Division Multiple Access (DT-WDMA).

DYNAMIC TIME-WAVELENGTH-DIVISION MULTIPLE ACCESS

In DT-WDMA, the number of nodes n equals the number of wavelengths W of the data being transmitted. W+1 control wavelengths are present for synchronization. Each node must be equipped with a fixed and tuned data transmitter and a tuned data receiver. In addition, each node must also have a fixed and tuned control transmitter and a control receiver operating at the control wavelength. On the data channel and the control channel, the time is divided into slots, but in this case, the data slot is n or W times the control slot. Unlike the SA/SA protocol, the data slots do not overlap in time. For each data slot, one of the n control slots is assigned to each node in the network, and the node transmits the control packet only in the assigned node. Figure 11.9 shows the basic DT-WDMA operation.

Figure 11.8
Collision of data and control packets in the SA/SA protocol because of simultaneous transmission.

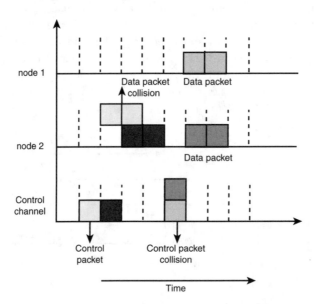

Figure 11.9
DT-WDMA with no collision of data packets.

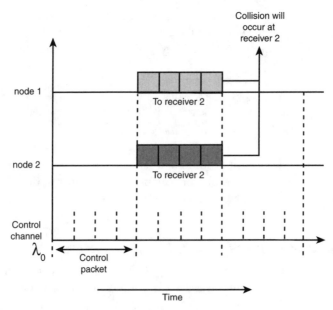

Each node operates on different wavelengths, so the collision of the data packets is impossible. The control packets are also transmitted on a different control slot, so they do not collide. However, if two nodes transmit data intended for the same receiver, the receiver can receive only one of these contending packets, because it is tuned to a single wavelength. The transmitting nodes use control channels to monitor the state of the packets received by the receiver. Therefore, the transmitting nodes that cannot transmit packets in the first attempt can retransmit the packets.

TYPES OF MULTIPLEXING AND MULTIPLE-ACCESS SCHEMES

The combination of two or more information channels onto a common transmission medium is called *multiplexing*. In electrical communications, the two basic forms of multiplexing are Time-Division Multiplexing (TDM) and Frequency-Division Multiplexing (FDM). In optical communications, the analog of FDM is called Wavelength-Division Multiplexing (WDM).

WAVELENGTH-DIVISION MULTIPLEXING

WDM is the technique of transmitting multiple optical signals on a single optical fiber. In other words, rather than sending a single signal at one specific wavelength, two or more signals are sent on different wavelengths. Figure 11.10 shows WDM technology.

Figure 11.10
Wavelength-division multiplexing with many wavelengths on a single fiber.

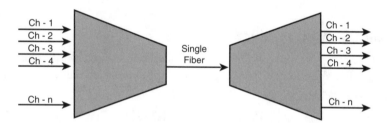

Equipment at the transmitting end converts the optical signal to a distinct, precise wavelength. These individual wavelengths are then optically multiplexed onto a single fiber. At the receiving end of the WDM system, the reverse process takes place. Individual wavelengths are filtered from the multiplexed fiber and are converted back to the original signals. WDM technology can be used to carry all types of optical signals, such as standard SONET/SDH, ATM, and Gigabit Ethernet.

Dense WDM (DWDM) refers to the ability to carry a large number of channels. DWDM equipment usually uses the 1530nm to 1565nm wavelength range with a light source such as a laser of high accuracy and temperature-controlled components.

Coarse WDM (CWDM) uses a much wider wavelength range of 1200nm to 1600nm with a minimum 20nm wavelength gap between any two channels. Optical components used for CWDM are less accurate and therefore are less expensive because of the 20nm wavelength gap.

Bidirectional WDM (BWDM) refers to the ability to carry two channels in different directions on a single fiber. Two distinct wavelengths might be used in BWDM technology, 1310nm and 1550nm. Figure 11.11 shows the wavelengths used by the various WDM technologies.

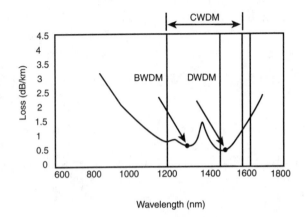

Figure 11.11
A graphical representation of the wavelengths used by WDM.

The obvious advantage of using DWDM for long-distance transmission is the increased bandwidth capacity that can be delivered on the existing infrastructure. DWDM has become increasingly popular for long-distance transmissions because the expenditure on DWDM equipment is less than that of laying down additional fiber-optic cables across oceans and continents.

TIME-DIVISION MULTIPLEXING

TDM is a type of multiplexing that combines data streams by assigning each stream a different time slot in a set. TDM repeatedly transmits a fixed sequence of time slots over a single transmission channel.

The basic concept of TDM is that bit streams from a number of channels and sources are combined at a higher aggregate speed on a single channel.

TDM has the following types:

- Fixed-length, preallocated time slots from channels all of the same speed, such as PDH systems
- Variable-length, but dynamically allocated time slots, such as TDMA
- Variable-length and allocated-on-demand, such as LAN techniques including CSMA/CD, token ring, token bus, and so on
- Fixed-length and allocated-on-demand, such as ATM

The latter two are sometimes called "statistical multiplexing." Traditional digital multiplexing systems have been based on 64Kbps channels derived from PCM voice signals, but they are also used for data.

→ To learn more about modulation techniques, **see** "Modulation," **p. 94** (Chapter 5)

Figure 11.12 shows basic TDM. Here, a commutator switches between the signals that are at lower rates and are converted into higher rates.

Figure 11.12
TDM with higher-rate channels aggregated from multiple lower-speed channels.

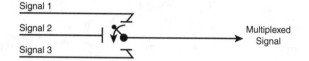

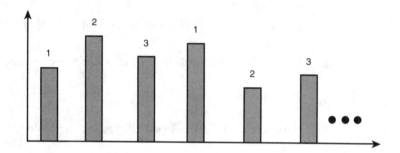

PLESIOCHRONOUS MULTIPLEXING

For long-distance high-speed systems, it is an advantage to multiplex several T1 or E1 channels into higher-speed channels. However, precise bit alignment is impossible, because the different channels can come from different sources with marginally different clocks and by different paths.

The solution is to add extra bits to cater to jitter. Each frame of 193 or 256 bits is placed in a larger slot and is preceded by a Frame Alignment Word (FAW) to signal its start. This approach is called *plesiochronous* (almost synchronous), and the hierarchy is called the Plesiochronous Digital Hierarchy (PDH). The disadvantage of this approach is that channels cannot be added or removed at the higher speeds. The higher-speed channel must be demultiplexed to the initial synchronous PCM frames first.

> **Note**
>
> *Jitter* is the deviation in or displacement of some aspect of the pulses in a high-frequency digital signal. The deviation can be in terms of amplitude, phase timing, or the width of the signal pulse.

SYNCHRONOUS MULTIPLEXING

It became clear by the late '70s and early '80s that the PDH structure was too restrictive to meet future network demands. It was also recognized that optical communication technology delivers more cost-effective bandwidth and that silicon technology provides capacity for more sophistication in multiplexing. This led to experimentation with purely synchronous

PART

II

CH

11

multiplexing systems that overcame the limitations of PDH. After trials, Bellcore Labs of AT&T proposed Synchronous Optical Network (SONET) in 1985.

The main features of SDH/SONET are as follows:

■ It has a basic transport rate of 155.52Mbps.

■ Lower-speed channels can be multiplexed onto this.

■ SONET has a 51.84Mbps subrate (OC-1).

■ All transport modules are synchronous with each other. This allows for drop and insert without demultiplexing.

■ Multiplexing is byte-interleaving.

■ Transport modules are based on a 125-microsecond frame, allowing direct handling down to 64Kbps.

■ It has many overheads for very flexible multiplexing structures, management messaging, voice channels, and so on.

■ It is compatible with the PDH.

→ To learn more about SONET and its various details, **see** Chapter 9, "Synchronous Optical Networks," **p. 167**

OPTICAL TIME-DIVISION MULTIPLEXING

TDM technology has limitations because of the data rates it can hold. The transmission rates that are available are around 10Gbps. To increase the data rate of TDM technology, research is in progress to carry this multiplexing and demultiplexing optically. This approach is called Optical Time-Division Multiplexing (OTDM).

→ To learn more about Optical Time-Division Multiplexing, **see** "Optical Time-Division Multiplexing," **p. 250** (Chapter 14)

MULTIPLE-ACCESS SCHEMES

In long-haul applications, optical links and networks consist of a multiplexed aggregate data stream, originating from the individual subscribers. These data streams are usually in a synchronized format. The TDM process was used to increase the usage of the enormous available fiber bandwidth. To increase this capacity even further, WDM techniques were employed. An alternative to WDM on a local area network (LAN) is Optical Code-Division Multiple Access (O-CDMA).

OPTICAL CODE-DIVISION MULTIPLE ACCESS

In its simplest configuration, CDMA achieves multiple access by assigning a unique code to each user. The two nodes communicate with each other by imprinting these codes onto the data. The receiver then decodes the data by locking onto the same code sequence.

Optical CDMA uses spread-spectrum techniques. These techniques have been widely used in mobile satellite and digital cellular communication systems.

The concept is to spread the energy of the optical signal over a frequency band that is much wider than the minimum bandwidth required for sending the information. For example, a signal that conveys information of 1Kbps is spread over a 1MHz bandwidth. The spreading is done by a code that is independent of the signal itself. Therefore, an optical encoder is used to map each bit of information into a high-rate information sequence.

The symbols in the spreading codes are called *chips*. The energy of the transmitted waveform is distributed more or less uniformly over the entire spread-spectrum bandwidth. The set of optical sequences becomes a set of unique address codes or signatures for individual network users. In this scheme, each 1 data bit is encoded into a waveform or a signature sequence consisting of *n* chips, which represent the destination address of that bit. In Figure 11.13, the signature sequence consists of three chips. When the data signal contains a 1 data bit, the three-chip sequence is transmitted. With the 0 bit, no chips are sent.

Figure 11.13
Optical CDMA with information transmitted using independent codes for the signal.

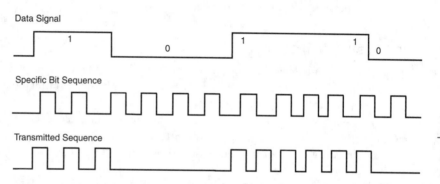

Therefore, the time-domain optical CDMA enables a number of users to access the network simultaneously through the use of common wavelength. However, there are limitations because as the number of users increases, the coding sequence becomes longer in order to maintain the performance.

Optical CDMA schemes can be synchronous or asynchronous. Synchronous access schemes produce higher throughputs than asynchronous ones, in which network accesses are random and collisions are possible. In applications requiring real-time transmissions, such as voice and video, synchronous schemes are efficient. When traffic is bursty in nature and there is not much real-time constraint, asynchronous multiplexing is used.

TIME-DIVISION MULTIPLE ACCESS

In Time-Division Multiple Access (TDMA), each user is allocated unique time slots within each channel. This allows a number of users to access a single radio frequency (RF) channel without interference. In this scheme, three signals are multiplexed over a single channel. Each user is assigned a specific time slot for transmission.

TEST BEDS

Extensive research is being conducted in the area of optical networking due to the network's capacity to carry large amounts of information. Although many optical networks have been proposed, only a few have been implemented. Here are some of the test beds used:

- Lambdanet
- NTT's test bed
- Rainbow
- STARNET
- BBC Television Studio test bed
- Lightning
- Supercomputer Supernet test bed

THE LAMBDANET TEST BED

Bellcore's Lambdanet uses both time- and wavelength-division multiplexing. Each node consists of a fixed-tuned transmitter. At the receiving node, a grating demultiplexer is used to separate the wavelengths and an array of receivers from each of the wavelengths. Experiments were carried out, demonstrating the transmission of 18 wavelengths spaced 2nm apart. Each wavelength was transmitted at 1.5Gbps over a distance of 57km. Experiments were also carried out for 16 wavelengths at 2Gbps.

THE NIPPON TELEGRAPH AND TELEPHONE CORPORATION TEST BED

The Nippon Telegraph and Telephone (NTT) Corporation's experiment uses 100 wavelengths spaced 10GHz apart, each having a capacity of 622Mbps. Only one receiver is used; it consists of a Mach-Zehnder Interferometric (MZI) filter. This filter is tuned by varying the temperature.

→ To learn more about the Mach-Zehnder Interferometer (MZI), **see** "Mach-Zehnder Interferometers," **p. 48** (Chapter 3)

THE RAINBOW TEST BED

IBM designed the Rainbow I and Rainbow II networks. They were intended to support about 32 wavelengths spaced 1nm apart in a star configuration. Each node transmits at a fixed-tuned wavelength, and a Piezo-tuned Fabry-Perot filter is used to get the desired channel. It uses both wavelength and time-division multiplexing. Thirty-two 200Mbps data channels can operate simultaneously.

→ To learn more about Fabry-Perot filters, **see** "Fabry-Perot Filters," **p. 57** (Chapter 3)

Each station is equipped with a fixed-frequency transmitter and a tunable receiver. Each station is allocated a unique wavelength from a band of wavelengths ranging from 1505nm to 1545nm. The tunable receivers are actually fixed-frequency incoherent detectors, each of which is preceded by a Fabry-Perot tunable filter with a tuning range of 50nm. The tuning rate is about 10usec/nm, which gives an average time to locate a channel as 250usec.

Simple OOK (On-Off Keying) modulation is used. The data rate is 200Mbps over a standard 8-micron single-mode fiber.

→ To learn more about on-off keying, **see** "On-Off Keying," **p. 94** (Chapter 5)

The system operates as follows: When node A wants to establish a connection with node B, it sends a setup request to node B. It is sent on node A's dedicated transmit wavelength. Node A then tunes its receiver to the wavelength of node B's transmitter. Even if node B is receiving data from another node, node A continues sending the setup request. When node B is not communicating with another node, it continuously scans the range of all wavelengths, looking for a setup request addressed to it. When node B receives a setup request, it locks its receiver onto the signal from node A and immediately sends a confirmation to the other node. It can do this because its transmitter is not tunable, and node A is already waiting for a response. Both nodes can then exchange data freely until they agree to disconnect. At this point, both nodes begin scanning all channels again, looking for the next setup request.

Due to the timing involved, up to 1 millisecond to make a connection, the system is circuit-switched rather than packet-switched. Figure 11.14 shows Rainbow I.

Figure 11.14
The Rainbow I connection process for very high data rates developed by IBM.

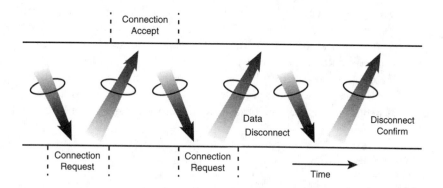

In Rainbow II, the bit rate per channel was upgraded to 1Gbps. It was built to tackle the problem of suitable higher-layer software and hardware to handle high bit rates offered by the physical layer.

Each node has an optical transmitter that emits light at a wavelength different from other transmitters in the network. From every node, a fiber leads to the network hub. This hub is an all-glass, totally passive star coupler with n inputs and n outputs, where n is the number of nodes in the network. The star coupler combines the transmissions from different nodes. At each output, you obtain approximately $1/n$th of the optical power from each transmitter. From the star coupler, a fiber leads to each node. Therefore, the network is broadcast in nature. All transmissions reach all the nodes. At each station, a tunable optical receiver selects one of the n wavelengths.

THE STARNET TEST BED

Optical Communications Research Laboratory at Stanford University has constructed and tested the broadband optical network STARNET. It avoids the requirement of fast tunability by creating two logical subnetworks over a single physical star topology network. It offers both a moderate-speed 125Mbps packet-switched subnetwork and a high-speed (up to 2.5Gbps) WDM circuit-switched subnetwork. Each node has a single fixed-wavelength transmitter that uses novel combined Amplitude Shift Keying (ASK) and Phase Shift Keying (PSK) modulation techniques to simultaneously send moderate-speed subnetwork traffic and high-speed subnetwork traffic on the same transmitter carrier wavelength. Each node is also equipped with a fixed-wavelength receiver for the packet-switched subnetwork and a wavelength-tunable receiver for the circuit-switched subnetwork. In this manner, the use of fast-wavelength tunability is avoided, because moderate-speed bursty data is sent using the fixed-tuned ring subnetwork, and high-speed continuous data is sent using the tunable circuit switch.

→ To learn more about phase shift keying, **see** "Phase-Shift Keying," **p. 96** (Chapter 5)

THE BBC TELEVISION STUDIO TEST BED

The Research and Technology Development in Advanced Communications Technologies, Europe (RACE) program developed the BBC test bed. In this case, each node in the network is a Local Routing Center (LRC). It is connected with up to 16 signal sources and destinations. LRCs are connected using a star coupler. Each LRC transmits at a specific wavelength and receives all 16 wavelengths from the coupler. The LRC uses gratings to demultiplex the wavelengths. A 16[ts]16 electronic switch operating at 2.5Gbps per port switches the data received by an LRC. Figure 11.15 shows the BBC topology.

Figure 11.15
The BBC topology with the transmission using local routing centers.

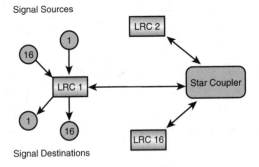

THE LIGHTNING TEST BED

The Lightning test bed was designed at SUNY-Buffalo to be used as the interconnecting network of an experimental distributed memory multicomputer. Lightning is based on a wavelength partitioner, a specialized switch that splits an incoming multiwavelength optical stream into two substreams such that one substream contains all light below a given wavelength and the other contains all light above it. This device is used to implement the so-called fat-tree topology that has been successfully applied to the design of parallel computers. The wavelength partitioners make possible the wide-scale reuse of wavelengths. Because Lightning is specialized for carrying processor memory and interprocessor traffic, two types of message transfer are supported—large block transfers and small control messages. The network also supports the reconfiguration of its virtual topology to adapt to changing traffic patterns. Figure 11.16 shows the wavelength partitioner used in Lightning.

Figure 11.16
A wavelength partitioner that allows the reuse of wavelengths.

THE SUPERCOMPUTER SUPERNET TEST BED

University of California, Jet Propulsion Laboratory, and Aerospace Corporation jointly developed the Supercomputer Supernet (SSN) Test Bed. This test bed employs WDM technology and high-speed transmission. Features that distinguish the proposed SSN test bed from other approaches include the combination of multiple single-hop, on-demand circuits with a multihop virtual embedded network to realize a two-level architecture. SSN also allows for the dynamic reconfiguration of the virtual topology of its multihop component by retuning its transceivers. The SSN two-level architecture, which combines a single-hop subnetwork for circuit-switched traffic and a multihop subnetwork for datagram traffic, has the benefits of both these networks, thereby compensating for their individual shortcomings.

SUMMARY

The topology design problem involves the design of two topologies—the physical or fiber topology and the logical or lightpath topology. The physical topology is of the wavelength-routing network, and the logical topology is the topology seen by a network that lies above the wavelength-routing network. By properly tuning the transceivers at the nodes, a logical ring topology can be embedded on a physical broadcast passive star network. In a wavelength-routed network, the routers use different switching configurations to incorporate different logical topologies. An optical network topology can be of two types—single-hop and multihop. A multihop network has two topologies—regular and arbitrary.

Three common regular topologies that are widely used in fiber optics are bus, star, and ring.

Various other topologies for multihop lightwave networks are Shuffle Net, de Bruijn graph, and toroidal Manhattan street network.

Protocols widely used for media access control include Slotted Aloha and DT-WDMA. The various multiplexing technologies used are TDM, WDM, plesiochronous multiplexing, synchronous multiplexing, and OTDM. Widely-used multiple-access schemes include O-CDMA and TDMA.

Test beds provide a proper scenario to implement optical networks. They are a stepping-stone toward high-speed data communication. Test beds such as Lambdanet, NTT's test bed, Rainbow, STARNET, BBC Television Studio test bed, Lightning, and Supercomputer Supernet test bed were discussed.

CHAPTER 12

ROUTING IN WDM NETWORKS

In this chapter

THE DESIGN OF WAVELENGTH-ROUTING NODES

Wavelength-Division Multiplexing (WDM) is such a widely used optical network because of the many advantages discussed in the preceding chapters. The design of the network nodes and the routing of data play a very important role in efficient operation of these systems. In this chapter, you will see the various strategies employed to route the wavelengths in a WDM network, the variations in the network architecture, and the parameters related to the design of such systems.

A wavelength-routing network with connections is shown in Figure 12.1. The nodes are interconnected by optical fibers, on which WDM signals are transmitted. The nodes are called *wavelength routers*. They can route an incoming signal to an outgoing port according to the signal's input port and wavelength. Wavelength-routing networks employ the spatial reuse of wavelengths. This enables many lightpaths to share the same wavelength in a network. A *lightpath* is a high-bandwidth pipe carrying a large amount of data. If the link between the lightpaths is common, wavelengths overlap and cause loss of optical information. This enables scalability of wavelength-routing networks. However, scalability is limited in nonreconfigurable networks, because the lightpath between the source and the destination is fixed and cannot be varied by a large measure.

Figure 12.1
A wavelength-routing network that reuses the wavelength to accommodate more channels.

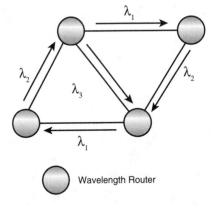

Wavelength Router

The general topology of a wavelength-routed network is a mesh network. It consists of nodes that are interconnected by fibers, as shown in Figure 12.2. The network provides lightpaths between pairs of network nodes. A lightpath is realized by assigning a wavelength on each link of the lightpath.

The main element of a network node is wavelength cross-connects (WXCs). Here, the node has trunk ports that connect to the other nodes. Each trunk port is bidirectional and is attached to an optical fiber pair. Tributary ports are present that manage the local traffic. These ports are either optical or electrical. The lightpaths start and end at the tributary ports. A network element manager is associated with a node to control and manage. When there are exactly two trunk ports, the node is called a wavelength add/drop multiplexer (WADM) node.

Figure 12.2
Elements of a wavelength-routed network.

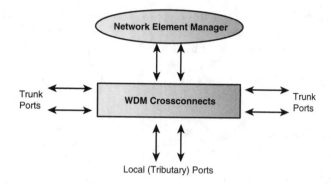

The main elements required for the proper operation of the nodes are wavelength multiplexers and demultiplexers, switches, and wavelength converters.

Depending on the functionality of the nodes, the networks are classified as static or reconfigurable. A *static* network is one in which there are no switches or dynamic wavelength converters. The routing pattern at the nodes is fixed, and they cannot be changed. A *reconfigurable* network contains switches and/or dynamic wavelength converters and thus can change routing patterns at the node.

WAVELENGTH CONVERSION

In simple wavelength-routing networks, a lightpath between two nodes along a particular route must use a single wavelength on all hops, or links, within the route. This requirement is called the wavelength continuity constraint. For instance, consider the two-link route shown in Figure 12.3. Imagine that a connection needs to be established between nodes 1 and 3 along a route that passes through a cross-connect at node 2. This connection can be established only if the same wavelength is available on the links between nodes 1 and 3. If wavelength λ_1 is available only on link 1, connecting nodes 1 and 2, and wavelength λ_2 is available on link 2, connecting nodes 2 and 3, the connection cannot be established. In Figure 12.3, the bold lines represent wavelengths that are unavailable. This constraint is overcome by converting the wavelength on one link to the wavelength present on the other so that the network connection is complete. This is achieved using wavelength converters.

Figure 12.3
Blocking in WDM networks.

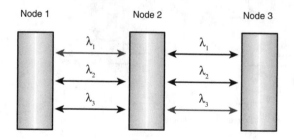

Wavelength conversion is used to improve network utilization. It is helpful when you need to interconnect equipment from different vendors that use incompatible wavelengths. Different types of wavelength conversion strategies are used in wavelength-routed networks:

- No wavelength conversion
- Fixed wavelength conversion
- Full wavelength conversion
- Limited wavelength conversion

NO WAVELENGTH CONVERSION

If the nodes in the network do not have any wavelength conversion capability, a lightpath is carried at the same wavelength from the source to the destination. Figure 12.4 shows a lightpath carried without wavelength conversion.

Figure 12.4
No wavelength conversion, with only one wavelength used between source and destination.

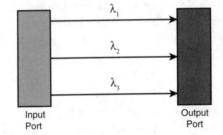

FIXED WAVELENGTH CONVERSION

In this case, the signal entering the node at any wavelength λ_a always leaves the node with the wavelength λ_b. The wavelength that enters a node is converted to a fixed wavelength at the node's output port. This is called fixed wavelength conversion, and it is represented by $\lambda_a(\text{input}) = \lambda_b(\text{output})$. Figure 12.5 shows fixed wavelength conversion.

Figure 12.5
Fixed wavelength conversion. The wavelength at the input port is converted to a fixed, specific wavelength at the output port.

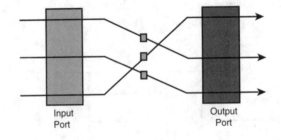

▦ - Wavelength Converters

FULL WAVELENGTH CONVERSION

In full wavelength conversion, the signal entering the node with a wavelength of λ_a can leave the node at any wavelength λ_b. The wavelength coming out of the node is not fixed, so the network is more flexible. Figure 12.6 shows a full wavelength conversion.

Figure 12.6
Full wavelength conversion, in which the wavelengths at the input and output are different.

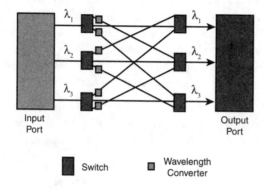

LIMITED WAVELENGTH CONVERSION

In limited wavelength conversion, the signal entering a node with a wavelength λ_a leaves the node at a wavelength that is a subset of the wavelengths that are available in the network. Figure 12.7 shows limited wavelength conversion.

Figure 12.7
Limited wavelength conversion, with wavelengths converted to subset wavelengths.

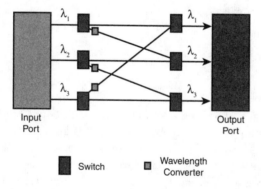

In terms of implementation, the simplest kind of wavelength conversion is no wavelength conversion. This is followed by fixed, limited, and full wavelength conversions. A certain degree of wavelength conversion is achieved using a combination of switches and wavelength converters.

NETWORK TRANSPARENCY

The degree of transparency can vary from one node to another. A fully optical implementation yields a high degree of transparency—that is, insensitivity to digital or analog data formats, bit rate, and modulation formats. In contrast, an implementation consisting of an electronic SONET digital cross-connect might have no transparency at all. If the implementation is completely analog, it can offer the same level of transparency as an optical network. If the implementation is digital, it clearly cannot support analog traffic.

Three regeneration techniques are used for digital data. The standard one is called regeneration with retiming and reshaping (3R). In this case, the bit clock rate is extracted from the signal, and the signal is reclocked. This technique produces a fresh copy of the signal at the regeneration step, thus allowing a large number of regenerators for the signals. However, it eliminates transparency to the bit rates and modulation formats, because the clock requires information about both of them. This can be provided using programmable clock recovery chips that work at a set of bit rates that are multiples of each other.

With the second method, 2R, the signal is regenerated and retimed without reshaping. This enables transparency of data without supporting the analog data or different modulation formats. Due to jitter accumulated at each regeneration step, the number of regeneration steps gets reduced.

The final form of regeneration is 1R, in which the signal is received and retransmitted without retiming or reshaping. This form can handle analog data well, but its performance is poorer than the other two forms of regeneration.

NETWORK REALIZATION

A wavelength cross-connect (WXC) is realized in various ways:

- With no wavelength conversion
- With wavelength conversion
- With electronic switching

WXC WITH NO WAVELENGTH CONVERSION

In no wavelength conversion, the WXC has M incoming and M outgoing links, each carrying W wavelengths. A demultiplexer demultiplexes the incoming links. There is a dedicated M*M optical switch for each wavelength. In other words, signals of wavelength λ_1 are sent to an optical switch that is dedicated to switch signals only on λ_1. For each outgoing link, the wavelength multiplexer combines all the different wavelengths from the switches to the outgoing fiber. Therefore, the configuration enables switching of wavelengths from any incoming link to any outgoing link, independent of other wavelengths. Here, the WXC does not enable the wavelengths to be converted. Figure 12.8 shows no wavelength conversion.

WXC WITH WAVELENGTH CONVERSION

This WXC has the same set of multiplexers and demultiplexers as in WXC without wavelength conversion, but it uses an MW*MW optical switch with MW wavelength converters. It can switch an incoming wavelength to any output port on any wavelength. It is more complicated than an optical WXC without wavelength conversion. Figure 12.9 shows wavelength cross-connects with conversion of wavelength.

Figure 12.8
WXC with no wave-
length conversion.

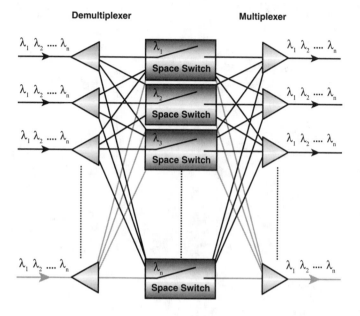

Figure 12.9
WXC with wavelength
conversion.

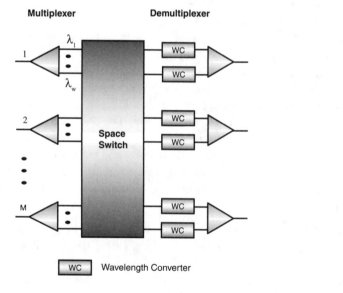

Many implementations of WXCs are not optical, but a combination of electronics and optics. One example is shown in Figure 12.10. In this case, WXC again uses optical wavelength multiplexers and demultiplexers. After the wavelengths are demultiplexed, the signal at each wavelength is converted from optical to electronic form and is switched to another port using an electronic switch. At each of the switch's output ports, the signal is again converted to optical form using a laser source.

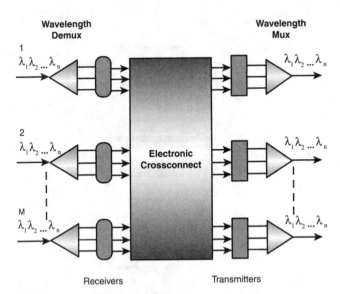

Figure 12.10
A WXC with electronic switching.

NETWORK DESIGN AND OPERATIONS

It is difficult to predict the bandwidth requirements and statistical properties of the traffic that will be carried by future wavelength-routing WDM networks. However, considering these factors is important for network design and analysis. For example, the bandwidth provided by a single lightpath is expected to far exceed the requirements of most individual calls. Therefore, lightpaths can be used to carry a single high-bandwidth call established between two individual users or to carry a stream of traffic from many different users who are electronically multiplexed in the time domain. The users of a WDM transport network can therefore use electronic switching equipment such as SONET/SDH cross-connects, ATM switches, IP routers, individual workstations, and video servers. The extent to which lightpaths are dynamically established due to time-varying fluctuations in traffic demand is an important issue in network design and analysis and is somewhat dependent on bandwidth requirements.

If the bandwidth of individual calls is significantly less than that of a single lightpath, a large number of calls are time-division multiplexed onto each lightpath. Depending on the rate at which the overall traffic demand varies, the lightpaths remain relatively fixed over time. There are occasional changes in the lightpath allocations to restore the network or to keep track of the mean traffic requirements through the course of a day.

Alternatively, in dynamic environments, such as in the transportation of multiplexed Internet traffic, lightpath requirements vary considerably over time, and lightpaths are established based on demand. Therefore, the traffic offered to a wavelength-routing network is either effectively static, with lightpath requirements fixed over time, or dynamic, with lightpaths established on demand.

Dynamic WDM networks perform online or offline routing. In offline routing, all the lightpath requests to be routed are known in advance, and the optimum routes and wavelength assignments are determined. If a new lightpath must be included in an existing set of lightpaths, the wavelength assignments for all lightpaths need to be recomputed and existing lightpaths rearranged. Optimized wavelength assignment is achieved through this process. However, it is impractical to rearrange established lightpaths. In contrast, networks, using online routing, establish new lightpaths without changing the wavelength allocations of existing lightpaths.

The main requirement when designing a network is to understand the type of traffic the network must support. Many different models have been used to describe traffic demands for the lightpaths. Each of these models has its pros and cons. Another dimension defines two types of lightpaths—permanent and temporary. A permanent lightpath is not released for connection, except for its dedicated path. A temporary lightpath is released.

A network can be *blocking* or *nonblocking*. A blocking network does not pass some of the lightpaths, whereas a nonblocking network services all the lightpath requests. The main aim when designing the network is to keep the *blocking* probability within acceptable limits.

It is impossible to design a network to meet arbitrary demands with limited resources. So you must assume some of the lightpath's properties while designing the network.

The various models that are considered for the design of the network are discussed here.

FIXED TRAFFIC MATRIX

In this case, the number of lightpaths that must be set up is in the form of a matrix $T=t(i,j)$. Here, $t(i,j)$ denotes the number of lightpaths to be set up between the nodes i and j. The network design is decided at the time of initial deployment and is static. Therefore, different situations encountered during network operation, such as setting and releasing lightpaths, cannot be reflected in the network design. The objective is to minimize the number of wavelengths and other parameters related to the equipment, such as the number of switches in a wavelength converter. This is an offline, nonblocking model.

PERMUTATIONS OF LIGHTPATHS

In this case, a pair of nodes is allowed to have a maximum of one lightpath between them, and each node is used to source or sink at that lightpath. When all nodes source or sink exactly one lightpath, the set of lightpath destination is a permutation of the set of lightpath sources. This model is used because it covers a wide range of traffic states. It is not a practical model to describe lightpath demands, but it is used to derive fundamental parameters such as the number of wavelengths, switches, and wavelength converters needed in the network. This model is used for online and offline, blocking and nonblocking traffic.

MAXIMUM LOAD IN THE NETWORK

Traffic is characterized by a parameter called load. It is the maximum number of concurrent lightpaths that are present on any link on the network. It is also a measure of link utilization. This is typically a nonblocking model. Its main objective is to maximize the load that the network can carry. This is used for both online and offline cases. The advantage of this method is that it requires very little knowledge of traffic demands and also provides knowledge of the resources needed to achieve certain network utilization.

STATISTICAL MODEL

In the statistical model, some knowledge of statistics is required for lightpath establishment and release. Most of the work in this case assumes Poisson's traffic. Some work is also carried out on non-Poisson traffic. This is usually an online, blocking model.

→ To learn more about Poisson's process, **see** "Poisson Distribution," **p.307** (Appendix B)

The network is of two types—static or reconfigurable. A *static network* uses no switches or wavelength converters inside the wavelength cross-connect nodes. It might use fixed or static wavelength converters. Nothing inside the network can change state. The static network is more economical and reliable than a reconfigurable network because it is completely composed of passive components. In other words, a signal entering the network at the input port at some wavelength is always routed to a specific output port. The routes are chosen when the network is built.

A *reconfigurable network* uses switches and/or dynamic wavelength converters. In case of reconfigurable networks, the routes can be changed at the time of network operation. These networks are made of active components that are expensive because they need a power supply, and their fabrication process is complex.

ROUTING AND WAVELENGTH ASSIGNMENT

The main objective of routing and assigning wavelengths is to service the lightpath requests using the shortest route available in the network and the smallest number of wavelengths. The network has a pair of unidirectional fiber links in the opposite direction between nodes. However, the lightpaths are bidirectional, with the same route and wavelength chosen for both directions of the lightpath. Therefore, all the lightpaths are full-duplex. For operational simplicity, the network operators assign the same route and wavelength in both directions. However, it is possible to reduce the number of wavelengths in some cases by assigning different wavelengths to different directions of the lightpath.

Sometimes you are given the routing, and you have to assign the wavelength. The wavelength assignment must obey the following rules:

- Two lightpaths must not be assigned the same wavelength on the link.
- If no wavelength conversion is available, the lightpath must be assigned the same wavelength on all the links in its route.

Given a set of lightpath requests and routing, let K_i denote the number of lightpaths on link i. Then you define the load request as $K = \max_i K_i$. Therefore, at least K wavelengths are required to accommodate this set of lightpath requests. As long as no more than K lightpaths use this link, K wavelengths are sufficient to accommodate this request. Without wavelength conversion, the number of wavelengths required is much larger.

WAVELENGTH ASSIGNMENT AND ALTERNATE ROUTES

The blocking probabilities experienced in a wavelength-continuous WDM network depend on the routing and wavelength assignment schemes used. Barry and Humblet suggested that a good routing algorithm in wavelength-continuous networks must consider route length in hops (H), interference lengths (L), and link congestion. They suggested that routes chosen to minimize H/L might provide better performance than other choices.

The route between the source and destination is fixed. Various wavelength assignment algorithms are considered to assign wavelengths as soon as the route has been selected. The wavelength assignment algorithms are as follows:

- **Random-1**—For a lightpath request between two nodes, choose, at random, one of the available wavelengths on the fixed shortest path between the nodes.

- **Random-2**—Fix two shortest paths between every pair of nodes. When there is a lightpath request between the nodes, one of the available wavelengths is chosen at random. If it is unavailable, the wavelength available on the second shortest path is chosen.

- **Max-used-1**—When there is a lightpath request between two nodes, of the available wavelengths, choose the one that has been used the maximum number of times in the network.

- **Max-used-2**—When there is a lightpath request between two nodes, of the available wavelengths, choose the one that has been used the maximum number of times in the network.

If no such wavelength is available, among the wavelengths on the second-shortest path, choose the one that is used the maximum number of times in the network at that point in time.

The wavelength assignment algorithm also plays an important role in determining the reuse factor. For the same number of available paths, the maximum used algorithms have an advantage over the random algorithm. Improved network performance is attained using the maximum used wavelength allocation algorithm. In networks with large numbers of wavelengths, where multiplexing occurs, a good wavelength assignment scheme can be effective. However, this algorithm must contain all details of the network state and the parameters affecting network performance.

ALTERNATE ROUTING

The majority of analyses of wavelength-continuous WDM networks are focused on networks with fixed routing, in which only a single route is defined between the source and the destination. If this route is unavailable when a lightpath request arrives, the lightpath is blocked. Significant performance improvements are often obtained in circuit-switched networks, and equivalently in networks with wavelength converters, if alternate routing is introduced.

Many researchers have investigated the performance of wavelength-continuous, single-fiber networks with alternate routing. They have considered various routing and wavelength assignment schemes and have shown that the performance of wavelength-continuous networks is strongly dependent on the schemes chosen. Some of these schemes are discussed in the following sections.

Karasan and Ayanoglu proposed Maximum H/L Routing (MHLR). In this scheme, a route is chosen from the k shortest routes that maximize the ratio of the route length to the interference length (H/L), thereby reducing interference. As the number of possible alternate routes, k, increases, H/L increases. Therefore, the blocking probability increases with increasing k. In contrast, the blocking probability with wavelength converters decreases with increasing k, due to the increased set of possible routes through the network for establishing a lightpath. Therefore, the performance improvements offered using wavelength converters increase. The MHLR algorithm is an example designed to increase the benefits of wavelength converters.

Karasan and Ayanoglu also considered Least-Loaded Routing (LLR). In networks with wavelength converters, the LLR algorithm chooses a route from the k possible alternate routes. This maximizes the minimum number of available wavelengths on any given link along a route. In a wavelength-continuous network, the route and wavelength are chosen together so that the number of fibers on which a wavelength is available in a link is minimized. The LLR algorithm decreases blocking. However, the performance improvements obtained with the introduction of wavelength conversion are comparable to those obtained using the MHLR algorithm and are significantly greater than with fixed routing. This is because having k alternate routes results in increased average route lengths and reduced interference lengths. This increases the blocking probability of the network due to an increased number of routes.

Ramamurthy and Mukherjeee showed that in networks employing fixed alternate routing, the benefits of wavelength conversion increase with an increase in the number of routes. In this type of routing, different alternate routes have a predefined order, and lightpaths are established on the first available alternate route.

Chan and Yum examined blocking in a fully meshed network with Least-Congested Path (LCP) routing, random wavelength assignment, and trunk reservation. When a connection request is made, the number of available wavelengths on each link of each possible route is determined. The connection is established on the route that has the maximum number of free wavelengths. The connection is broken after the most-used links have been examined.

A direct link exists between each source and destination in a fully-meshed network, with alternate routes consisting of two links. Wavelength converters provide no performance improvements in a fully-meshed network with fixed routing, because all routes consist of only a single hop. However, Chan and Yum showed that if alternate routing is introduced, wavelength converters reduce blocking probabilities at low loads. However, the performance improvements are relatively small due to the short route lengths.

There are two modes of operation. In the first mode, the traffic is alternately routed, requiring two links per connection. In the second mode, the traffic is directly routed, requiring only a single link. However, research proved that wavelength-continuous networks that use

LCP routing and fixed alternate routing with connections established on direct routes have lower blocking probabilities than networks that use wavelength converters. This is because when the number of wavelengths used on a link increases, the probability of blocking for a two-hop route also increases. The wavelength continuity constraint imposes this limitation, thereby reducing the number of alternately routed connections. In directly routed networks, one-hop connections are established, thereby reducing the overall blocking probability.

ARCHITECTURAL VARIATIONS

Nodes that are independent of the wavelength are cheaper and easier to build. Networks that are independent of the wavelength are called Linear Lightwave Networks (LLNs). The current work on lightwave network architectures is largely based on the following:

- Using fixed passive power combiners in a broadcast mode
- Using point-to-point optical links with electronic switching and multiplexing

All operations on signals within the network are performed optically. Therefore, it contains no electronic equipment and related problems. As opposed to the star network, the LLN can have any arbitrary mesh-type topology, thereby achieving greater reliability and better load distribution. The network is assumed to operate in a circuit-switched mode at the optical level.

The structure and properties of an LLN are described in the following sections.

THE STRUCTURE OF A LINEAR LIGHTWAVE NETWORK

The heart of the LLN is a Linear Divider-Combiner (LDC), which is present at each node. Its function is to direct combinations of the inbound signals at the node to each outbound fiber in a controlled manner. Larger LDCs with more input and output fibers can be built that can direct a portion of the power from each input link to any output link.

Although some power attenuation occurs in traversing each LDC and each fiber, it is assumed that the signal level at all receivers is maintained sufficiently high by optical amplification for satisfactory reception.

Consider a network manager and a signaling system that sets up calls on request from the user stations. This is achieved by establishing end-to-end or circuit-switched optical paths between transmitter and receiver. The network manager determines the physical path to be allocated to the call, sets the respective LDC parameters along the route, and finally assigns the physical route that is allocated to the call. The physical route allocated to the call is assumed to remain unchanged throughout its duration.

PROPERTIES OF THE LLN

LLN has the following properties:

- Each signal is transported optically in unmodified form from transmitter to receiver. In other words, there is no frequency conversion, regeneration, buffering, or any other nonlinear operation within the network.
- More than one signal is combined linearly on each fiber. These are called interfering signals.
- A multiple-access scheme is implemented, allowing the signals interfering on any link to be distinguishable at the receivers.

The structure of the LLN imposes some special constraints on the routing problem. These are discussed in the following sections.

CHANNEL CONTINUITY

A call must be allocated the same channel on all the links that it traverses within the network.

DISTINCT CHANNEL ASSIGNMENT

All interfering calls must be assigned distinct channels, and the same wavelength is reused by calls using disjointed paths.

INSEPARABILITY

Signals combined on a single fiber cannot be separated within the LLN. This is because LDC operates on the aggregate power carried on each inbound link without distinguishing between signals on different channels. Inseparability tends to create unintended multicast connections where point-to-point connections were intended. This is inevitable and leads to wasted power and bandwidth.

MUTUALLY INDEPENDENT SOURCES COMBINING

Only signals from mutually independent sources are combined on the same fiber. In other words, a signal is not allowed to split, taking multiple paths in the network and then recombining on a link. If a routing violates this condition, it results in a source interfering with itself.

COLOR CLASH

A color clash arises when a routing decision on a new call results in two or more calls combining on the same fiber. These calls are already in progress on disjointed paths that were previously assigned to the same channel.

Routing involves the following steps:

- Choosing a path for a requested call
- Checking for violations of the LLN constraints
- Assigning an appropriate channel to the call

Consider a simple LDC that has three inputs and three outputs (see Figure 12.11). It consists of splitters and combiners with a switch in between. Depending on the switch settings, the power coming to an input port can be transmitted on the subset of the output ports. The switch settings determine the specific set of output ports.

Figure 12.11
A linear splitter/divider and combiner node.

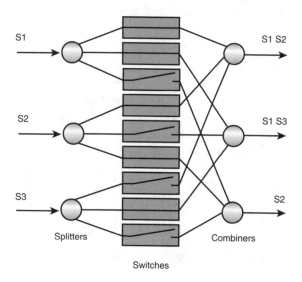

Many algorithms have been proposed to overcome the constraints imposed by LLNs. The advantage of the LLN is that it makes multicasting very easy. The concept of LLN is extended to cases in which the LDCs in the network are partially wavelength-selective. It implies that they can separately switch groups of wavelengths called *wavebands*, but cannot distinguish between the wavelengths in the waveband. The added complexity of routing, along with dividing and combining losses, prevents LLNs from being practical. LLNs can, however, incorporate good multicast capabilities in wavelength-routed networks. An efficient way to do this is to use an LDC on the desired multicast wavelength instead of a switch.

PART
II

CH
12

WAVELENGTH-ROUTING TEST BEDS

Many wavelength-routing test beds have been built in the last few years because of cooperation from several companies. Various research organizations, such as Defense Advanced Research Projects Agency (DARPA) and Research and Development in Advanced Communications Technologies in Europe (RACE), came to the forefront and funded research and development activities. By using these test beds, you can set up networks that provide good performance and also point out issues that need to be resolved before the entire network is deployed. Some of the widely used test beds are described in the following sections.

AFRICA ONE/SEA ME WE-3

The Africa Optical Network (Africa ONE) is a project proposed by AT&T and Alcatel Submarine networks. It was planned to design an underwater WDM ring around Africa. Sea Me We-3 has the same architecture as Africa ONE and is deployed in Europe, the Middle East, and Asia. The network consists of about 40 nodes spread over a distance of 40,000km.

The network is made up of hub and access points. Figure 12.12 shows the architecture of Africa ONE.

Figure 12.12
An Africa ONE network with connectivity of nodes.

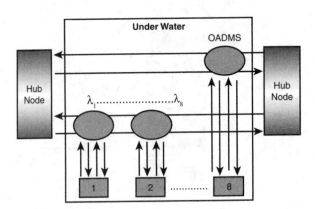

The hub nodes are connected using two fiber pairs to form a ring structure. Each fiber carries eight wavelengths of STM-16 having a rate of 2.5Gbps. The link between the hub nodes is all-optical and extends up to 5,000km. The optical amplifiers are placed in the path at periodic intervals. Optical Add/Drop Multiplexers (OADMs) are used to add and drop one predetermined wavelength to or from the fiber. The access nodes are connected to the countries and are placed at the shores. The OADMs are connected to these access points using two fiber pairs. Most of the fiber is present under water. The OADMs are advantageous because, unlike electronic ADMs, they are very simple, passive, and reliable. The access nodes cannot interfere with the signals destined for other nodes if an OADM is used. This is an essential requirement for the network.

ALL-OPTICAL NETWORK TEST BEDS

The All-Optical Network Consortium is a static wavelength-routing test bed. The architecture has a two-level hierarchy. Level 0 corresponds to local-area networks (LANs) and level 1 corresponds to metropolitan-area networks (MANs). Level 0 uses a broadcast star architecture, whereas level 1 uses a wavelength cross-connect consisting of an Arrayed Waveguide (AWG) router.

This test bed uses 20 wavelengths spaced 50GHz apart. The odd-numbered wavelengths are used for level 0, and the even-numbered ones are used for level 1. The wavelength is allocated using filters—in this case, a Mach-Zehnder filter. The wavelength is allocated when the network is built.

Three types of services are provided by AON. The A service is a transparent circuit-switched service. It is used for high-bit-rate applications.

The B service uses TDM within an optical channel to provide a scheduled, time-slotted service that is transparent within its time slots. In the test bed implementation, the B service uses 250ms frames with 128 slots per frame. The user can choose the modulation rate and format to use within an assigned slot. The optical terminals therefore can use the B service to provide services such as OC-3 connections and Ethernet or FDDI virtual networks. The B service enables any wavelength channel to be transparently shared between 128 lower-bandwidth applications.

Both services enable point-to-point or point-to-multipoint connections, and they share the 20 available wavelength channels. In addition, the optical network provides a third service that serves as a common control link between all users of the optical network. This C service is a datagram service that enables optical terminals to transmit control packets in a specific data and modulation format. Therefore, this service is not transparent. The C service operates out-of-band at 1,310nm.

NIPPON TELEGRAPH AND TELEPHONE CORPORATION RING

The Nippon Telegraph and Telephone Corporation (NTT) test bed consists of a unidirectional ring with one fiber for connection and the other for protection. The network has hub and access nodes. The hub node is called the center node, and the access nodes are called remote nodes. The hub node sends the signals multiplexed onto a single fiber at W different wavelengths. The number of access nodes possible is W. At any access node k, the wavelength k is added or dropped. An AWG is used to add and drop wavelengths. Certain protection circuits are also incorporated to protect against link failures.

This test bed has six wavelengths spaced 100Ghz apart at 622Mbps.

MULTIWAVELENGTH TRANSPORT NETWORK

The European RACE Multiwavelength Transport Network (MWTN) project provides an interconnection between a wavelength-routed optical layer and a conventional electronic layer. This was one of the earliest reconfigurable wavelength-routing test beds.

The MWTN project has four main objectives:

- To demonstrate that an optical network layer forms a logical extension to a network hierarchy and can be integrated with network service and management systems
- To demonstrate transparency of optical networks and the ability to carry multiple transmission formats
- To identify evolutionary paths for implementing an optical network layer
- To identify the needs for standards dealing with wavelength allocation and use

This test bed uses four wavelengths spaced 4nm apart, with each wavelength carrying data at 622Mbps. A feature to detect and isolate failures is used in which the wavelength is carried by a superimposed pilot tone. This tone is monitored to detect failures.

PART

II

CH

12

OPTICAL NETWORK TECHNOLOGY CONSORTIUM TEST BED

The Optical Network Technology Consortium (ONTC) test bed has a reconfigurable wavelength-routing architecture. The test bed has two unidirectional rings that are interconnected. Each ring has two nodes. A common node interconnects these rings. The test bed has four wavelengths spaced 4nm apart. Four analog subcarrier multiplexed video channels are carried by one of these wavelengths. The wavelength is carried by a single-mode fiber with a total distance of 150km at 155Mbps. It carries the ATM traffic.

This test bed demonstrates the use of ATM virtual topology over the optical layer. The transparency of WDM networks where different forms of data are transmitted over different lightpaths is also determined.

ALCATEL'S WDM RING

Alcatel's WDM ring has three nodes. It uses four wavelengths that are spaced 200GHz apart to carry SDH data at a rate of 2.5Gbps. The test bed consists of a two-fiber ring network with OADMs. It consists of both optical and electronic components. The signal is electronically regenerated at each node, so the number of nodes that can be cascaded is large. The physical layer design is also simplified, because it consists of only point-to-point links.

MULTIWAVELENGTH OPTICAL NETWORK

Multiwavelength Optical Network (MONET) was developed to produce wavelength-routed networks that can be deployed commercially. MONET demonstrated the transmission of eight wavelengths at 10Gbps over 2000km. A single-mode fiber with dispersion compensation at appropriate intervals was used. MONET provided a thorough understanding of various issues of network management.

SUMMARY

In this chapter, you studied basic wavelength-routing networks, their various configurations, and test beds. A wavelength-routing network consists of wavelength cross-connects (WXCs) with interconnected fibers. The nodes are called wavelength routers because they route the traffic from one point to another.

This chapter covered factors such as degree of wavelength conversion, degree of transparency, and network realization of wavelength-routing networks.

Many different algorithms are used to overcome the problem of routing and assigning wavelengths to lightpaths. These algorithms reduce the number of wavelengths.

You also explored the architectural variations of a wavelength-routed network that are suitable for multicast operations.

Finally, you studied the test beds that are widely used in optical networks and the objectives for their implementation. The test beds give you a fair idea of what kind of networks will be implemented in the near future.

CHAPTER **13**

THE OPTICAL ACCESS NETWORK

In this chapter

THE ARCHITECTURE OF AN ACCESS NETWORK

Currently, optical networking technologies such as Dense WDM (DWDM), optical cross-connects, optical integrated circuits, optical amplifiers, and others are being deployed for long-distance networks. With demand increasing for Internet access, remote access, interactive multimedia, and digital video services, multiwavelength networks provide a transparent solution that supports all these digital formats and services.

The optical access network promises limitless bandwidth, a high degree of flexibility and configurability, increased security, and privacy and integration with existing transport and switching systems. Its deployment in regional and metropolitan networks has also increased recently. Today, a local access network handles a wide range of services, ranging from a few KHz to several MHz. Table 13.1 lists a few services expected to be delivered through the access network in the near future. Upstream transmission is from customers to a central office (CO), and downstream is from a CO to customers.

TABLE 13.1 SERVICES AND THEIR DATA RATES

Service	Downstream Bandwidth	Upstream Bandwidth
Telephony	4KHz	4KHz
ISDN	144Kbps	144Kbps
Broadcast video	Analog or 6Mbps	0
Interactive video	6Mbps	Small
Internet access	A few Mbps	Small initially
Videoconferencing	6Mbps	6Mbps

An optical access network is divided into two sections, *feeder* and *distribution*, as shown in Figure 13.1. Feeder networks aggregate the traffic from distribution networks and transport them to the corresponding backbone networks or to other distribution networks through egress or exit nodes. Distribution networks transport the traffic from customers to feeder networks. The cost of maintaining a feeder network is shared among many customers. However, relatively few customers share a distribution network, making cost the main issue in designing an optical access network. Within a distribution network, a hub or an egress node serves customers through remote nodes (RNs) or access nodes (ANs) and Network Interface Units (NIUs). An RN/AN can serve several NIUs. An NIU can be located either in a house or outside a service provider that serves several users. The portion of the network between the hub (CO) and the RNs/ANs is the feeder network, and the portion between the RNs and NIUs is the distribution network.

Figure 13.1
A basic access network with feeder and distribution networks for traffic organization.

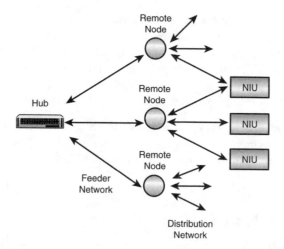

In the initial stages of optical fiber deployment, the major issue was determining how close to the customer the fiber should penetrate. This is highly dependent on the bandwidth requirement. Fiber To The Building (FTTB) is implemented in high-end users such as companies and campuses, and Fiber To The Curb (FTTC) is for home users. For FTTC, data is transmitted over optical fiber from the hub to Optical Network Units (ONUs), as shown in Figure 13.2. The network between the central office and the ONUs is the feeder network, and the distribution network is between the ONUs and the NIUs. FTTC is also called Baseband Modulated Fiber Coaxial Bus (BMFCB).

Figure 13.2
Fiber deployment strategies in access networks.

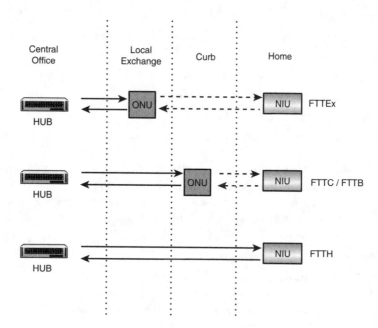

The network architectures proposed for optical access must be kept simple, so they involve no active components. This is because passive components require no switching and therefore no control. The ONU must also be very simple so that the cost gets reduced. This also increases the reliability. The ONU must be able to operate without requiring any temperature control. The CO equipment is sophisticated because it resides in a controlled environment and the cost gets distributed when the CO provides service to many customers.

Therefore, passive optical networks (PONs) are used. The main advantage of using passive networks is that the fiber infrastructure itself is transparent to the bit rates and modulation formats and thus can accommodate future enhancements without changing the infrastructure.

PASSIVE OPTICAL NETWORK

Passive optical network technology is called passive because the electrical cables that carry communications signals are replaced by fiber-optic links that carry the same signals using laser light. No electrical signals flow through or are needed in the fiber, and electronic equipment is needed only at the fiber's end points. Optical fibers can carry data much faster and more efficiently than electrical wires. With the goal of reducing the costs of installing optical fiber and bringing broadband services to homes, developers invented PON. These networks distribute the costs of fiber and much of the equipment located at the service provider among several customers. They also eliminate the need for expensive powered equipment between the service provider and these customers.

A basic PON consists of the following elements:

- One or two shared optical fibers connecting a service provider to an output device located near the customers
- Dedicated optical fibers between each output device and customer
- Fiber connectors or splices as required
- An optical line terminator (OLT) present at the provider end
- An optical network terminator (ONT) present at the customer end

No component in a PON requires electrical power, except at the ends. That's why the network is called passive. In a PON serving n customers, the output device is either a 1-to-n optical power splitter or a 1-to-n wavelength-division demultiplexer. Sometimes it is a combination of both. PON is transparent to bit rate, modulation format (digital or analog format), and protocols such as SONET/SDH, IP, and Ethernet. A PON is shown in Figure 13.3.

In PONs, the components installed between the service provider and the customers need not be specific to bit rates, modulation format, and so on because of the inherent transparency. PONs therefore enable services to be mixed or economically upgraded in the future as needed. New services and/or new customers can be added by changing service-specific equipment only at the ends of the network and for affected customers. Other network architectures do not provide such flexibility.

Figure 13.3
A typical passive optical network architecture.

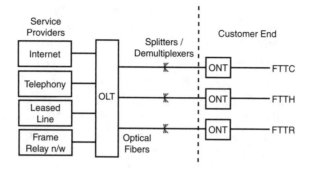

When using a power splitter, the transmission channels, and therefore the bandwidth given to the customers, are shared. By using a wavelength-division router (demultiplexer), dedicated channels are created between the service provider and the customer. Although the channel and bandwidth are dedicated, the optical fiber and output device remain shared, thus reducing costs. Dedicated wavelengths are combined with a shared power-split wavelength in some PONs for added capabilities. The alternative to a single-splitter 1-to-n tree topology is a PON that uses a combination of smaller splits to achieve the 1-to-n splitter. However, they are arranged in a different, more-convenient topology. PONs can also be configured as rings and buses.

The splitter or router can be moved closer to or farther from the service provider to optimize costs. Future upgrading without affecting the active terminations or protocols becomes easy. Because of the lack of electronics, the reliability is high and there is no requirement for reserve or standby powering, except at the ends of the network.

OPTICAL ACCESS ARCHITECTURES

The simplest architecture of a passive optical network consists of a separate fiber pair from the CO to each ONU. The cost of the CO equipment increases with the number of ONUs. It is also necessary to install and maintain these fiber pairs. Ring architecture is used for these networks. These fibers have limited deployment and are mostly used in high-speed services. This network is shown in Figure 13.4.

Figure 13.4
A point-to-point fiber network.

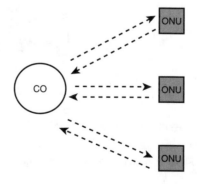

PART

II

CH

13

A single fiber can be used for bidirectional transmission, thus eliminating the requirement of fiber pairs. However, this does not enable transmission on one wavelength over both directions because of back reflections in the fiber. Another solution is to use two different wavelengths in different directions.

Another architecture is the Telephony Passive Optical Network (TPON). A laser transmitter at the CO broadcasts the traffic going downstream, as shown in Figure 13.5. The transmitter broadcasts to all ONUs using a passive star coupler, similar to broadcast-and-select networks. Switched services based on the time slot are provided according to demands. For the upstream, the ONUs share a channel that is combined using a coupler. These channels use fixed TDM or any multiaccess protocol. Because the CO equipment is shared among all ONUs, there is a substantial reduction in the cost of the equipment. The CO equipment can be a light-emitting diode (LED) or a Fabry-Perot laser. The pin receivers and Fabry-Perot lasers or LEDs are used within the ONUs. The splitting loss of the star coupler limits the number of ONUs that are supported. In TPONs, each ONU has the electronic equipment running at the bit rate that is the aggregate bit rate of all the ONUs. This architecture can support a few hundred Mbps as the total bandwidth.

Figure 13.5
A broadcast-and-select PON.

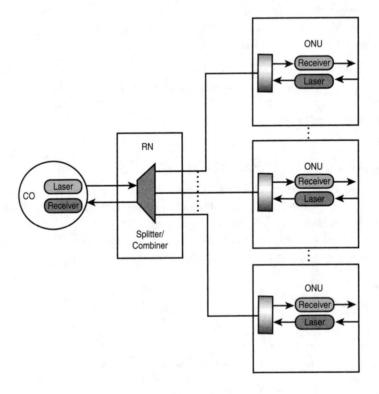

The single transceiver at the CO in a broadcast-and-select PON is replaced with a WDM array of transmitters or a single tuned transmitter to yield a WDM PON. This method enables each ONU to run only at the rate at which it receives data, not at the aggregate bit rate. The splitting losses still limit the maximum number of ONUs that can be supported. Figure 13.6 shows the architecture of WDM PON.

Figure 13.6
A broadcast-and-select WDM PON.

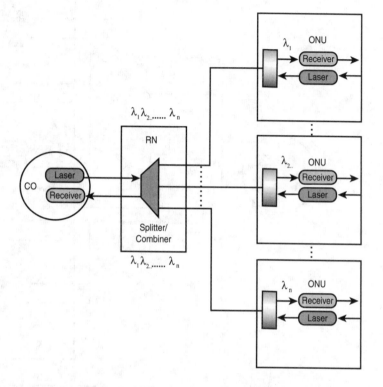

Wavelength routing solves the problem of splitting losses, keeping the other advantages of WDM PON intact. Various types of Wavelength Routing Passive Optical Networks (WRPONs) have been proposed. They all use wavelength routers in between. The most typically used wavelength router is an Arrayed Waveguide Grating (AWG). The router directs the different wavelengths to different ONUs. It uses 16 channels in the 1310nm band for downstream transmission and 16 channels in the 1550nm band for upstream transmission. This setup becomes uneconomical, because it involves the use of two lasers for each ONU—one situated in the ONU and the other at the CO. Figure 13.7 shows a WRPON.

Various architectures in WRPON provide economic sharing of resources at both the ONU and the CO. The RITE-net architecture, shown in Figure 13.8, uses a laser at the central office. The frame sent by the CO to the ONU consists of two parts—the data and the return traffic. The CO transmits the data. The return traffic part is when no data is transmitted but the CO laser is left turned on. Each ONU is provided with an external modulator. The light signal is modulated during the return-traffic part of the frame. This eliminates the need to have a laser at the ONU. The upstream traffic from the ONU is combined using a wavelength router at different wavelengths, and it is sent to a common port at the CO's receiver. This requires only a single laser to be shared at the NIUs but requires an external modulator at each ONU.

PART

II

CH

13

Figure 13.7
WRPON reduces splitting losses.

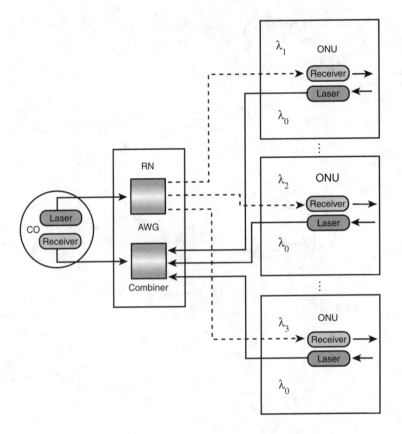

Figure 13.8.
The RITE-net WRPON architecture.

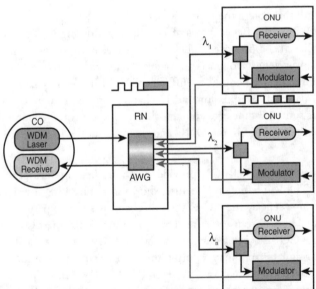

To reduce the cost, an LED replaces the external modulator at the ONU. This is the LAR-net WRPON, shown in Figure 13.9. The LED emits a broadband signal that gets sliced as it passes through the wavelength router. The part of the power in the LED that corresponds to the passband of the wavelength router only gets transmitted. When there are many ONUs, a fraction of the power is lost. This loss is known as *splitting loss*.

Figure 13.9
The LAR-net WRPON architecture.

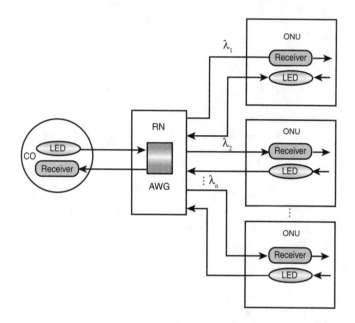

A LED can also be incorporated at the CO where the signal sent by the CO's LED is broadcast to all the ONUs. Two transmitters can be used at the CO. One of them is an LED, fixed and tuned to 1,310nm, that broadcasts to the ONU. The other is a tunable laser at 1550nm, selectively transmitting to the ONU.

WRPON components are expensive when compared to those used in simple broadcast PONs. However, WRPONs offer much higher capacities and provide a nice upgrade path over the existing infrastructure.

PART
II

CH
13

SUMMARY

Optical access networks promise nearly limitless bandwidth, a high degree of flexibility and configurability, increased security, privacy, and integration with existing transport and switching systems.

An optical access network is divided into two sections—the feeder and distribution parts.

The FTTC and FTTB are used to penetrate deep for deploying optic fiber and providing a long-term solution.

Passive optical networks have been widely used for optical access networks because they use passive components and eliminate the need for active electronic components that are costly and that require more maintenance and control.

Network architectures such as TPON, WDM PON, and WRPON and its types (RITE-net and LAR-net) play a major role in improving the quality of networks.

CHAPTER 14

OPTICAL SWITCHING NETWORKS

In this chapter

OPTICAL TIME-DIVISION MULTIPLEXING

In Optical Time-Division Multiplexing (OTDM), optical signals representing data streams from multiple sources are interleaved in time to produce a single data stream. Ultrafast optical time-division multiplexed (TDM) networks have the potential to provide truly flexible bandwidth on demand at burst rates of 100Gbps. The total capacity of single-channel local area networks and metropolitan area networks (LANs and MANs) is the same as the number of WDM lower-rate channels. They also provide potential improvements in network performance in terms of user access time, delay, and throughput, depending on the user rates and statistics. In addition, end-node equipment is conceptually simpler for single-channel versus multichannel approaches.

PHOTONIC SWITCHING ARCHITECTURE

OTDM is similar to electronic TDM, except that all the operations in the network are performed optically at very high rates. OTDM systems have a bit rate of about 100Gbps. OTDM uses very short-width pulses that are generated using single-mode locked laser. Due to small pulse width, the pulse-broadening effect caused by chromatic dispersion is large. Therefore, special care must be taken to reduce this effect. You can do this using soliton pulses that can travel over large distances without pulse broadening. Shaping the output of the mode-locked laser is not required, because any pulse shape gets transformed into the shape of a soliton after traveling for some distance within the fiber. However, the pulse must be launched with appropriate peak power. This peak power is directly proportional to the bit rate of operation. Soliton pulses must be sufficiently isolated from each other to maintain their shape. Soliton pulses therefore occupy only a fraction of the bit interval so that it does not interfere with the adjacent bit interval. These pulses therefore use short-pulse format.

Note

Peak power is the maximum power with which the pulses need to be launched so that they are successfully received.

→ To learn more about mode-locked lasers, **see** "Mode-Locked Lasers," **p.78** (Chapter 4)
→ To learn more about soliton pulses, **see** "Solitons," **p.40** (Chapter 2)
→ To learn more about short-pulse format, **see** "Short-Pulse Format," **p.97** (Chapter 5)

TYPES OF MULTIPLEXING

Two types of multiplexing techniques are used in OTDM—*bit interleaving* and *packet interleaving*.

In optical bit interleaving, the pulse train generated by the mode-locked laser is split, and each data stream to be multiplexed is given a copy of this pulse. Then delay is induced in the data stream by passing the pulse train through the corresponding length of the optical fiber. The delayed pulses, therefore, do not overlap with each other. The pulses that are not delayed serve as the framing pulses. The data stream externally modulates the delayed pulse stream. The bit-interleaved OTDM stream is then obtained by combining the outputs of the external modulator and the framing pulses. The framing pulses carry additional information about data and help retrieve data during the demultiplexing operation. Figure 14.1 shows a block diagram of bit-interleaved multiplexing. Figure 14.2 shows the multiplexing of bits.

Figure 14.1
A block diagram of bit-interleaved multiplexing.

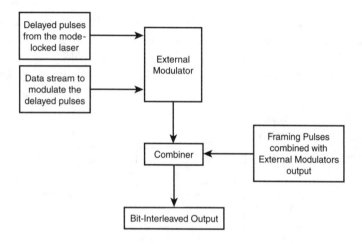

Figure 14.2
Bit-interleaved multiplexing with the data stream modulating the pulses delayed by the mode-locked laser.

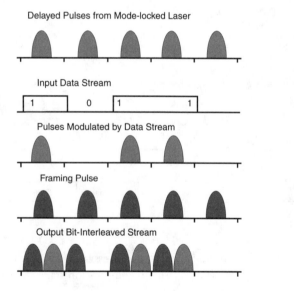

In demultiplexing, the multiplexed input is split into different streams by a coupler. If the ith stream in a signal is to be demultiplexed, one of the streams is delayed by $i\tau$, where τ is the interpulse width. The framing pulses are introduced with high power for easier demultiplexing. A thresholding operation is performed on the delayed pulses. In a thresholding operation, only pulses above a certain value are extracted. Therefore, the framing pulses are multiplexed with higher power so that they can be extracted easily during demultiplexing.

PART
II

CH

14

The extracted framing pulses coincide with the pulses that are not delayed. The pulses that are not delayed correspond to the input data stream to be demultiplexed. A logical AND between the framing pulses and the bit-interleaved multiplexed pulse stream is used to extract the ith stream. Two devices that are used for the logical AND operation are Nonlinear Optical Loop Mirror (NOLM) and soliton-trapping gates. NOLM is discussed in the next section.

In packet interleaving, as shown in Figure 14.3, the data stream externally modulates the periodic stream of narrow pulses. The width between the successive pulses is the same as the bit interval t. The bit interval must be reduced to the interpulse width τ so that signals with high rates can be multiplexed. Figure 14.4 shows the multiplexing of the bits in packet interleaving.

Figure 14.3
A block diagram of packet interleaving multiplexing.

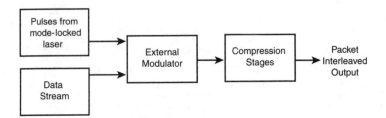

Figure 14.4
Multiplexing of bits with data compressed and sent in the time slot as burst packets.

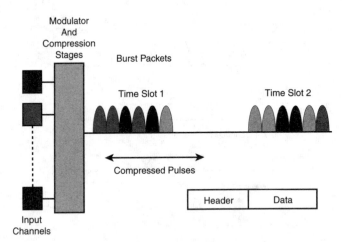

This is achieved by passing the output through compression stages so that if the size of each packet is n bits, the output goes through $k = \log_2 n$ compression stages. For the ith compression stage, the delay has the following value:

$$2^{i-1}(t-C)$$

Demultiplexing involves retrieving the data packets from the compressed stream. This is achieved by passing the compressed packets through a series of decompression stages. The number of stages required is again $k = \log_2 n$. The switches required here need to have switching times that are of the order of the interpulse width T. In photonic switching, very small values of τ are needed, so this approach becomes impractical.

Another solution to overcome this problem is to use AND gates that convert the single high-speed data to many parallel lower-speed streams. These data streams can be processed electronically. They have components that can handle lower data rates, eliminating the need for expensive optical components.

OPTICAL DEMULTIPLEXING

Many mechanisms have been proposed to achieve logical AND operations at high speeds. In this case, the AND operations are performed by an on-off switch, where one signal is given as input to the switch and the other is used to control it.

Candidates for ultrafast demultiplexing include soliton gates, NOLM, and Semiconductor Laser Amplifier in a Loop Mirror (SLALOM). Recently, an ultrafast all-optical demultiplexer, Terahertz Optical Asymmetric Demultiplexer (TOAD), was studied.

NOLM is shown in Figure 14.5. It is composed of a 3dB coupler, a fiber connecting the coupler's outputs, and a nonlinear element (NLE). The NLE is located anywhere in the fiber loop. In the absence of an NLE, if the signal is present at one of the inputs (arm X of the directional coupler), the coupler's two outputs are equal. The phase shift of the outputs is also the same. Therefore, the signals coming from both the clockwise and counterclockwise directions are reflected onto input arm X, and no signal comes from arm Y. This configuration is therefore called fiber loop mirror.

Figure 14.5
Nonlinear Optical
Loop Mirror.

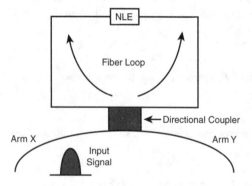

If one output signal undergoes a different phase shift, the output emerges from arm Y. For all the energy to come from arm Y, the phase shift must be π or 180°. The NLE is present to induce a phase shift as a nonlinearity that is dependent on the intensity of light. Initially, the intensity-dependent phase shift induced by silica fiber was itself used as a nonlinearity. However, this is a weak nonlinearity, and it is not possible to produce the desired effect for pulse switching. The length of the fiber required in this case is also long. The NLE enables the use of shorter fibers and logical ANDing. This is because NLEs are easily controlled using control pulses.

TOAD, shown in Figure 14.6, provides a strong nonlinearity and also easy control. Here, another directional coupler is introduced in the fiber loop that provides the control pulses. These control pulses alter the optical properties of NLE when they pass through it.

PART

II

CH

14

Figure 14.6
Terahertz Optical
Asymmetric
Demultiplexer.

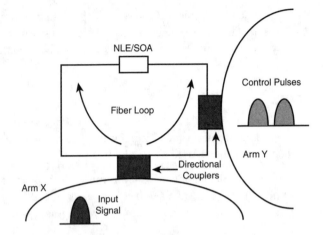

In other words, the phase of the signal passing through this NLE during the interval when the control pulse is passing changes. One example of such an NLE is a Semiconductor Optical Amplifier (SOA). The timing between the control and the signal pulses must be correct for efficient operation. The output signal contains both the signal and the control pulse. The control pulse can be eliminated either by using different wavelengths for signal and control pulse so that only the wavelength for the signal pulse is selected, or by using orthogonal polarization. This enables discrimination between the signal and control pulses. In TOAD, the polarization state is maintained even in single-mode fibers. This is due to the short length of the fiber loop.

Note

Orthogonal polarization is the alignment of lightwaves at right angles to each other.

→ To learn more about semiconductor optical amplifiers, **see** "Semiconductor Optical Amplifiers," **p.66** (Chapter 3)

CLASSIFICATION OF PHOTONIC SWITCHING ARCHITECTURE

Photonic switching networks can be broadly classified into two types—broadcast and switch-based OTDM networks.

With broadcast OTDM networks, two topologies are present—star and bus. In a star network, the nodes are connected to a central star coupler. If the network having x nodes uses bit interleaving, each frame consists of x+1 bits, with 1 bit present for each node and 1 bit added for framing. A star coupler does the multiplexing. The demultiplexing is performed at each receiver. Another star coupler again performs the splitting. If each node has one receiver, only 1 bit per frame is received. A media access protocol is therefore required for the nodes to know how to tune their transmitters and receivers. Packet interleaving eliminates the need for media access protocols.

Star networks offer better link budget features than bus networks, but bus networks enable easier synchronization, and media access protocol can be designed easily at high speeds. Broadcast networks have the problem of splitting loss and do not reuse the network capacity efficiently. Therefore, photonic packet-switched networks were proposed.

Two types of photonic packet-switched networks are in use today. The first one is a broadcast network, in which a media access protocol is required to share the broadcast medium's bandwidth. FDDI, Ethernets, and token rings are examples of this type of network. The second type of network, shown in Figure 14.7, is store-and-forward. It is based on an arbitrary mesh topology.

Figure 14.7
A store-and-forward network with data packets stored.

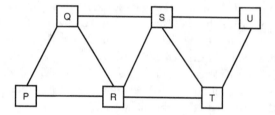

In Figure 14.7, the nodes P to U are the routing nodes or the switching nodes. If node P must send a packet to node U, various routes are possible:

- P-Q-S-U
- P-R-T-U
- P-Q-R-S-T-U

The route to be chosen is specified by the packet, or the decision is left to the nodes on the routing path. In the following discussions, it is assumed that the packet header field in the packet makes the routing decisions. In photonic packet-switched networks, the links run at very high speeds, and the routing node handles the signals optically within the node.

ACTIVITIES OF A ROUTING NODE

A routing node must perform routing and switching functions optically. The functions that are carried out at the nodes are synchronization, header recognition, and buffering.

SYNCHRONIZATION

In photonic switching networks, synchronization refers to the alignment of an input signal with the clock or to the alignment of two input signals. To synchronize the two streams, they must be delayed. The delays considered for optical multiplexers and demultiplexers are fixed delays. However, because the amount of delay is not known beforehand, the synchronizer and the other photonic applications use tunable delays. These tunable delays reduce the problem of synchronization to determining only the phase between the two pulses. A

PART

II

CH

14

logical AND operation is used to compare all the shifted versions of one data stream to another. Because the approach of ANDing is costly, another approach called optical phase lock loop is used. In an optical phase locked loop, the phase and frequency of the local clock source (the mode-locked laser) are adjusted to that of the incoming pulse stream. An electronic oscillator controls the output pulses by providing a feedback loop.

RECOGNIZING THE HEADER

The processing of header bits at the nodes is controlled either optically or electronically. When the control is electronic, if the switch has two inputs and two outputs, a lookup table is used to determine in which state the switch must be set for each input packet—cross state or bar state. If both the inputs have a packet destined for the same output, a conflict arises as to how to route the packet. Therefore, the routing node has buffers.

The header bits can be read if the destination packet carries them. This is done using AND gates that demultiplex the header bits. This is an expensive way to do header recognition. Another technique is to transmit the header bits at a much lower speed than the packet data so that they can be processed and retrieved with ease. It is also possible to transmit the packet header at a different wavelength from the packet data. It can be transmitted on the same wavelength on a separate subcarrier channel. This allows the header to be recognized easily, because it has a lower bit rate than the high-speed data packet.

BUFFERING

Buffers are used to store the packets of the incoming links before they can be forwarded on the outgoing links. Buffers can be present at the inputs, outputs, or both. Buffers are integrated within the switch itself. There are three reasons for having buffers in an optical network:

- When the decision is being made about how the packet must be routed, the incoming packet needs to be buffered.
- The input switch might not be free, thus requiring the packets to be queued at the switch's input buffer. The input switch might not be free because either the packets that have reached earlier are being serviced or the packets from other ports are being switched to this switch.
- After the packet is transmitted to the output port, this port might be busy transmitting other packets. Therefore, the packet must wait its turn.

The best way to build an optical buffer is to use an optical fiber and a delay signal within it. The packet in the buffer cannot be accessed at an arbitrary point in time; it can exit the buffer only after a fixed interval. This is because the packet must traverse the length of the fiber. This is not the case with electronic buffers. Photonic switching uses buffers only to process packet headers. It is avoided otherwise.

Buffering is avoided in photonic switching in many ways. The switch operates at the same rate as the input and output links, causing the transmitted packets to arrive at the output at the same rate. Therefore, the packets are immediately transmitted on arrival, and no buffering is necessary at the output.

If two packets are destined for the same output, only one can be transmitted, because the switch runs at the same speed as the input links. Three options are available in this case. First, one of the packets must wait. This requires a buffer. However, buffering is unnecessary if headers are transmitted. The second option is to drop the packet. This option occurs too often unless the number of packets in the network is low. The source must then retransmit the packet, causing link utilization to further decrease. The third option is to misroute the packet by the switch. This misrouting of packets is called *deflection routing*.

DEFLECTION ROUTING

Deflection routing, also called hot-potato routing, was invented by Paul Baran in 1964. With deflection routing, packets are intentionally misrouted so that they take longer paths to reach their destination. This results in higher delays and less throughput. This method eliminates the need for a buffer in the network. Regular topologies such as Manhattan networks and Shuffle Nets incorporate deflection routing.

The delay experienced in deflection routing is larger than in store-and-forward networks. As a result, both network topologies and statistics between each node pair are fixed. The delay experienced basically consists of two parts. The first part is the queuing delay, in which the packets have to wait at each routing node during transmission. Deflection routing has no queuing delay. The second component is propagation delay—the time taken by the packet to travel all the paths from the source to the destination node. Deflection routing has a larger propagation delay, because the packets are directed away from their destination nodes. This delay compensates for the lack of queuing delay in deflection routing, and the total average delay is higher.

The network's throughput is decreased because of deflection routing. Throughput is maximized when the number of new packets introduced in the network is greater. This depends on the data rates, connection topology, traffic pattern, and so on. The traffic pattern must remain fixed when the throughput is defined. Theoretically, a uniform traffic pattern is used to evaluate the throughput in which the packets arrive at the same rate at the source and the destination. Deflection routing achieves 55%–70% of the throughput as compared to routing with buffering.

In irregular networks, two factors need to be considered while designing photonic packet-switching networks—the diameter and the deflection index. Diameter is the largest number of hops between any two nodes in the network. If the diameter is large, the number of hops required to reach the destination is greater. In the Manhattan street network, the diameter is proportional to $\sqrt{n}$, where n is the number of nodes in the network. In Shuffle Net, the diameter is proportional to $\log_2 n$. Therefore, if both these networks have the same number of nodes, the throughput of the Manhattan street network is lower when routed using buffers than when routed using Shuffle Net. Therefore, generalizing this, you can say that the smaller the diameter, the greater the throughput for routing with buffers.

When deflection routing is used, another property called the deflection index comes into the picture. For the shortest path between any two nodes, the deflection index is the largest number of hops that a single deflection adds to the path. Therefore, network topologies with a small diameter and small deflection indices increase the network's throughput. For further improvements in network performance, deflection rules are specified. The random rule, a type of deflection rule, states the manner in which the packets that need to be deflected must be chosen from the contending ones. Another rule known as closest-to-finish states that when two packets contend for the same output, the one that is farther away is deflected.

A limited number of buffers are also sometimes used in deflection routing so that as soon as the buffer is full, the packets are deflected. This increases the network's throughput.

In deflection routing, it is possible for the packet to be deflected forever and never reach its destination. This condition is called *livelock* or *deadlock*. One of the methods to eliminate livelocks is to simply drop the packets that have exceeded a certain number of hop counts.

DELAY LINE ARCHITECTURES

Two architectures, feed-forward and feedback, are used to incorporate buffers in deflection routing, thereby increasing network throughput.

In the feed-forward architecture, shown in Figure 14.8, three 2×2 switches are used to construct a two-input, two-output routing node. They are interconnected using two delay lines. If two packets arrive simultaneously at both inputs, one of the packets is routed to the correct output, and the other is stored in the delay line. If no packets arrive in the next slot, the stored packet can be routed to the desired output by switching the appropriate switches.

Figure 14.8
The feed-forward architecture.

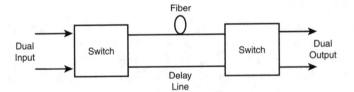

In the feedback architecture, shown in Figure 14.9, the switch's outputs are connected to the inputs using the delay lines. If two packets are sent, one of them can be stored in the delay line. If the length of the delay line slot is one slot, the stored packet is routed to the desired output in the next slot.

The feed-forward architecture is preferred over the feedback architecture because the signals pass through the switch and all the signals are attenuated almost equally, regardless of the path taken through the routing node.

Figure 14.9
The feedback architecture.

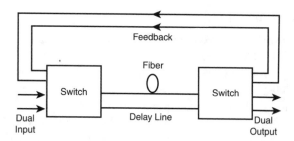

OTDM TEST BEDS

Many OTDM test beds have been developed in recent years. Their key focus is on optical functions such as synchronization, multiplexing/demultiplexing, routing/switching, header recognition, pulse storage, and so on.

ASYNCHRONOUS TRANSFER MODE OPTICAL SWITCHING TEST BED

Asynchronous transfer mode optical switching (ATMOS) was developed to enhance ATM switching capabilities to obtain high speeds. In this test bed, a combination of WDM and TDM is used, and the switches route the packets based on the wavelength and destination address. The demonstrations were carried out at a bit rate of 2.5Gbps. The switches demonstrated were semiconductor amplifier gates, Mach-Zehnder interferometers, and directional couplers. This project also developed the all-optical wavelength converter with speeds of about 20Gbps.

BRITISH TELECOM LABS TEST BED

The British Telecom (BT) laboratory demonstrated a prototype broadcast LAN network based on a bus topology called *synchrolan*. The multiplexed channels operate at 2.5Gbps, and bit interleaving is used. A total bit rate of 40Gbps is transmitted on the bus. Clocking is provided for the bit-interleaved streams, eliminating the need for optical clock recovery techniques. The clock signal is transmitted with a polarization separate from the data signal. A separate time slot is not used. The clock and data signals are passed on two single-mode fibers so that there is no need to have costly polarization-maintaining components.

The BT laboratory also demonstrated routing in photonic switch-based networks, in which an AND gate was used to compare the address of the incoming header with the local address of the routing node. The remaining packet is stored in the fiber delay line when the comparison is performed.

PRINCETON UNIVERSITY TEST BED

The Lightwave Communication Laboratory at Princeton University demonstrated a single routing node operating at a rate of 100Gbps. Packet interleaving is used. Packets from the electronic sources at 1.25Gbps are optically compressed to 100Gbps. Optical demultiplexing is achieved using AND gates. The TOAD architecture is used to convert the serial packet header to a parallel electronic header.

ALL-OPTICAL NETWORKS TEST BED

The All-Optical Networks (AON) consortium developed an all-optical TDM LAN/MAN operating at a rate of 100Gbps. The basic topology is a bus topology in which the users transmit from the upper half and receive from the lower half. Two proposed services are bandwidth on demand and guaranteed bandwidth. The topology has a helical shape and is therefore called helical LAN (HLAN). Experiments demonstrating optical phase loop were carried out in which the frequency and phase of 10Gbps electrically controlled mode-locked laser are locked to that of the incoming stream of 40Gbps. The other technologies demonstrated using this test bed were pulse compression, pulse storage, and wavelength conversion.

CONTENTION RESOLUTION BY DELAY LINES TEST BED

The Contention Resolution by Delay Lines (CORD) test bed consists of two nodes transmitting packets of the size of ATM at 2.488Gbps with different transmit wavelengths. This is actually a WDM test bed, but it also demonstrates important aspects of photonic switching. Every node generates a packet that is destined for itself and the receiving node. The headers are carried at distinct subcarrier frequencies. Tapping a small portion of the power from the incoming signal retrieves these headers. One of the nodes uses a feed-forward architecture. This node can resolve contention better. Thus, the name given to the test bed is Contention Resolution by Delay Lines. This test bed was built using components such as lithium niobate switches, SOA, and polarization-maintaining fibers.

TEST BED FOR OPTICAL NETWORKS

Test Bed for Optical Networks (TBONE) uses crossbar switches to establish direct optical connections between the network nodes. This test bed is being developed by Optivision, Mitre, and TASC and is funded by DARPA. This test bed is mainly intended for high-bandwidth applications such as image transfer and HIPPI communication. The wavelength of operation chosen is 1310nm, which is the zero-dispersion wavelength for single-mode fiber. This wavelength was chosen because analog services must be supported by this test bed. Analog services are very sensitive to dispersion. Various control mechanisms for requesting lightpaths are also studied using this test bed.

SUMMARY

Photonic packet-switched networks provide higher capacities of data than what is possible with electronic networks. The technology needs to improve in terms of the techniques used for optical buffering and for overcoming the difficulty of propagating over long distances on the fiber. The optical switches used now have large losses. This must not be allowed when realizing large switches. The components are also temperature-dependent, and that causes problems in multiplexing/demultiplexing and synchronization. Many companies are developing different test beds. Research is being conducted to develop a complete optical network.

MANAGING OPTICAL NETWORKS

CHAPTER 15

VIRTUAL TOPOLOGY NETWORKS

In this chapter

DESIGN OF VIRTUAL NETWORKS

In the past few years, there has been a growing interest in All-Optical Networks (AONs) with Wavelength-Division Multiplexing (WDM), which uses wavelength routing. The huge bandwidth inherent in optical fibers and the use of WDM to match user and network bandwidths make the wavelength routing architecture an attractive option for future backbone transport networks. In second-generation optical networks, an optical layer provides services to the higher layers, such as the SONET and ATM. The higher layers utilize these services. These layers receive connection requests from the optical layer and also use the optical layer to establish the connections. A connection using lightpaths is set up when a request is made. The connection is released after the request is served. This kind of connection is used when the higher layers are circuit-switched.

You can also set up a lightpath connection for higher-layer services by treating each lightpath as a physical link between two nodes. The lightpaths are permanent. To further introduce the concept of establishing connections using lightpaths, I will define two topologies—physical and virtual. Physical topology is the topology above the optical layer, which is the lowermost layer. Virtual topology, also called logical topology, is obtained by logically mapping the physical topology at the higher layers. A virtual topology over a WDM wide area network (WAN) consists of clear channels between nodes called lightpaths, with traffic carried from source to destination with a minimum of electronic switching. The virtual topology design tries to combine the best of optical switching and electronic routing techniques. By extending the optical network to the lower levels, you not only increase the speed of the bulk data transfers, but also reduce the overall latency of the network. You can design a virtual topology on a physical network by choosing the lightpaths to be set up in terms of their source and destination nodes, and by assigning wavelengths.

DIFFICULTIES IN VIRTUAL TOPOLOGY IMPLEMENTATION

Two problems are present in designing an optical network. First, when designing the physical layer, you must consider factors such as the overall traffic distribution, the link's cost, and the location of the nodes. You must also know the design of the virtual topologies that need to be supported by the physical topology. Therefore, the physical topology needs to be designed with some knowledge of the traffic it must support. This, in turn, depends on how the virtual topology is designed. You also need to consider the constraints imposed on the physical layer while designing the virtual layer. When designing the physical and virtual/logical topology in a network, you must design each topology independently. Figure 15.1 illustrates this two-level design problem.

I will now discuss some of the scenarios in which the design needs to be broken up. The first scenario consists of a physical topology owned by a service provider. The provider can be a telephone company, an Internet service provider (ISP), or a service provider that takes services on lease from other service providers. The service is provided using lightpaths, and it can be an ATM or SONET service. A service provider must support a large number of lightpath requests from customers. You must design the network to meet the demands of both the physical topology and the routing and wavelength assignments of the different lightpaths. The design must attempt to minimize the cost, because the wavelength cross-connects and the fibers connecting them add to the system's cost.

Figure 15.1
The virtual topology design problem.

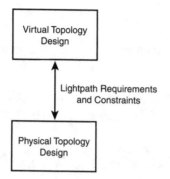

Virtual Topology
Design

↕

Lightpath Requirements
and Constraints

Physical Topology
Design

In the second scenario, the service provider can spread a SONET or ATM network above the physical topology or the optical layer. The provider must have an idea of the traffic requirements and then decide on the lightpaths that need to be established between the nodes. In this case, you can solve the problem using a combined two-level design. However, it is easier to consider the physical and virtual layer designs independently.

In the following discussions, consider the first scenario in which the physical topology is available and only the logical or virtual topology needs to be designed. This design considers the cost and efficiency of the network. The tariff charged by the network is the cost of setting up the lightpath.

There are various implementations of the virtual topology design, a few of which are explained in the following sections.

COMBINED DESIGN OF SONET AND WDM NETWORKS

A network consisting of SONET with WDM rings has many variants. A typical example is of a service provider interested in deploying SONET in a ring structure for fault tolerance. Some of these links use WDM, and others use simple physical fiber links without WDM. You have to determine which set of SONET interconnected rings will carry this traffic when the location of the nodes and the traffic to be carried in Mbps is given. The links of SONET rings are implemented using lightpaths that are routed over existing fiber links. The rings are made up of SONET add/drop multiplexers (ADMs). Multiple ADMs are present in any node. They are interconnected so that the traffic can be switched between the rings at that location. The main objective is to minimize the cost of the entire network, which includes the cost of the SONET, the WDM link, and the fibers connected between the links.

→ To learn more about add/drop multiplexers, **see** "Add/Drop Multiplexers," **p. 183** (Chapter 9)

This problem consists of several related tasks:

1. Identify the set of lightpaths that carries the traffic.

2. Group the lightpaths into rings by adding some dummy lightpaths to complete the rings.

3. Route the traffic onto the lightpaths.

4. Check if any existing rings need to be supported. They can be running at different bit rates.

Tools are available for designing SONET, ATM, and IP networks. You can modify them to design WDM networks by incorporating the constraints imposed in WDM networks.

A SOLUTION TO THE VIRTUAL TOPOLOGY DESIGN PROBLEM

You will now consider a virtual topology design that assumes that there are no constraints on the physical layer design. Consider an ATM network that has a simplex lightpath. This means that if there are two nodes, a and b, and there is a lightpath connection from a to b, it is not necessary to have a lightpath connection from b to a. This is possible because the higher-layer traffic is asymmetrical in many applications. You can make the network full-duplex by adding more constraints. Therefore, a simplex mode is assumed in this discussion.

Let δ be the number of ports in the switch that connect to the other switches. At each node, you can use only a single $(\delta+1)(\delta)+1)$ ATM switch. This imposes a constraint. The remaining switch ports are used to route the ATM packets from the source to the destination. Another constraint is that, for a total of δ lightpaths, only one lightpath per port in each node can be set up to and from the node. If the network contains n nodes, a total of $n\delta$ lightpaths are possible in the network. This is given by the degree constraint, discussed in a moment.

The problem of routing lightpaths over the virtual topology also needs to be considered, because network performance depends on both the topology and the routing algorithm that is used.

Let's consider a numerical analysis of the ATM traffic. The rate of arrival for packets between the source and destination is λ_{sd}, where s is the source and d is the destination. Here, the values s,d=1,2,3...n. u_{ab} is a binary value variable. a,b=1...n. If a virtual link is possible from node a to node b, the value of $u_{ab}=1$. If no link is available, $u_{ab}=0$. The traffic between the same pair of nodes can be split over different paths.

Let the fraction of the traffic that is routed between the source-destination pair be given by x_{ab}^{sd}. Then, $\lambda_{ab}^{sd}=x_{ab}^{sd}\lambda_{sd}$ is the traffic that is routed over link (a,b) between the source-destination pair. The total traffic routed over link (a,b) from all the source-destination pairs is given by the following equation:

$$\lambda_{ab}=\Sigma_{sd}\lambda_{ab}^{sd}$$

Congestion is an important parameter that needs to be considered in this context. It is defined as follows:

$$\lambda_{max}=max_{ab}\lambda_{ab}$$

Congestion is the blocking of data over the lightpaths. It must be minimized to increase network throughput. In an ATM network, congestion occurs because the packets are of a fixed length and are not distributed exponentially.

The problem can now be stated in mathematical terms. The main objective is to minimize congestion. That is, λ_{max} must be at a minimum. The following factors affect congestion:

- Flow conservation at each node:

  $\Sigma \lambda_{ab}^{sd} - \Sigma \lambda_{ba}^{sd}=\lambda^{sd}$ if s=a,
  $-\lambda^{sd}$ if d=a
  0 otherwise

  The packets that are routed between the source and destination are identified by their flow. In equation 1, if the node is the source, the net flow is equal to λ_{sd}, which is the arrival rate at the node. The net flow is zero if the node is neither the source nor the destination. If the node is the destination, the net flow is given by $-\lambda_{sd}$.

- Total flow on a logical link:

  $\lambda^{sd}=\Sigma_{s,d}\lambda_{ab}^{sd}$ for all a,b
  $\lambda^{sd} \leq \lambda_{max}$ for all a,b
  $\lambda_{ab}^{sd} \leq u_{ab}\lambda^{sd}$ for all a,b,s,d

  The constraint $\lambda^{sd} \leq \lambda_{max}$ and the fact that λ_{max} is minimized, ensure that the minimum value of congestion is obtained. The constraint $\lambda_{ab}^{sd} \leq u_{ab}\lambda^{sd}$ ensures that if $u_{ab}=0$, $\lambda_{ab}^{sd}=0$. That is, if there is no link (a,b) in the topology, there is no routing. If there is a link (a,b) in the topology, the constraint $\lambda_{ab}^{sd} \leq u_{ab}\lambda^{sd}$ is always true and therefore imposes no constraint on the values of λ_{ab}^{sd}.

- Degree constraints:

  $\Sigma_a u_{ab} \leq \delta$ for all b
  $\Sigma_b u_{ab} \leq \delta$ for all a

  This constraint ensures that the topology does not have more than δ nodes. This means that in a network with a total of δ lightpaths, only one lightpath per port at each node is possible.

- Nonnegativity and integer constraints:

  $\lambda_{ab}^{sd},\lambda_{ab},\lambda_{max} \geq 0$ for all a,b,s,d
  u_{ab} 0,1 for all a,b

  This constraint restricts u_{ab} to the values 0 and 1.

The task of designing the virtual topology is easy if these constraints are overcome. The constraints discussed and the objective function (minimum λ_{max}) are linear functions of the variables ($\lambda_{ab}^{sd},\lambda_{ab},\lambda_{max,}$ b_{ab}). A program with this linear property is called a linear program. All the variables can take only integer values. Therefore, the program is called

Integer Linear Programming (ILP). If there is no such restriction on the values the variables can hold, the program is called Mixed Integer Linear Programming (MILP). The solution to any mathematical program is to get a set of values that satisfy all these constraints. Various algorithms are used to solve these design problems. LP relaxation and rounding is one algorithm that is used to solve the mathematical problem discussed.

REGULAR VIRTUAL TOPOLOGIES

A topology is regular when all the virtual topologies have the same degree. Regular topologies make the routing of traffic simpler and therefore provide high throughputs and low delays. The parameters that determine the performance of regular topologies are discussed here.

Let $\lambda=\lambda^{sd}$ for uniform traffic between source and destination routed over the link (a,b). l_{ab} is called loading on the link. The average queuing delay is then given by the following equation:

$$d_{ab}=1\div\mu-l_{ab}\lambda$$

The average queuing delay for a network of N nodes is given by the following equation:

$$d_{q}(\lambda)=1\div N(N-1)\ \Sigma l_{ab}\div\mu-l_{ab}\lambda$$

The average link loading in the network is given as follows:

$$l'=1\div M\Sigma_{a,b}\ l_{ab}$$

where M is the number of links in the virtual topology.

Note   l′ is pronounced "l dash."

The average number of hops between the source and the destination pair is given by the following equation:

$$H'=1\div N(N-1)\Sigma_{a=0\ to\ D}\ a\ n(a)$$

where D is the diameter of the virtual topology and n(a) denotes the number of node pairs that have the shortest path length, a, between the nodes in the virtual topology.

There are a number of popular regular virtual topology configurations, such as GEMNet and Manhattan Street Network. We will have a brief look at these topologies.

GEMNet is a regular virtual topology that enables you to factor your network configuration in a number of different ways. The diameter, D, of a GEMNet is

$$D=[\log_{p}M]+K-1$$

Where M refers to the number of rows and K refers to the number of columns, as shown in Figure 15.2.

Figure 15.2
Design of a GEMNet topology.

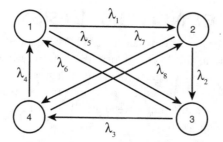

> **Note**
>
> A GEMNet can be arranged in one column with any number of arbitrary nodes added to such one column GEMNets.

Manhattan Street Network was developed by Maxemchuk in 1985. It represents a unidirectional, mesh-configured network, which resembles the layout of the streets and avenues of Manhattan. There are two incoming and two outgoing links to each node (see Figure 15.3) and the routing decisions are made at each node.

Figure 15.3
A 16-node Manhattan Street Network.

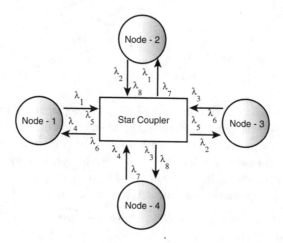

In the Manhattan Street Network, the labeling of the nodes is crucial for the routing functions. Two types of node addressing are followed, absolute addressing and relative addressing. In absolute addressing, the nodes are addressed on the basis of the physical position of the nodes in the network. On the other hand, in relative addressing, a node is considered to be the center of the network and all the other nodes are assigned addresses that mark their relative position from the central node.

→ To learn more about optical network topologies, **see** "Optical Network Topologies," **p. 202** (Chapter 11)

BROADCAST-AND-SELECT NETWORK DESIGN

Virtual topologies were initially proposed for use over a WDM broadcast-and-select network so that the need for rapidly tunable WDM transmitters and receivers could be eliminated. Consider the implementation of a regular topology of degree λ over a star network, as shown in Figure 15.4. Each node has an equal number of transmitters and receivers. Each transmitter and receiver is tuned to a different wavelength. The virtual topology is dictated by the tuning of the transmitter and receiver.

Figure 15.4
A regular virtual topology design.

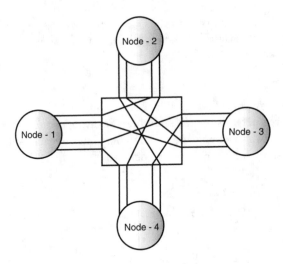

Consider the virtual topology shown in Figure 15.5. The assignment of wavelengths to transmitters and receivers is shown in Figure 15.6. Then obtain the virtual topology of a four-node broadcast-and-select WDM network by using eight wavelengths. Nd wavelengths are needed to implement a virtual topology with degree d. Time-sharing each wavelength between multiple nodes reduces the total number of wavelengths. You can change the virtual topology by tuning the transmitters and receivers to different wavelengths.

In Figure 15.6, each node has two non-WDM transmitters and receivers. The link in the virtual topology is established by a direct point-to-point optical fiber link. The fibers can also be brought to the central hub, if desired, and the interconnections made. This design is less expensive, because it requires nonwavelength-specific lasers and no splitting losses.

However, depending on the circumstances, a particular kind of virtual topology is used.

Figure 15.5
A broadcast-and-select virtual topology implementation.

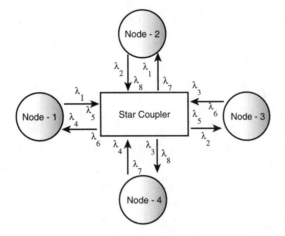

Figure 15.6
Wavelength assignment in a broadcast-and-select network.

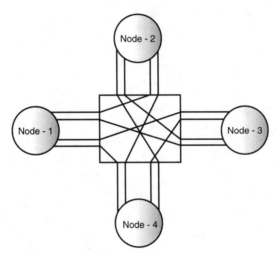

SUMMARY

This chapter covered the design of virtual topologies. In a virtual topology, the connection is made using lightpaths. This makes the network flexible and enables the interconnection pattern to be changed. This feature is not available in conventional point-to-point networks. The network problem is now a two-layer problem and, depending on the scenario, the network is designed. Various algorithms are used to solve the problem of this design. You also read about regular topologies that are good for supporting uniform traffic. The virtual topology design simplifies the connections, and the network can also be reconfigured. Further studies are going on in this field to improve performance using virtual topology.

CHAPTER 16

MANAGING OPTICAL NETWORKS

In this chapter

PERFORMANCE TUNING

First-generation optical networks were point-to-point arrangements that needed little network management. Second-generation systems offered the ability to provide high data rate services along with raw bandwidth.

Performance management basically involves functions that identify the behavior of telecommunications devices and their efficiency. A report is then generated that consists of information about network statistics, a log of the various processes in the network, determining system performance under various conditions, and so on.

Here are some factors that are forcing service providers to incorporate better optical performance management into their next-generation systems:

- Optical performance monitoring and management are necessary to guarantee reliable service in networks that have a large number of optical channels.

- The hurried deployment of optical networks leads to lower-quality installations.

- In the current competitive environment, proper conduits must be installed, or the fiber will be damaged, causing a loss of revenue.

Test beds have identified several difficulties leading to performance limits in the form of network instabilities, limits on network transparency, high error rates, and limits on the minimum error rate. The dominant factors affecting network performance are power loss in the network, accumulated channel cross talk, and nonuniform gain between channels.

POWER LOSS MANAGEMENT

The loss of optical power in the channels during transmission and routing through the network must be compensated for using amplifiers. However, amplifiers add spontaneous emission noise to the signals, reducing the signal-to-noise ratio, thereby limiting the transmission distances. The majority of the power loss in the network occurs at the demultiplexers and switches. The link losses are significant for long-distance transmission. The demultiplexers in the test-bed networks use passive splitters in conjunction with optical filters. This reduces the optical power of each channel by a factor of $1/n$, where n is the number of carrier wavelengths. Alternatives such as bulk optic-grating demultiplexers have typical losses on the order of 6dB. They are not very easily scalable with the number of wavelengths and have narrower overall bandwidths.

CROSS TALK REDUCTION

Cross talk occurs in a WDM optical network either within a channel (intrachannel) or between channels (interchannel). Poor filter performance because of imperfect extinction ratios and no flat passband causes interference between different wavelength channels. Cross talk limits the spacing of channels and therefore limits the overall number of available carrier wavelengths. Poor optical switch performance or optical reflections can cause intrachannel cross talk between multiple subcarriers within the same band. Furthermore, because phase-modulated signals and amplitude-modulated signals have different sensitivities to cross talk, these effects currently restrict the transparency to modulation formats of the test beds. Future developments in types of switches, such as indium phosphide switches, can help reduce cross talk.

GAIN MANAGEMENT

The varying route lengths of the channels, polarization-dependent losses, and the non-uniform gain spectrum of Erbium-Doped Fiber Amplifiers (EDFAs) cause the power level in the optical channels to differ. These effects get cascaded as the signals traverse the network. To ensure that the power level in the channels is uniform, the channel power must be compensated for. Providing a feedback control where the output is fed back to the input ensures this. The feedback keeps the output power at a constant level. When the optical amplifiers are operated near saturation, the power levels in the channels depend on the number and power of the channels being amplified. Existing channels undergo gain variations if a new channel is added to the network. Again, these effects can be compensated for using feedback loops. However, because the feedback is not instantaneous, transient variations in the channel powers occur. These variations spread through the network and result in network instabilities. An alternative is to demultiplex the channels before amplifying each channel power level individually to a common threshold. The demultiplexing and the recombining stage add more complexity to the network and can cause additional signal-to-noise ratio degradation.

With the ability to constantly monitor and manage traffic levels, service providers guarantee levels of service to their customers. Using an integrated performance-management solution, service providers effectively demonstrate their ability to deliver high-performance services in terms that their customers will understand. The service providers use the QoS (Quality of Service) model to maintain their competitive edge in the market. With the use of performance management applications, providers can monitor ongoing physical network performance effectively, analyze its data to correlate end-to-end service performance, and take action based on a complete understanding of network behavior. The use of these applications enables the service providers the ability to guarantee the service levels and ensure that the network performance is at the optimal best.

Service providers/vendors incorporate service-level agreements (SLAs) to ensure that their customers' needs are fulfilled. SLAs involve all aspects of managing the network infrastructure, including the physical layer. Therefore, the physical layer equipment used by service providers must have error-monitoring and performance-monitoring capabilities. Proper communication with the customers and consistent high performance can improve the management and therefore the revenue of the service providers/vendors.

MANAGING THE NETWORK STRUCTURE

This is also called configuration management. It deals with managing network changes such as maintaining a log of the connections that are established and terminated. It consists of two parts—*device management* and *connection management*.

DEVICE MANAGEMENT

The devices used in optical networks operate at very high speeds. The system consists of many devices, and you must keep a count of them. You must know the total wavelengths used by the network. You should maintain a log of activities of the other network devices, such as the transmitters, receivers, line amplifiers, power amplifiers, and preamplifiers.

In a network, when new devices or wavelengths need to be added, the existing system operation must not be disrupted. The networks are usually deployed as point-to-point links and are later upgraded to other configurations, such as ring or star. Therefore, the devices must have the flexibility to add new ports and wavelengths. Arrayed waveguide (AWG) is cheaper and accommodates a large number of wavelengths. When AWGs are used, the entire device must be replaced if one array fails. This replacement is expensive and disturbs the wavelengths that are operating. The user is given access to only a specific wavelength range for security reasons. In case of device failure, a backup must always be present. The efficient management of network devices provides a guarantee and good quality of service to its users.

MANAGING NETWORK CONNECTIONS

In a network, it is important to keep track of when a connection is established or released. You can increase network efficiency by releasing connections when they are unneeded. These resources are then used to establish other connections. A lightpath is used in wavelength-division multiplexing (WDM) networks. The lightpath connection is either centralized or distributed. Centralized connections are used in networks where connections are not made or broken too often. Distributed protocols are used to manage the connection when connection establishment and takedown are frequent. Wavelength contention, when many nodes compete for the same lightpath, is a problem in distributed networks. The topology also needs to be consistent over the entire network so that it is easy to handle failures.

In some cases, unavoidable loops are formed at particular wavelengths that affect the normal operation of the network. You can prevent loops by carefully controlling the network. To control laser gain, sometimes a loop with optical amplifiers is intentionally introduced in the network. If the gain is not controlled, lasing might occur.

> **Note**
>
> A *loop* is condition in which a signal travels in one particular path forever without reaching its destination.

FAULT DETECTION AND MANAGEMENT

Fault management is an area of network management that is concerned with detecting, isolating, and recovering from network faults. It consists of providing backup facilities. The network must be able to detect failures and switch over to backup paths in case of failure. Optical networks pose new challenges in fault management, mainly because many optical network implementations are passive. In other words, no processing is done on the data when it is transported through the network. In conventional systems such as Fiber Distributed Data Interface (FDDI) and Asynchronous Transfer Mode (ATM), a link failure is detected and reported by the nodes at either end of the link. However, in passive optical networks, the optical nodes have no processing capabilities. Thus, other fault-detection techniques must be used. Another difficulty of fault management in passive optical networks is that they use devices whose failure modes and reliability are not well-characterized because the network equipment is passive and has no monitoring capabilities. Thus, the well-developed fault-management techniques used in digital electronic networks are not necessarily applicable to passive optical networks.

The typical topology of a passive broadcast network is a star or tree. Internally there are no active processing elements. Optical amplifiers are installed within the network, generally at the center of the star. They are active but have no processing components. Amplifier backup strategies, with fault monitoring and switchover, are used. Fiber cuts are a major threat in metropolitan area networks (MANs). This is because it is difficult to detect, locate, and recover a cut in a fiber plant that is spread across several hundred miles. The location of the cut is not easy to determine, because internal nodes such as splitters and couplers have no link failure detection capabilities. Therefore, an important research area is the development of topology redundancy strategies that permit the switchover to a backup topology if the primary topology is damaged. The backup strategy must provide smooth switchover and also enable the fault manager to identify the location of the cut to repair the fault.

Virtual topology reconfiguration can be used effectively in passive networks. After the faulty station or router is isolated, the wavelengths affected by the failure are identified, and a new virtual topology is deployed that excludes the faulty elements.

Wavelength routing networks have all the fault-management problems that are present in passive broadcast networks. In addition, the nodal backup problem is more acute here, because the node contains more active equipment, such as tunable filters, switches, amplifiers, and so on. The problem of fiber-cut detection is also more complex due to multipath routing. The challenge is to develop a strategy, either centralized or distributed, that permits identification and isolation of link failure based on end-to-end user failure reports. Then the users affected by such failure are switched to an alternative path.

Note

When a node fails in the network, backup nodes must be present to switch the control of the network to a backup node. This process is called *nodal backup*. In wavelength routing networks, switching is difficult and expensive, because it requires active components to be present at the backup nodes.

Some of the protection techniques are discussed in detail in the following sections.

POINT-TO-POINT LINK-PROTECTION TECHNIQUES

A point-to-point link is one in which the connection between the source and the destination consists of a single direct link. The main protection techniques that are used in point-to-point links are 1+1 protection and 1:1 protection. The other protection techniques are discussed based on point-to-point protection techniques.

1+1 PROTECTION

Figure 16.1 shows a typical point-to-point link. In this kind of protection, the signal is transmitted on two fibers from the source to the destination. One of the fibers is the main fiber, and the other one is the redundant fiber. If the main fiber is cut, the signal is transmitted by the redundant, backup fiber. 1+1 protection switching is very fast, and no protocols are involved for signaling. This type of protection is called *nonreverting* because the traffic is not reverted to the working fiber from the protection fiber after the failure is repaired.

Figure 16.1
1+1 protection switching.

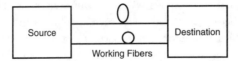

1:1 PROTECTION

In 1:1 protection, shown in Figure 16.2, the signal is transmitted on only one fiber. When this fiber is cut, both the source and the destination switch over to another fiber—the backup fiber. The Automatic Protection Switching (APS) protocol is used in unidirectional systems, because in such systems the fiber cut is identified only at the destination and not at the source. The advantage of this system is that the backup fiber can be used to carry low-priority traffic when it is not used as the main fiber. However, 1:1 protection is not as fast as the 1+1 system.

Figure 16.2
1:1 protection switching.

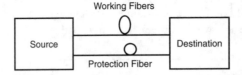

1:N PROTECTION

In the 1:*n* protection scheme, shown in Figure 16.3, *n* working fibers share one protection fiber. The APS protocol is used to switch the traffic from the failed node to the protection fiber. When the failure is repaired, the traffic is switched back to the original fiber so that the protection fiber can handle traffic from other failed nodes. The protection fiber can also carry low-priority traffic. This type of protection is also called *reverting*.

Figure 16.3
1:*n* protection, with one protection fiber for many working fibers.

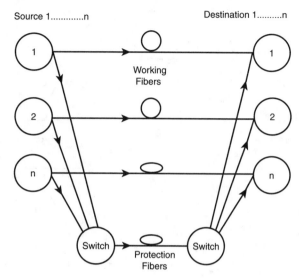

Two ways of protecting traffic intended for different sources from different destinations are path switching and line switching. In path switching, the corresponding source and destination of the individual traffic stream handle the traffic. In case of failure along the route, the source and destination reroute the traffic. In line switching, neither the source nor the destination handles the traffic; the node at the failed link end does this.

RING NETWORK PROTECTION

Ring networks are widely used because they have two separate paths between any node pair, making the ring networks resistant to failures. SONET/SDH rings are used in most networks. These architectures are called *self-healing* because they have mechanisms to overcome failures very quickly. Two ring architectures that are widely used for protection are discussed in the following sections.

UNIDIRECTIONAL PATH-SWITCHED RING

The Unidirectional Path-Switched Ring (UPSR) network, shown in Figure 16.4, is designed for channel-level protection in two-fiber rings. UPSRs designate one fiber as the working fiber and the other as the protection fiber. Traffic is sent along both fibers (1+1 protection). UPSR's working traffic travels clockwise, and protection traffic travels counterclockwise. This implies that bidirectional connections consume resources on all working and protection fibers, thereby restricting ring throughput to that of a single fiber. UPSRs have simpler designs and do not require any signaling mechanisms for switchover between ring nodes, because receiver nodes perform the switchovers. However, they do not use resources efficiently because the fiber capacity between working and protection paths is not reused.

PART
III

CH
16

Figure 16.4
A UPSR network with one fiber as the working fiber and the other as the protection fiber.

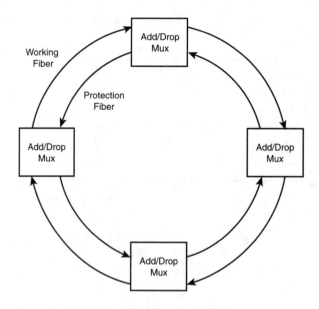

BIDIRECTIONAL LINE-SWITCHED RING

Bidirectional Line-Switched Rings (BLSRs) are designed to protect at the line level. They are of two types—two-fiber rings (BLSR/2) and four-fiber rings (BLSR/4). BLSR/2 is designed to overcome the spatial reuse limitations associated with two-fiber UPSRs. UPSR provides only path protection.

The BLSR/2 scheme, shown in Figure 16.5, uses two fibers. In each fiber, the capacity is divided evenly between working and protection channels/paths. This means that half of the fiber capacity has working traffic, and the other half is used for protection. This allows for load sharing and reuses the fiber capacity. In the event of failure, the nodes of the ring adjacent to the failed node loop back the affected traffic to the ring's protection path. Therefore, there is no dedicated protection path as in UPSR, but a lot of spare capacity is shared among multiple working paths. This is commonly called loopback protection. However, loopback protection increases the channels' distance and transmission delay. The BLSRs perform line switching at intermediate nodes, so more complex signaling functionality is required. Furthermore, bandwidth utilization improvements can also be made by enabling low-priority traffic to traverse on idle protection fibers.

Four-fiber BLSRs extend the BLSR/2 concepts by providing added fiber-switching capabilities. In BLSR/4 rings, two fibers are used for working traffic and two for protection traffic (see Figure 16.6). Again, working traffic is carried in both directions, and there is better resource utilization for bidirectional connections. Line protection is used when both working and protection fibers are cut. However, if only the working fiber is cut, less switching is required at the fiber level. Here, all failed channels are switched to the corresponding protection fiber in the same direction as the working fiber. Overall, the BLSR/4 ring capacity is twice that of the BLSR/2 ring, and it can handle more failures. Also, it must be noted that both two- and four-fiber rings provide node failure recovery for traffic passing through them. All the channels on fibers passing the failed node are line-switched away from the node.

Figure 16.5
A BLSR network enabling sharing of resources and reuse of the fiber capacity.

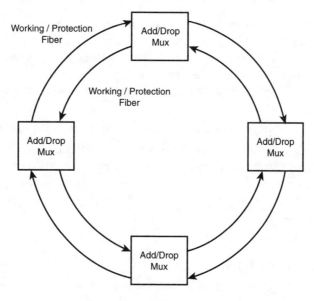

Figure 16.6
A BLSR network with two protection fibers and two working fibers.

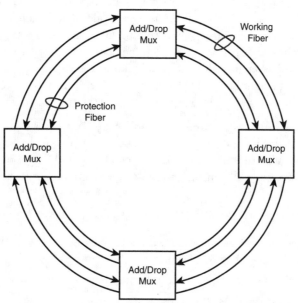

BLSRs require a protection signaling mechanism. Because the protection channels are shared, each node must keep track of the state of the other nodes. Signals are sent over both fiber directions of the ring. This is achieved using an APS protocol running on the K1/K2

bytes in the SONET frame overhead. This protocol uses a 4-bit node identifier in the K1 byte, so it allows only 16 nodes per ring. Additional bits are designated to identify the type of function requested, such as bidirectional or unidirectional switching and the fault condition.

With SONET/SDH technology, rings are available in discrete steps of ring capacity. However, with the increased capacity requirements, the available maximum ring capacity is insufficient to transport the demanded traffic on a single ring. Therefore, multiple rings, stacked on top of each other, are required. The number of rings required in a stack is determined by the ring capacity, the demand pattern, the routing within the rings, and the type of ring used.

→ To learn more about SONET, **see** Chapter 9, "Synchronous Optical Networks," **p.167**

Add/Drop Multiplexers (ADMs), needed to access the traffic in the ring's nodes, are available only in discrete steps of add/drop capacity. Some types of ADMs, called compact ADMs, cannot access all the traffic passing on the ring. Therefore, it is necessary to install multiple ADMs in tandem in a node to achieve full nonblocking configurations in the ring's nodes.

SAFETY MANAGEMENT

You need to consider the safety issues with fiber optics. Careless handling of the light source in a fiber, such as a laser, can result in permanent damage to your eyes. Most fiber-optic systems have power levels too low to cause damage. In addition, the light coming out of the fiber is in the form of an expanding cone, causing the light to disperse. Therefore, there is less danger to your eyes if you are away from the fiber end. Most systems operate with light over the 1000nm wavelength, where the liquid in the eye absorbs light, preventing retinal damage. Most of the light is invisible to the human eye. If the power emitted is high, the damage is likely to be irreversible. You can use a power meter to see if power is present.

The two major safety issues are proper disposal of the glass pieces that are created by cleaving or accidentally breaking the fiber, and the appropriate use of cleaning chemicals and adhesives. You must be careful about fiber particles lying on the floor or sticking to your clothes. Chemicals can be flammable and can cause respiratory problems or allergic reactions.

Here are some of the precautions you need to take when working with fiber:

- Keep food and beverages out of the work area, because if fiber particles are ingested, they can cause internal hemorrhaging.
- Do not smoke while working with fiber-optic systems.
- Always wear safety glasses with side shields.
- Never look directly into the end of fiber cables until you are sure that there is no light source at the other end. Use a fiber-optic power meter to ensure that no light is transmitted over the fiber.

- After ascertaining that there is no light, you can look at the fiber from an angle at least 6 inches away from your eye.

- Wash your hands thoroughly before touching your eyes or handling contact lenses.

- Keep all combustible materials at a safe distance.

- Work in well-ventilated areas.

- Wear disposable aprons if possible to minimize fiber particles on your clothing. Fiber particles on your clothing can later get into food and drinks and/or be ingested by other means.

- Keep all cut fiber pieces in a safe place, and ensure that they are disposed of properly.

- Thoroughly clean your work area when you have finished your work.

UPGRADING OPTICAL NETWORKS

The transmission capacity of today's first-generation optical networks is about 2.5Gbps. Network operators are trying to increase this capacity fourfold without a substantial increase in network cost. Three basic approaches are used to upgrade fiber's transmission capacity:

- Space-Division Multiplexing

- Time-Division Multiplexing

- Wavelength-Division Multiplexing

SPACE-DIVISION MULTIPLEXING

In Space-Division Multiplexing (SDM), the bit rate is kept the same, but the number of fibers is increased.

SDM is a very simple upgrading alternative. This approach has two major drawbacks. First, the large number of fibers required leads to increased cost. The cost of laying new conduits is greater because of the extra fibers made available for future upgrading on the required routes. If no fibers are available on the required route, fiber must be laid. The second drawback is that even if fiber is available, a separate set of optical amplifiers is required, leading to increased cost. Therefore, SDM is used when fibers are available in abundance and the distances are short so that no amplifiers are required.

TIME-DIVISION MULTIPLEXING

In Time-Division Multiplexing (TDM), the transmission rate of the bit on the fiber is increased. The TDM approach is used to increase data rates beyond 10Gbps. The main constraints in TDM systems are chromatic and polarization mode dispersion (PMD). Dispersion-shifted fibers are used to reduce chromatic dispersion. The limit for chromatic dispersion is about 60km at 10Gbps and 1000km at 2.5Gbps. Beyond these distances, you must regenerate the signals by using repeaters or by applying chromatic dispersion compensation.

The PMD values in older links are on the order of 2ps/√km. For long distances, electronic regeneration is required. PMD also limits the distance because of splices, connectors, and other components. In the newer links, the PMD is kept as low as 0.1ps/√km. Therefore, in TDM, the speed is limited by the electronics. OTDM is used to push the data rates beyond the capabilities of electronic networks. An important factor is that the SDM and TDM approaches are compatible with today's network management techniques, and additional learning for installation and deployment is not required.

WAVELENGTH-DIVISION MULTIPLEXING

Another method for expanding fiber capacity beyond TDM without the bottlenecks and complexity is Wavelength-Division Multiplexing (WDM). This is achieved by allocating a particular wavelength to a given channel. Each wavelength, or channel, can then transmit its own data independently of the other wavelengths. Passing the wavelengths through a prism or diffraction grating where they are then combined into a single fiber multiplexes the different wavelengths. At the receiving end of the fiber, the individual signals are then separated using optical filters. Each wavelength supports the high speeds that once required entire optical fibers. In other words, on WDM systems, multiple channels can be transmitted over a single fiber, because they are sent at different wavelengths.

WDM wavelengths can each independently carry OC-3 voice on one wavelength, analog video on another wavelength, and OC-12 ATM on yet another. Currently, WDM systems can carry as many as two dozen channels. In the future, the capacity will increase to 128 channels or more on a single fiber. A system with 24 channels, each running at OC-48, has a total capacity of 60Gbps, and a system with 40 such channels can carry 100Gbps.

Note

Some devices, manufactured by Lucent, are available in the market that can carry over 128 channels using the DWDM technology.

→ To learn more about Wavelength-Division Multiplexing, **see** "Wavelength-Division Multiplexing," **p.190** (Chapter 10)

→ To learn more about OC-3 signals, **see** "SONET Frame Structures," **p.169** (Chapter 9)

WDM is used in fiber-optic networks for communications and data transmission such as cable TV and telephony.

Using WDM can double the transmitting capacity per optical fiber and lead to cost reduction.

AREAS OF OPERATION

The systems discussed in the preceding sections are deployed depending on network traffic, the application, bandwidth of operation, and cost. The cost trade-offs are important when you're deciding which systems to use. Some of the applications are discussed here.

Companies that provide very high-speed data communication using optical fibers are called interexchange carriers (IXCs). Some of the major carriers in the industry are AT&T, Sprint, and MCI. WDM is an attractive option for IXCs because of the advantages offered and because their deployment is carried out on a large scale. High-speed TDM systems having dispersion-shifted fiber are also deployed. Nonzero dispersion fiber links are installed for deployment of both WDM and TDM systems.

Optical fibers deployed for short-distance communication are called local exchange networks. These systems mostly use TDM or SDM systems. However, WDM systems are used to increase network capacity. These systems support high transmission capacity and different modulation formats and protocols. Wavelength routing is also used, because different network services are segregated. Customers might also require dedicated services.

SUMMARY

The chapter provided a view of efficient network management. Network performance involves considering many factors, such as output power, cross talk, and the limitations of the equipment in the network. This is achieved by maintaining a log describing the network's daily activities. The management of the equipment must be efficient for the network to provide good service. In case of network failures, various protection techniques such as 1+1, 1:1, UPSR, and BLSR-2/4 are employed. The safety considerations when handling an optical system must be deployed mainly in areas where users are unaware of the hazards caused by carelessness. These factors cause limitations in the network design. However, efforts are made and the transmission capacity of the fiber is improved using techniques such as SDM, TDM, and FDM.

CURRENT TRENDS AND TECHNOLOGIES

In this chapter

OPTICAL ADD/DROP MULTIPLEXERS

The need for more bandwidth led to the introduction of optical technologies in the transmission world. Point-to-point optical links, wavelength-division multiplexing networks, and all-optical networks are now a reality. Switching technologies are trying to match the progress of transmission technologies. Research and experiments are being performed to figure out how switching can be accomplished in the optical domain. The devices that are being developed to realize an all-optical network include optical add/drop multiplexers (OADMs), optical cross-connects (OXCs), and optical gateways. To provide fault tolerance in the optical domain, optical bidirectional line-switched rings (OBLSR) are also being developed. Technological progress allowed the combination of optics with acoustic and thermal engineering. The use of liquid crystals with optics has also been of great interest to researchers. This chapter discusses the latest trends and technological progress in optical networks.

An OADM, shown in Figure 17.1, enhances WDM terminals. OADM systems have a capacity of up to 40 optical wavelengths. It is now possible for ATM, frame relay (FR), local area networks (LANs), high-bandwidth Internet Protocol (IP), and others to connect directly to the network using a wavelength in the optical layer. OADM is also the foundation of OBLSRs. OADM adds and drops traffic without converting the entire optical data stream into electrical signals. OADM accommodates local and long-distance traffic and provides transparency, increased service velocity, and reduced site costs without compromising the network's flexibility.

Figure 17.1
An OADM adds and drops signals without optical conversion.

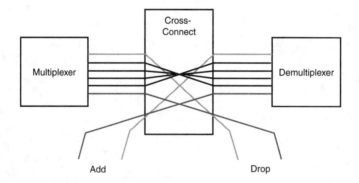

OPTICAL CROSS-CONNECTS

An Optical Cross-Connect (OXC), shown in Figure 17.2, is a space-division switch that switches an optical data stream on an input port to an output port. Such a switch has opto-electric conversion at the input port and electro-optic conversion at the output port. It is also possible to have an all-optical switch. An OXC has a processor that implements signaling and routing protocols necessary in an optical network.

Figure 17.2
An OXC switches optical data with either electro-optic conversion or all-optical switching.

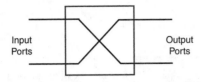

Input Ports

Output Ports

The components required for optical switching are optical switches, optical cross-connects, and any combination of cross-connects, switches, routers, or another box that performs the switching function. Studies have shown that in today's data-centric networks, only 20% of traffic terminates at any given node. This means that even though only 20% of the traffic requires electrical conversion, OXCs convert 100% of the traffic to electrical, and then 80% back to optical. This adds to the cost of the network. The scalability of the OXC depends on the volume of traffic and the bit rate.

PART

III

CH

17

OPTICAL BIDIRECTIONAL LINE-SWITCHED RINGS

The optical ring uses the same principles as the fiber ring to provide protection against equipment and network failures. In case of failure or a break in the fiber connection, the traffic is routed automatically in the opposite direction around the fiber ring. The network elements have intelligent software to do this. The optical network automatically reroutes the traffic of up to 40 optical signals in less than 50 milliseconds. Optical rings are most cost-effective over large networks.

OPTICAL GATEWAYS

The optical gateway is used to access the optical network efficiently, maximize bandwidth capacity, and enable protocol transparency. A common transport structure must be present for the traffic entering the optical layer. The basic format used widely for high-speed transport is Asynchronous Transfer Mode (ATM). Optical gateways enable a mixture of standard SONET and ATM services. The optical gateway is the key element to enable a smooth transition to optical networks. With the addition of more intelligence to the optical layer, costs are reduced in the SONET layer. For example, the optical gateway can interface the lower-cost 1:n protected SONET system with the optical ring. By partitioning wavelengths, existing rings are kept intact, and new systems are integrated in the optical layer.

MICROELECTRO MECHANICAL SYSTEMS

A Microelectro Mechanical System (MEMS) is an integrated micro device or system that combines electrical and mechanical components that can sense, control, and function on the micro scale. These devices function individually or in groups to generate effects as produced on the macro scale. MEMS technology finds its place in future computer networks and modern machinery. It is fabricated using integrated circuit- (IC) compatible batch-processing techniques. The small size of MEMS makes it ideal for use in aerospace, automotive, biological/medical, fluidics, military, optics, and many other areas. MEMS uses a combination of circuits and micromachinery.

> **Note**
>
> *Fluidics* is the technology of using the flow and pressure of fluids to sense, control, and process information in systems.

Using the same fabrication techniques as those used in microprocessors, you can build sensors and actuators on the same microscopic level as the processor chip. Measured in microns, thermal sensors, pressure sensors, inertial sensors, flow and viscosity sensors, resonators, levers, gears, transmission systems, micromirrors, valves, pumps, and motors are batch-produced together on the same chip along with the processing unit. The MEMS fabrication process is discussed here in detail.

Being miniature embedded systems themselves, MEMS devices are batch-fabricated using a process similar to that used in IC technology. They use silicon wafers as the material and etching techniques to build components. MEMS fabrication and IC fabrication share characteristics such as mass production and low cost. The products fabricated are assembled as a single system. MEMS has mechanical parts and electromechanical parts integrated with electronic parts, so the fabrication process is complicated. These systems usually have complex shapes and moving joints and pivots. Therefore, MEMS systems need to have more material strength and require lubrication because of the moving parts.

Common processing techniques that are used to form these mechanical structures include bulk micromachining, wafer-to-wafer bonding, surface micromachining, and high aspect ratio micromachining. Here is a brief list of MEMS processing techniques:

- In bulk micromachining, a variety of etching procedures such as anisotropic etching, isotropic etching, and Deep Reactive Ion Etching (RIE or DRIE) selectively remove material with a chemical etchant. The etching properties are dependent on the crystallographic structure of the bulk material.

> **Note**
>
> *Etching* is the process of removing the lines or surfaces left unprotected in metal, glass, and other similar materials. Chemicals such as acids are usually used for etching and are called *etchants*.

- Bulk micromachining also uses wafer-to-wafer bonding, in which different silicon wafers are brought together and permanently joined. The two most common bonding techniques are anodic bonding and silicon fusing bonding. Many bulk-micromachined wafers are bonded to obtain a wide range of complex mechanical structures.
- High aspect ratio micromachining is a newer technique that enables the fabrication of thickness to usually be greater than hundreds of microns and up to centimeters thick to give a high-precision high aspect ratio MEMS structure.

> **Note**
>
> A *high aspect ratio* MEMS structure is a structure that has nearly vertical sides.

- The surface micromachining (SMM) technology creates thin micromechanical devices on the surface of a silicon wafer. Large numbers of devices are created inexpensively, and this technology integrates well with electronics. On the surface of a silicon wafer, thin alternate layers of structural and sacrificial material are deposited and patterned. At the end of the processing, the sacrificial material is removed, and only completely assembled micromechanical devices remain. Surface micromachining enables the fabrication of complex and multicomponent integrated electromechanical structures. It gives you the freedom to fabricate devices and systems without constraints on materials, geometry, assembly, and interconnections.

> **Note**
>
> A *sacrificial layer* is used to fill in the empty areas on the surface and make it smooth. It is usually made using silicon dioxide.

Polysilicon is the main material used to construct both the electrical and mechanical parts of MEMS devices. It is used in the structural layer. It is the most abundant solid element in the earth's lithosphere and has great strength. Material strength is not a key limiting factor in the performance and reliability of MEMS. This means that fracture and wear and tear of the material are not the dominant causes of MEMS failure. The material can endure high stress and is used in joints, beams, and springs. However, failures induced by wear are found in parts involving sliding motion and operating under stress. Fretting wear occurs when machine elements experience fluctuating loads, leading to microcracks, and fatigue failure. This is not observed in MEMS material.

> **Note**
>
> *Fretting wear* occurs due to friction or rubbing between parts, leading to corrosion and reducing the strength.

THERMO-OPTICS

Thermo-optical technology is used to make small optical switches, typically in the 1×1, 1×2, and 2×2 range. Integrating basic 1×2 components on the same wafer forms larger switches. The two basic types of thermo-optic switches are interferometric switches and digital optical switches (DOSs). Interferometric switches are advantageous because they are compact, but they are also wavelength-sensitive. Therefore, they require some form of temperature control.

Most switches made in silica are interferometric. They consist of a Mach-Zehnder Interferometer (MZI) with a thin-film phase shifter deposited on the waveguide arms of the interferometer. By heating the waveguide, the phase of the optical waves traveling in the interferometer is varied. When the heater is on, the upper and lower arm waves recombine out of phase, because the waveguide's refractive index is slightly modified by the thermal electrons. This is known as the thermo-optic effect. It causes the input signal to exit the switch on the lower output port (the bar state). With the heater off, the two waves travel in the interferometer arms at the same speed and recombine in phase at the output coupler. The input signal exits the switch at the upper output port (the cross-state).

→ To learn more about MZIs, **see** "Mach-Zehnder Interferometers," **p.48** (Chapter 3)

The DOS is more robust, because it has a step-like response. In other words, if more power is applied to the heater, the switch stays in the same state. The simplest device, a 1×2 switch, is called a Y-splitter. When heat is applied to one arm of the Y, it changes the refractive index, which blocks the light traveling down that arm. DOS is made from silica or polymer. The latter draws about 100 times less power, but optical losses are higher.

> **Note**
>
> In a system that has a step response, the change in the signal level is in steps; it is not gradual.

The reason why most silica switches are interferometric is simple. Silica has a relatively high thermal conductivity, and this architecture ensures that the heaters are at least 100 micrometers apart so that they do not influence neighboring switches.

The main characteristics of a thermo-optic system are as follows:

- The scalability of these systems is limited by their heat loss. Presently, the biggest device is a 16×16 port switch from NTT Electronics.
- The main factor affecting the switching speed is the heat rate on the switch material. This means that if the material heats up fast, it is potentially good.
- Although no moving parts are present, continuous heating and cooling causes fatigue and dislocations on the material that can shorten its life. Therefore, it is less reliable.
- The light loss is potentially high because of polymer-based switches. Vendors are trying hard to reduce this loss.
- The cost is low, because similar technology is in mass production already.
- The power consumption is low, because polymer-based switches require 100 times less power than silica-based switches.

LIQUID CRYSTALS AND OPTICS

Liquid crystals are an intermediate phase of matter between the solid and liquid phases. A liquid crystal is a substance that flows reasonably freely. It has lost some degree of translational order, but retains some orientation order in the distribution of molecules. This means that the molecules of the liquid crystal are all aligned in a particular direction, but are randomly distributed. The mean direction along which the liquid crystals are aligned is called the *director*. In a normal liquid, the molecules are not aligned in the way that they are in the liquid crystal, so all the properties of the liquid, both optical and physical, are *isotropic*. The properties of the liquid crystal are *anisotropic*.

Note

Liquid crystals are found in things such as soap film. The Egyptians used them as part of the mummification process to form impermeable layers. Friedrich Reinitzer made the first observations of phase changes in liquid crystals as a function of temperature in 1888.

Note

Anisotropic materials have properties that vary depending on the direction of measurement. In liquid crystals, this is due to the alignment and shape of the molecule.

An *isotropic material* has properties that remain the same regardless of the direction in which they are measured. In the isotropic state, all directions are indistinguishable from each other.

Note

With *translational motion,* the molecules of a body move parallel to one another and are at the same distance from every other molecule in the body.

Note

The *orientation* of the molecules in a body is defined as the alignment of molecules in a specific manner.

PART

III

CH

17

LIQUID CRYSTAL CATEGORIES

Liquid crystals are obtained in two distinct ways. The first category is *lyotropic*. Absorption of a liquid into an organic solid forms the liquid crystal phase in lyotropic materials. The liquid penetrates the molecules of the solid and weakens the intermolecular forces so that the molecules move easily with respect to one another. These liquid crystals are found in many living systems, and they are important for the manufacture of some organic compounds.

The second category of liquid crystal is *thermotropic*. These liquid crystal phases occur between the liquid and solid phases of certain materials. The solid crystal melts into a liquid crystal. These crystals retain the molecular order to some extent because of the highly anisotropic Van der Waals forces between the molecules. As the temperature increases, the liquid crystal melts into a regular liquid. Thus, there is a specific temperature range over which the liquid crystal phase exists. Thermotropic liquid crystals are commonly used for optical devices. You will now consider their properties.

Thermotropic liquid crystals are divided into three classes according to their ordering in the liquid crystal phase. The simplest ordering, known as *nematic* ordering, is shown in Figure 17.3. Here, the molecules are randomly distributed, but they point in the same direction.

Figure 17.3
Nematic ordering of molecules with random molecular distribution but regular orientation.

Cholesteric ordering, shown in Figure 17.4, is even simpler than nematic ordering. This form of ordering is shown by esters of cholesterol. The director for each layer of the liquid is angled with respect to the last layer, forming a helical pattern. The pitch of the helix is altered by changing the molecules or by applying external forces to the system.

Figure 17.4
Cholesteric ordering of molecules, which forms a helical pattern.

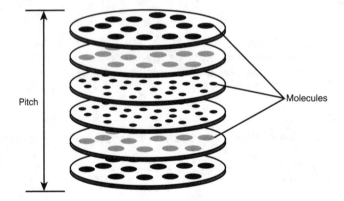

Pitch

Molecules

The third type of ordering, *smectic* ordering, is shown in Figure 17.5. Smectic ordering is divided into phases that are then subdivided into groups A through O. There is some degree of translational and orientational order. None of the ordering discussed is perfect. Figures 17.3, 17.4, and 17.5 show the tendencies of the molecules and not their real positions.

LIQUID CRYSTALS AS OPTICAL DEVICES

The optical properties of liquid crystals are anisotropic. For example, cholesteric liquid crystals are optically active. The rotational power of a typical cholesteric liquid crystal is about 40,000°/mm. This is large compared to the rotational power of quartz crystal, which is 22°/mm.

Figure 17.5
Smectic ordering, showing the ordering of phase A.

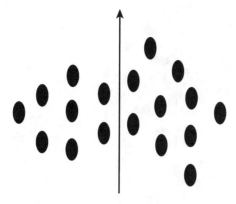

Thermotropic liquid crystals are used as temperature sensors, because they operate over a particular temperature range. This is the range in which the liquid crystal phase is formed. Examples of thermotropic liquid crystals include thermometers for refrigerators and thermometers for people. They are based on different kinds of liquid crystals having different phase transition temperatures. Applying an external field, usually an electric field, controls the properties of liquid crystals. The liquid crystal molecules align themselves with an applied electric field, because the molecular structure of these crystals has a permanent *electric dipole moment*. Attempts to produce optoelectronic devices from liquid crystals are discussed next.

DYNAMIC SCATTERING EFFECT

A nematic liquid crystal is introduced in an ionic liquid to make it conduct, and a cell is formed. If no electric field is present, the crystal is transparent. However, when an electric field is applied, the ionic currents flow, and the liquid crystal scatters light and looks white. Many problems are associated with this effect, so it is not in use.

GUEST-HOST EFFECT

The guest-host effect, shown in Figure 17.6, is obtained using pleochroic dyes. A *pleochroic dye* is anisotropic. It absorbs light only when it is polarized parallel to its long axis, not polarized perpendicular to its axis. A small percentage of such a dye is added to a nematic or cholesteric liquid crystal. If the dye aligns with the liquid crystal, it absorbs light of one polarization and color. The light emerging from the cell is colored and linearly polarized.

An electric field is applied to the liquid crystal so that the axes of the liquid crystal molecules rotate by 90°. Then the axes of the electric field are parallel to the liquid crystal molecules. Therefore, the light hitting the dye molecules rotates with the liquid crystal molecules and is polarized in such a way that the dye is not absorbed. Therefore, the cell is transparent. Thus, you have a switchable colored filter. This effect can be used for color displays.

PART
III

CH
17

Figure 17.6
The guest-host effect enables you to obtain linearly polarized light.

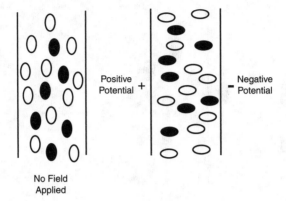

Positive Potential + − Negative Potential

No Field
Applied

TWISTED NEMATIC EFFECT

In the twisted nematic effect, two plates are treated so that they contain tiny ridges in a particular direction. When these two plates are aligned at 90° to each other, and if the nematic crystals are placed between the plates, the alignment of the nematic layers gradually rotates by 90°. This causes the polarization of the light traveling between the plates to be rotated by 90°. Therefore, when a cell is placed between two parallel linear polarizers, no light is transmitted. This effect is called the twisted effect. If a field is applied to the cell, the liquid crystal molecules align with the field, and the cell does not affect the polarization state of light passing through. Thus, the cell with field applied appears transparent. The twisted effect of not allowing the light when the cell is placed is therefore eliminated. A transparent electrode is needed to make this work. These electrodes are formed using a very thin layer of indium tin oxide. The setup needed to generate this effect is shown in Figure 17.7.

Figure 17.7
The twisted nematic effect changes the alignment of the crystals when placed between the treated plates.

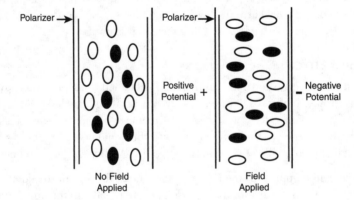

Polarizer→   Polarizer→

Positive Potential + − Negative Potential

No Field
Applied

Field
Applied

The twisted nematic type of display is the most commonly used liquid crystal device. Most calculators, watches, and monochrome computer displays are of this type. The advantages of the twisted nematic display are as follows:

■ Low fields are needed, so not much power is dissipated.

■ Only a small reorientation of the molecule is needed.

The speed of the display is still not fast, as in case of the display of liquid crystal televisions. However, this is still a very successful technology. Displays such as liquid crystal TV screens are called Spatial Light Modulators (SLM) and are one of the most important advances in the technology of displaying information since the cathode ray tube. Liquid crystals are also necessary if information must be input into several of the kinds of optical computers that are designed to process image information. Liquid crystals with twisted effect are widely used as optical gratings.

ACOUSTO-OPTICS

An approach to modulator technology uses the interaction between light and sound waves to produce changes in optical intensity, phase, frequency, and direction of propagation. Acousto-optic modulators are based on the diffraction of light by sound in a suitable interaction medium. Several materials are available for use in the visible and near-infrared regions, and germanium is useful in the far-infrared region.

When a sound wave travels through a transparent material, it causes periodic variations in the index of refraction. The sound wave is a series of compressions and rarefactions moving through the material. In regions where the sound pressure is high, the material is compressed. This compression leads to an increase in the index of refraction. The increase is small, but it can produce cumulative effects on a lightwave that has passed some distance through the compressed material.

An acousto-optic device requires a material with good acoustic and optical properties and high optical transmission. Several types of material that are available are fused silica/quartz, gallium arsenide, gallium phosphide, germanium, lead molybdate, tellurium dioxide, and lithium niobate.

A piezoelectric transducer produces the sound wave. *Piezoelectric* materials exhibit slight changes in physical size when voltage is applied to them. An example of one such material is crystalline quartz. If the piezoelectric material comes into contact with the acousto-optic material and a high-frequency oscillating voltage is applied to the piezoelectric material, it expands and contracts as the voltage varies. This, in turn, exerts pressure on the acousto-optic material and launches an acoustic wave that travels through the material. The frequency, f, of the acoustic wave is the same as the frequency of the applied voltage. The acoustic wave has a wavelength λ given by

$\lambda = c/f$

where c is the velocity of sound in the material. Therefore, varying the acoustic frequency changes the acoustic wavelength, which in turn changes the characteristics of the acousto-optic interaction.

A typical structure for an acousto-optic device is shown in Figure 17.8. It consists of piezoelectric materials and metal layers deposited on the acousto-optic material. A radio-frequency field is applied across the piezoelectric material using the metal layers as electrodes. The acoustic wave is then launched into the acousto-optic medium by the piezoelectric material. Acoustic waves propagating from a flat piezoelectric transducer into a crystal form plane wavefronts traveling in the crystal. The opposite end of the material from the transducer has an acoustic termination to suppress reflected acoustic waves.

Figure 17.8
An acousto-optic device with a piezo-electric crystal between the metal layers.

When an acoustic wave passes through a crystal, regions of high and low refractive index are formed. These regions form a grating within the material, which can act like a regular diffraction grating. The grating can be switched on and off by turning the acoustic wave on and off. Therefore, it can switch or redirect the light. The speed at which the grating is turned on and off depends on the speed of the wave traveling through the crystal. No light is deflected unless the acoustic wave is present. These devices react in times of 100 nano-seconds. Figure 17.9 shows the principle of operation of an acousto-optic modulator.

Figure 17.9
Operating principle of an acousto-optic modulator.

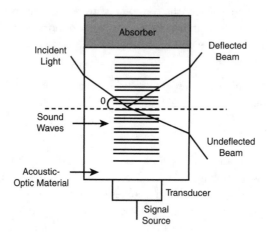

For a material with a fixed acoustic velocity, the acoustic wavelength or grating spacing is a function of the radio-frequency drive signal. The acoustic wavelength controls the light beam's angle of deflection. The amplitude of the disturbance is a function of the radio-frequency power applied to the transducer, and it controls the fraction of the light that is deflected. Thus, the power to the transducer controls the intensity of the deflected light. The light beam is modulated by maintaining a constant radio frequency, allowing only the deflected beam to emerge from the modulator. Thus, the modulator is in its off state when no acoustic power is applied and is switched to its transmission state by the presence of acoustic power.

The diffraction of the light beam by the periodic array of acoustic waves is similar to the scattering of X-rays by periodic planes of atoms. This scattering of X-rays is called Bragg's scattering, and the diffraction of lightwaves is called Bragg's reflection. In X-rays, Bragg's scattering occurs at the planes of atoms in a crystal, which are spaced at regular intervals. Therefore, the Bragg angle gives the angle at which the most efficient scattering occurs. The phenomenon of optical reflection from the regular *wavefronts* of the acoustic waves is similar to X-rays, with the acoustic wavelength replacing the distance between the planes of atoms.

The Bragg angle, Q, is defined as the angle the incident beam makes with the reflecting waves. It is given by the following equation:

$$sinQ = 1/2n\lambda$$

Acousto-optic light beam modulators have many important features. The electrical power required to excite the acoustic wave is small. *High extinction ratios* are obtained easily, because no light emerges in the direction of the diffracted beam when the device is turned off. A large fraction of the incident light is diffracted into the transmitted beam. Acousto-optic devices are compact and offer an advantage for systems where size and weight are important. As compared to electro-optic modulators, they tend to have lower bandwidth but do not require high voltage.

PART

III

CH

17

SUMMARY

All-optical switching products form the core systems for next-generation optical networks. Some of the optical switching products used are OADMs, OXCs, and optical gateways. OBLSR provides efficient failure protection in the same way as fiber ring. MEMS is based on solid-state switch components. These components provide high performance, reliability, small size, and photonic matrix devices that have low power consumption at a significantly lower cost per channel. Thermo-optics helps so that switching is done in a better way. Research into the field of liquid crystals continues. As new applications are developed, they play an important role in modern technology. Acousto-optic switches use sound waves to deflect beams of light from one fiber to another.

PART IV

APPENDIXES

THEORIES RELATED TO OPTICS

In this appendix

SNELL'S LAW AND RAY THEORY

When light traveling in one medium passes into a second medium, the speed of the light changes. When the incident ray is normal to the boundary between the two media, the change in the light speed causes bending of the light rays at the boundary. This process is known as *refraction*.

The angles of incidence (θ_i) and refraction (θ_r) are related by Snell's Law. If n_1 and n_2 denote the refractive indices of the two media, Snell's Law is stated as follows:

$$n_1 \sin\theta_i = n_2 \sin\theta_r$$

If n_1 is less than n_2, such as when light passes from air into glass, Snell's Law states that the angle of refraction will be less than the angle of incidence, and the light beam is refracted toward the normal, as shown in Figure A.1.

Figure A.1
A refracted ray bending toward the normal when light travels from a rarer medium to a denser medium.

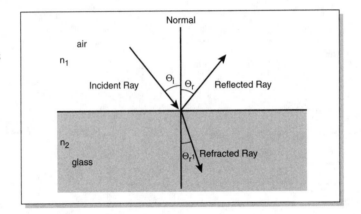

However, when light travels from a denser medium to a rarer medium—that is, when n_1 is greater than n_2—the angle of refraction is greater than the angle of incidence. The refracted ray is bent away from the normal, as shown in Figure A.2.

Figure A.2
A refracted ray bending away from the normal when light travels from a denser medium to a rarer medium.

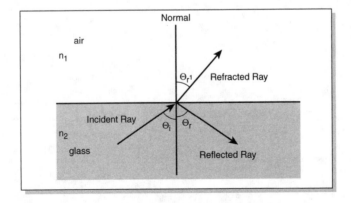

THEORIES IN COMMUNICATION

In this appendix

RANDOM VARIABLES

A random variable X is characterized by a probability distribution function given as follows:

$$F_x(x)=P\{X \le x\}$$

The derivative of $F_x(x)$ is the probability density function given by the following equation:

$$f_x(x)=dF_x(x)/dx$$

In many cases, you might be interested in obtaining the associated ensemble average using the probability function. The ensemble average of a function g(x) is defined as follows:

$$E[g(X)]=\int_{-\infty}^{+\infty}fx(x)g(x)dx$$

The mean of X is defined by the following equation:

$$E[X]=\int_{-\infty}^{+\infty} xfx(x)dx$$

The mean square (second moment) of x is given as follows:

$$E[X^2]=\int_{-\infty}^{+\infty}x^2fx(x)dx$$

The variance of X is defined as follows:

$$\sigma_x^2=E[X^2] - E[X]$$

In many cases, you might be interested in determining the statistical properties of two or more random variables that are not independent of each other. The joint probability distribution function of the two random variables X and Y is defined as follows:

$$F_{x,y}(x,y)=P\{X \le x, Y \le y\}$$

The conditional distribution of X given y is denoted as follows:

$$F_x|_y(x|y)=P\{X<x|Y<y\}$$

An important relation between these distributions is given by Bayes' theorem as follows:

$$F_x|_y(x|y)=F(x,y)/F_y(y)$$

MAXWELL DISTRIBUTION

Maxwell's probability density function is useful to calculate penalties caused by polarization mode dispersion (PMD). A random variable X is said to follow a Maxwell's distribution if its probability density function is given as follows:

$$f_x(x)=\sqrt{}/(\alpha^3\sqrt{\pi})x^2e^{-x2/2\alpha2}$$

where $x \ge 0$

where α is a parameter associated with the distribution. The mean is computed as follows:

$$E[X]=2\alpha\sqrt{(2/\pi)}$$

The mean-square value is given by the following equation:

$$E[X^2]=3\alpha^2=3/8(\pi)(E[X])^2$$

Therefore, the variance is given as follows:

$$\sigma_x^2=E[X^2]-(E[X])^2=\alpha^2(3-(8/\pi))$$

You can also show the following condition:

$$P(X>3E[X])=4\times10^{-5}$$

GAUSSIAN DISTRIBUTION

A random variable X is said to follow a Gaussian distribution if its probability density function is as follows:

$$f_x(x)=1/\sqrt{(2\pi)}\sigma e^{(x-\mu)2}/\sigma^2$$
$$\text{where } -\infty\leq x\leq+\infty$$

where

μ is the mean.

σ^2 is the variance of X.

To compute bit error rates, you need to compute the probability that $X \geq v$, defined as the function given by the following equation:

$$Q(v)=\int_v^\infty fx\ (x)\ dx$$

This function can be evaluated. If X and Y are jointly distributed Gaussian random variables, it can be proven that

$$E[X^2\ Y^2]=E[X^2]E[Y^2]+2(E[XY])^2$$

POISSON DISTRIBUTION

A discrete random variable X takes on a value from a discrete, but possibly infinite set S={x_1, x_2, x_3, ...}. It is characterized by a probability mass function P(x), which is the probability that X takes on a value x. The expectation of a function g(X) is defined as follows:

$$E[g(X)]=\Sigma_{\ I\mid xiES}\ g(x_i)P(x_i)$$

X is a Poisson random variable if the following condition is satisfied:

$$P(i)=e^{-r}r^I/I!$$
$$\text{where } i=0, 1, 2, ...$$

r is a parameter associated with the Poisson distribution. It is easily verified that $E[X]=r$ and $\sigma_x^2=r$.

RANDOM PROCESSES

Random processes are used for time-varying stochastic events. A random process $X(t)$ is a sequence of random variables $X(t_1)$, $X(t_2)$, ..., one for each instant of time. The first-order probability distribution function is given by the following equation:

$$F(x,t)=P\{X(t)\leq x\}$$

Note

A *stochastic* event is one that involves random variables and processes.

The first-order density function is as follows:

$$f(x,t)=\delta F(x,t)/\delta x$$

The second-order distribution function is the joint distribution function, given as follows:

$$F(x_1,x_2,t_1,t_2)=P\{X(t_1)\leq x_1, X(t_2)\leq x_2\}$$

The corresponding second-order density function is defined as follows:

$$f(x_1,x_2,t_1,t_2)=\delta^2 F(x_1,x_2,t_1,t_2)\delta x_1 \delta x_2$$

The mean of the process is given as follows:

$$\mu(t)=E[X(t)]=\int_{-\infty}^{+\infty} xf(x,t)dx$$

The autocorrelation of the process is given as follows:

$$R_x(t_1,t_2)=E[X(t_1)X(t_2)]=\iint x_1 x_2\, f(x_1,x_2,t_1,t_2)dx_1 dx_2$$

The autocovariance of the process is defined as follows:

$$L_x(t_1,t_2)=R_x(t_1,t_2)-E[X(t_1)]E[X(t_2)]$$

The random process is wide-sense stationary if it has a constant mean given as follows:

$$E[X(t)]=\mu$$

The autocorrelation and autocovariance depend only on $\tau=t_1-t_2$. In other words:

$$R_x(\tau)=E[X(t)X(t+\tau)] \text{ and } L_x(\tau)=R(\tau)-\mu^2$$

For a wide-sense stationary random process, the power spectral density is the Fourier transform of all autocovariance and is given by the following equation:

$$Sx(f)=\int_{-\infty}^{+\infty} Lx(\tau)e-i2\pi f\tau d\tau$$

The variance of the random process is given by the following equation:

$$\sigma_x^2=R_x(0)=\int_{-\infty}^{+\infty} S_x(f)df$$

In many cases, you represent noise introduction in the system as a stationary random process. In this case, the spectral density is useful to represent the spectral distribution of the noise. For example, in a receiver, the noise X(t) and signal are sent through a low-pass filter with an impulse response h(t). The transfer function of the filter H(f) is the Fourier transform of its impulse response. In this case, the spectral density of the output noise process Y(t) can be expressed as follows:

$$S_y(f) = S_x(f) |H(f)|^2$$

Suppose the filter is an ideal low-pass filter with bandwidth B_e. In other words, $H(f)=1$, $-B_e \leq f \leq B_e$, and 0 otherwise. The variance of the noise process at its output is given as follows:

$$\sigma_y^2 = R_y(0) = \int_{-B_e}^{+B_e} S_x(f) df$$

POISSON RANDOM PROCESS

A Poisson process X(t) is characterized by a rate parameter λ. For any two time instants t_1 and $t_2 > t_1$, $X(t_2) - X(t_1)$ is the number of arrivals during the time interval (t_1, t_2).

The number of arrivals during this interval follows a Poisson distribution that is given as follows:

$$P(X(t_2)\ X(t_1)=n) = e^{-\lambda(t2-t1)}\ (\lambda(t_2-t_1)^n / n!$$

where n is a nonnegative integer.

Therefore, the mean number of arrivals during this time interval is given as follows:

$$E[X(t_2) - X(t_1)] = \lambda(t_2 - t_1)$$

A Poisson process has many important properties that make it easier to analyze systems with Poisson traffic than other forms of traffic.

GAUSSIAN RANDOM PROCESS

In many cases, you can model noise as well as wide-sense stationary Gaussian random process X(t). It is also common to assume that at any two instances of time, $t_1 \neq t_2$. The random variables $X(t_1)$ and $X(t_2)$ are independent Gaussian variables with mean μ.

For such a process, you can use random variables and write the equation as follows:

$$E[X^2(t)X^2(t+\tau)] = (E[X^2(t)])^2 + 2(E[X(t)]E[X(t+\tau)])^2$$

Alternatively, it can be expressed as follows:

$$E(X^2(t)X^2(t+\tau)] = R_x^2(0) + 2R_x^2(\tau)$$

This equation is an odd transform.

FOURIER TRANSFORMS

Linear transforms, especially Fourier transforms, are widely used to solve problems in science and engineering. The Fourier transform is used in linear systems analysis, antenna studies, optics, random process modeling, probability theory, quantum physics, and bound-ary-value problems. It has been successfully applied to the restoration of astronomical data. The Fourier transform is used in many fields of science as a mathematical tool. It can be used as a physical tool to change a problem into one that can be more easily solved.

A Fourier transform separates a waveform or function into sinusoids of different frequencies that sum to the original waveform. It distinguishes the sinusoids of different frequencies and their respective amplitudes. The Fourier transform of $f(x)$ is defined by the following equa-tion:

$$F(s) = \int_{-\infty}^{+\infty} f(x) \exp(-i2\pi xs)\, dx$$

Applying the same transform to $F(s)$ gives the following equation:

$$f(w) = \int_{-\infty}^{+\infty} F(s) \exp(-i2\pi xs)\, ds$$

- If $f(x)$ is an even function of x—that is, $f(x)=f(-x)$—$f(w)=f(x)$.
- If $f(x)$ is an odd function of x—that is, $f(x)=-f(-x)$—$f(w)=f(-x)$.
- When $f(x)$ is neither even nor odd, it can be split into even or odd parts:

$$f(x) = \int_{-\infty}^{+\infty} F(s) \exp(-i2\pi xs)\, ds$$
$$F(s) = \int_{-\infty}^{+\infty} f(x) \exp(-i2\pi xs)\, dx$$

  The value of $f(x)$, therefore, is as follows:

$$f(x) = \int_{-\infty}^{+\infty} \left[\int_{-\infty}^{+\infty} f(x) \exp(-i2\pi xs) \right] \exp(-i2\pi xs)\, ds \text{---------(1)}$$

The equation (1) holds true as long as the integral exists and any discontinuities are finite.

SOURCES OF NOISE IN OPTICAL SYSTEMS

In an optical communication system, a photodiode at the receiving end must be able to detect signals having very low strength. Therefore, the photodiode must be optimized so as to have a good signal-to-noise ratio. The signal-to-noise ratio of an optical system is given as follows:

S/N = power due to photocurrent/(photodetector noise power + power generated due to amplifier noise)

To understand the relationship between the different types of noise, a model of the receiver and its equivalent circuit are shown in Figures B.1 and B.2. It consists of a photodiode hav-ing a series resistance R_s; total capacitance C_d, comprised of junction and packaging capaci-tances; and load resistor R_l. The amplifier's input capacitance is C_a, and the resistance at the input is R_a. The value of R_s is small when compared to R_l and therefore is neglected.

Figure B.1
A receiver using a
photodetector.

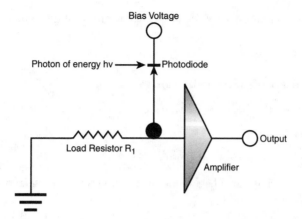

Figure B.2
An equivalent circuit.

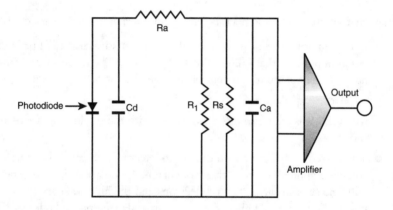

When the input modulated signal P(t) falls on the photodiode, the primary photocurrent produced is given as follows:

$$i_{ph}(t) = \eta q / hv P(t)$$

where

η is the efficiency of the photodetector.

q is an electron's charge.

h is Planck's constant.

hv is the photon energy.

The primary current consists of two parts:

- A DC value current I_p, which is the average current due to the signal power
- The component of the signal $I_p(t)$

In pin receivers, the mean square value of the signal current is given by the following equation:

$$i_s^2 = \sigma_{spin}^2 = i_p^2(t)$$

where σ is the variance of the photodetector.

For avalanche diodes, the mean square signal current is given as follows:

$$i_s^2 = \sigma_{s.APD}^2 = i_p^2(t)M^2$$

where M is the gain of the avalanche photodiode.

For a sinusoidally varying signal having modulation index m, the signal component $i_p^2(t)$ is given by the following equation:

$$i_p^2(t) = \sigma_p^2 = (m^2/2)Ip^2$$

The main noises in photodetectors having no internal gain are as follows:

- Quantum noise or shot noise caused by the statistical nature of production and accumulation of photons that follows Poisson's process. The mean square value of the shot noise or the quantum noise current is given by the following equation:

$$i_Q^2(t) = \sigma_Q^2 = 2qIpBM^2F(M)$$

where F(M) is the noise figure associated with the random nature of avalanche multiplication.

- The current flowing through the photodetector in the absence of light (when no bias voltage is applied) is called the dark current. The dark current is generated because of bulk and surface currents. The electrons and the holes that are thermally generated at a pn-junction produce bulk current (i_{db}). In avalanche photodiodes (APDs), these bulk current carriers get accelerated because of the electric field present at the pn-junction. Surface defects, surface area, and bias voltages produce the surface dark current (i_{ds}). The mean-square value of the bulk dark current is given as follows:

$$i_{db}^2 = \sigma_{db}^2 = 2qI_dM^2F(M)B$$

where I_d is the primary dark current without multiplication. The mean-square value of the surface dark current is given as follows:

$$i_{ds}^2 = \sigma_{ds}^2 = 2qI_lB$$

where I_l is the surface leakage current.

Avalanche multiplication does not affect the surface dark current because multiplication is a bulk process.

- The total photodetector noise current is given as follows:

$$i_N^2 = \sigma_N^2 = i_Q^2 + i_{db}^2 + i_{ds}^2 = \sigma_Q^2 + \sigma_{db}^2 + \sigma_{ds}^2$$
$$i_N^2 = 2q(I_p+I_d)M^2F(M)B + 2qI_lB$$

- The amplifier's input impedance is assumed to be greater than the load resistor so that the noise current caused by the thermal noise at the input amplifier is less. The photodetector's load resistor also contributes to thermal noise or Johnson's noise. The mean square value of this noise current is given by the following equation:

$i_t^2 = \sigma_t^2 = 4k_b tB/R_1$

where

k_b is Boltzman's constant.

t is the absolute temperature.

R_1 is the load resistor.

Using a high-value load resistor reduces thermal noise. This value must also provide optimum performance and must be consistent with the receiver's bandwidth requirements.

GLOSSARY

acceptance angle   The maximum angle at which light launched into the core of an optical fiber is efficiently guided. See also *core*.

access network   The part of a telecommunications network that connects the central office (CO) to individual homes and businesses. It consists of remote nodes (RNs) and network interface units (NIUs). See also *CO*.

angle of incidence   The angle between the incident ray and the normal to the core-cladding boundary.

angle of reflection   The angle between the reflected ray and the normal to the interface.

angle of refraction   The angle between the refracted ray and the normal.

anisotropic   Materials having properties that vary with the direction of measurement. In liquid crystals, anisotropic properties are exhibited due to the alignment and the shape of the molecule.

attenuation   A reduction in signal strength caused by the impurities present in glass and improper fabrication techniques. Attenuation is an important factor to consider when you're deciding which type of fiber to install.

avalanche multiplication   When an intense electric field is applied to a semiconductor, electrons are are excited from valence band to conduction band. The resulting electron-hole pairs are called secondary electron-hole pairs. These in turn generate more electron-hole pairs. This multiplication is called avalanche multiplication.

avalanche photodiode   A photodiode exhibiting avalanche multiplication. See also *avalanche multiplication*.

baseband   Baseband communication allocates the entire capacity of an optical fiber to one channel of transmission.

B8ZS   A scheme in which every bit is used for transmission. Therefore, it has a rate of 64Kbps per channel.

bidirectional transmission   The ability of a system to transmit and receive on a single fiber.

binary block line code   See *line coding*.

bipolar with 8-zero substitution   See *B8ZS*.

birefringent   A medium having different refractive indices along two different directions.

bit stuffing   The process of adding dummy bits. See also *justification bit*.

blocking network   A network that does not pass some of the lightpaths.

blocking probability   The possibility of successful and simultaneous communication among multiple ports.

bounded media   Includes cable types such as coaxial cable, twisted-pair cable, and fiber-optic cable. Also called cable media. See also *STP* and *UTP*.

boundless media   Includes all forms of wireless communication.

broadband   Broadband communication enables two or more channels to share the fiber's bandwidth.

central office   See *CO*.

CEPT-1   Conference of European Posts and Telecommunication-level 1. The CEPT-1 signal consists of 30 voice signals and two channels—that is, 0 and 16 for framing and signaling. Therefore, it has a rate of 2.048Mbps. CEPT-1 uses the HDB3 coding technique.

channel   A closed, direct, hardware-intensive connection that connects external peripheral devices to the workstation.

chipping code   A redundant bit pattern for each bit that is transmitted. It increases the signal's resistance to interference.

cholesteric ordering   A form of ordering that is shown by esters of cholesterol. The director for each layer of the liquid is with respect to the last layer, forming a helical pattern. See also *director*.

chromatic dispersion   Occurs when signals at different wavelengths travel with different velocities and reach the receiver at different times. Chromatic dispersion causes the spreading of the signal. Also called material dispersion.

cladding   A layer of material having a higher refractive index. It surrounds the core to contain the light within the core. See also *core*.

CO   Central Office. The main part of the public network. COs are located in all regions from where a telecommunication carrier operates and from where switching is performed.

Conference of European Posts and Telecommunication-level 1   See *CEPT-1*.

confinement factor   A fraction of the power traveling the core of the waveguide.

core   The central region about the longitudinal axis of an optical fiber through which the optical signal is guided.

credit   The number of frames the destination can handle. This is sent to the source beforehand.

critical angle   The angle of incidence that provides an angle of refraction of 90° so that all the incident light passes through the core. See also *core*.

cross talk   The undesirable interference of signals on the desired signal.

deflection routing   A variation of shortest-path routing in which some packets are intentionally misrouted to prevent congestion. Also called hot-potato routing.

demodulation   The process of extracting the transmitted data at the other end by converting the optical signal back to electronic form.

demultiplexer   A device that helps retrieve the original signal from the multiplexed stream.

demultiplexing   The process of recovering the original channels from a multiplexed signal. See also *multiplexing*.

Dense Wavelength-Division Multiplexing   See *DWDM*.

depletion region   When a pn junction is created by doping, free electrons near the junction migrate or diffuse from the n-type material into the p-type material to fill holes. At the same time, holes in the p-type material migrate or diffuse into the n-type material, where they capture electrons. This causes the n-type material near the junction to become positively charged and the p-type to become negatively charged. The junction, therefore, becomes relatively free of majority charge carriers and is known as the depletion region.

diffraction grating   A collection of reflecting or transmitting elements separated by a certain distance.

Digital Signal 1   See *DS1*.

direct sequence spread spectrum   Combines a data signal at the sending station with a higher data rate bit sequence called a chipping code (also called processing gain), which spreads the user data according to a spreading ratio. See also *processing gain* and *chipping code*.

director   The mean direction along which liquid crystals are aligned.

dispersion   The phenomenon that occurs when different components of the signal travel at different velocities in the fiber. Dispersion causes degradation of the electromagnetic signal propagating in a fiber.

distribution network   The network between the remote node and the network interface units.

dopant   An element added to a semiconductor material during its manufacture to increase its conductivity.

DS1   Digital Signal 1 has a basic data rate of 1.544Mbps and corresponds to the T1 signaling rate of North America and Japan.

dual-attached station   A station present in a ring having at least two ports—port 1, where the primary ring comes in and the secondary ring goes out, and port 2, where the secondary ring comes in and the primary ring goes out.

dual-ring topology   A topology that contains two token rings rotating in opposite directions. An extra ring is set up for backup in case the primary ring fails. If the secondary ring is not needed for backup, it is used to carry data, thereby extending the capacity of data transmission.

DWDM   Dense Wavelength-Division Multiplexing allows a single fiber to have very high density of wavelengths. See also *WDM*.

efficiency   A photodetector's efficiency is the ratio of the energy of the optical signal absorbed to the photocurrent generated.

electric dipole moment   A system is said to have a definite electric dipole moment when it has two equal charges of opposite signs placed a small distance apart.

electric flux density   The number of electric field lines on a given surface.

electric polarization   The orientation of the lightwaves in a particular direction caused by the electric field generated.

evanescent wave   A lightwave that penetrates into the optical fiber's cladding for a short distance. The evanescent wave's energy flow is parallel to the core's surface and is in the same direction as the flow of energy.

extinction ratio   The ratio of the power (P_1) transmitted during the 1 bit period to the power (P_0) transmitted during the 0 bit period.

fabric   A fabric topology is used to connect devices in a crosspoint switched configuration. The switch connecting these devices is called a fabric.

facet   The two end faces of the cavity in a Fabry-Perot laser.

feeder network   The network between the central office (CO) and the remote nodes (RNs). See *CO*.

fiber channel   A set of standards defined by the American National Standards Institute (ANSI).

first-generation optical network   A network in which optical fibers function solely as a transmission medium and serve merely as a substitute for copper cable. Here, the electronic equipment present in the network performs the data processing.

frequency hopping   Takes the data signal and modulates it with a carrier signal that hops in a random fashion. Frequency hopping reduces interference.

gain   The amount of amplification that takes place, usually expressed in decibels (dB). Calculated as one-tenth of the logarithm of the output power divided by the input power.

grating plane   Multiple narrow slits are placed equally apart on the grating plane. When light is incident on the grating plane, it is diffracted into discrete directions.

ground state   Electrons in an atom exist in various energy levels. The lowest energy level is called the ground state.

guided ray A lightwave that undergoes total internal reflection at the core-cladding boundary.

hot-potato routing See *deflection routing*.

impulse response When a function describes an output waveform that is excited by a unit impulse input.

interchannel cross talk Cross talk that occurs when the interfering signal is at a wavelength that is very different from the desired signal, such that their difference is greater than the receiver's electrical bandwidth.

interexchange network A network that interconnects cities or major traffic hubs.

intermodal dispersion Caused when light rays in a multimode fiber follow several paths of different lengths and do not reach the end of the fiber at the same time. This difference in propagation delay broadens the pulse.

intrachannel cross talk Arises if the interfering signal is at a wavelength that is within the receiver's electrical bandwidth.

isotropic An isotropic material has properties that remain the same regardless of the direction in which they are measured. In the isotropic state, all directions are indistinguishable from each other.

jitter The deviation in or displacement of some aspect of the pulses in a high-frequency digital signal. The deviation can be in terms of amplitude, phase timing, or the width of the signal pulse.

justification bit When two channels are bit-interleaved, they must be brought to the same bit rate by adding dummy bits called justification bits.

LAN Local area network. A network that has a group of computers that share resources and network communication devices within a small geographical area.

laser line width The spectral width of a laser beam.

lasing threshold The lowest excitation level at which the laser's output is dominated by stimulated emission rather than by spontaneous emission.

lightpath An end-to-end connection established across an optical network.

line coding The process of encoding data into bits.

livelock or deadlock A condition in which the packet is deflected forever and never reaches its destination.

local area network See *LAN*.

local exchange network The part of a public network that connects all the COs in a metropolitan area. See also *CO*.

lyotropic   In lyotropic materials, the liquid crystal phase is formed by the absorption of a liquid into an organic solid.

MAC   Medium Access Control. A mechanism that provides coordination to avoid contention and collisions between the different nodes in the network.

magnetic flux density   The number of magnetic field lines on a given surface.

magnetic polarization   The alignment of lightwaves in a specific direction.

MAN   Metropolitan area network. A network that interconnects users with computer resources in a geographic area or region larger than that covered by a large local area network, but smaller than the area covered by a wide area network.

Medium Access Control   See *MAC*.

metropolitan area network   See *MAN*.

mode hopping   The sudden shift of the laser diode output beam from one longitudinal mode to another during single-mode operation. It is due to an unexpected rise in laser frequency because of a change in the injected current above the threshold value.

mode shift   A change in laser frequency due to changes in temperature.

modulation   To transmit data over an optical fiber, the data in electronic form is converted into an optical form. The process of converting data into an optical form is called modulation.

multiplexer   The device used to combine signals from different sources into a single stream.

multiplexing   A technique that combines two or more data channels for transmission on a common medium. Multiplexing lets broadband media support multiple data channels.

multiplication gain   An avalanche photodiode's multiplication gain is the mean value of the number of secondary electron-hole pairs generated by the primary electron. See also *avalanche photodiode*.

NAS   Network Access Station. A station that connects the optical network to the non-optical systems in the electronic domain. The electronic domain is the equipment that is outside the network's purely optical segment.

nematic ordering   An ordering in which crystals have some orientational order but have lost their translational order to some extent.

network   An aggregation of connected nodes, such as workstations or file servers, that has its own protocol for managing the interaction between the nodes.

Network Access Station   See *NAS*.

nonblocking network   A network that services all the lightpath requests. See also *lightpath*.

optical layer   Provides lightpaths to the higher layers. See also *lightpath*.

optical network   A telecommunications network with optical fiber as the transmission medium.

optical network node   Connects the fibers within the optical network.

Optical Time-Division Multiplexing   See *OTDM*.

oscillator   See *positive feedback*.

OTDM   Optical Time-Division Multiplexing. The signal is multiplexed in the optical domain using time-division multiplexing to increase the data rate beyond the maximum TDM rate. See also *TDM*.

PAM   Pulse Amplitude Modulation. A modulation scheme that generates a sequence of pulses with the amplitude proportional to the amplitude of the sampled analog signal at the sampling instant.

Passive Optical Network   See *PON*.

Phase-Shift Keying   See *PSK*.

photoemission   When electrons fall from a higher energy level to a lower energy level, a photon is emitted. This release of energy is called photoemission.

photonic switching fabric   A collection of active switches connected by fiber links to form an arbitrary physical topology.

piezoelectric effect   An electromechanical effect by which mechanical forces acting on a ferro-electric material produce an electrical response, and electrical forces produce a mechanical response.

pleochroic dye   A dye that is anisotropic. It absorbs light only when it is polarized parallel to its long axis, not perpendicular to its axis. See also *anisotropic*.

plesiochronous   The dummy bits introduced during multiplexing are discarded during the demultiplexing of signals to get back the original signal. This operation is called plesiochronous, meaning "almost synchronous" in Greek.

polarization   The alignment of lightwaves in a particular direction.

PON   Passive Optical Network. No electrical signals are flowing; only optical signals are present. The electronic equipment is present only at the fiber's end points.

population inversion   A nonequilibrium condition in which the majority of electrons are in the higher excited state than the lower state of a particular transition. This unusual distribution among the excited state is unstable and tends to decay to thermodynamic equilibrium, which consists of more electrons in the lower states.

positive feedback   The process of light emerging from the lasing medium and being reflected for more amplification. The device used to perform this amplification is called an *oscillator*.

pre-emphasis The process of improving the overall signal-to-noise ratio in which the magnitude signals of some higher frequencies are increased with respect to the magnitude of signals with lower frequencies.

private network A network that is set up in a private enterprise. The private enterprise owns the tools and links that make up the network.

processing gain The difference in the signal-to-noise ratio of the signal before and after spreading. See also *direct sequence spread spectrum* and *chipping code*.

PSK Phase Shift Keying. A technique for switching phases in response to the signal.

public network A network owned by a telecommunication service provider.

Pulse Amplitude Modulation See *PAM*.

pulse broadening The spreading of the pulse in a multimode fiber caused by intermodal dispersion.

Pulse Width Modulation See *PWM*.

PWM Pulse Width Modulation. The width of the pulse is determined by the amplitude of the signal.

QPAM Quadrature Pulse Amplitude Modulation. Two sinusoidal carriers exactly 90° out of phase with each other are used to transmit data over a given physical channel.

Quadrature Pulse Amplitude Modulation See *QPAM*.

reconfigurable network A network containing switches and/or dynamic wavelength converters that can change routing patterns at the node.

reflected ray The part of the incident light passing through the core.

reflection grating The grating superimposed on a reflective surface.

refracted ray The part of the incident light that passes through the cladding.

resonant wavelength The wavelength of the reflected part of the signal, which is an integral multiple of the length traveled. This wavelength is in phase and therefore increases the signal strength.

ring network A network in which each node in the unidirectional ring can transmit on a specific signature wavelength, and each node can recover any other node's wavelength signal by means of a wavelength-tunable receiver.

scrambling A process in which bits are transferred from one data stream to another by generating a random sequence of bits of a known bit sequence at the transmitting end by a scrambler.

SDM Space-Division Multiplexing. The bit rate is kept the same, but the number of fibers is increased. SDM uses statistical techniques to dynamically allocate transmission space depending on the traffic pattern.

self-healing   Self-healing networks can overcome failures very quickly. They are also called ring networks. See also *ring network*.

shielded twisted-pair cable   See *STP*.

shortest-path routing   Packets are routed using the available shortest path to the destination.

shot noise current   The photodetector at the receiving end generates electrons randomly even if the intensity of input light remains constant. This current caused by the random generation of electrons produces current that is called shot noise current.

side-mode suppression ratio   The amount to which the longitudinal modes other than the main mode are suppressed.

single-hop network   A network in which an uninterrupted optical path between the originating and terminating nodes is provided.

smectic ordering   Ordering in which there is some degree of translational and orientational order. It is divided into phases that are then subdivided into groups A through O.

soliton   A stable particle-like solitary wave. These waves provide a solution to certain equations of propagation. Solitons occur in many areas of physics and applied mathematics, such as plasmas, fluid mechanics, lasers, optics, solid-state physics, and elementary particle physics.

Space-Division Multiplexing   See *SDM*.

splitting ratio   The amount of power for each output of a coupler.

spontaneous emission   The emission of a photon by an atom as it makes a transition from an excited state to the ground state. This occurs independently of any external electromagnetic radiation. Examples of spontaneous emission include radiation from an LED and radiation from an injection laser below the lasing threshold.

static network   A network that has no switches or dynamic wavelength converters. The routing pattern at the nodes is fixed and cannot be changed.

stimulated emission   An emission that occurs when an atom is excited by a photon of the right energy and this atom then emits a photon. This results in two photons that have the same energy and are in phase with each other. This phenomenon is essential for the operation of lasers.

stimulating photon   The photon that induces emission of the new photon.

STP   Shielded Twisted Pair. A special kind of copper telephone wiring used in some business installations. It consists of an outer covering or shield added to ordinary twisted-pair telephone wires. The shield functions as a ground.

subcarrier modulation   In subcarrier modulation, the data first modulates an electric carrier signal in the microwave frequency range. The modulated microwave carrier then modulates the optical transmitter. The microwave signal is the subcarrier—hence the term subcarrier modulation.

susceptibility   The degree to which a piece of equipment is affected by radiated electromagnetic energy.

TDM   Time-Division Multiplexing. A technique that increases the bit rate by sending signals over a channel divided into time slots. The signals are received and restructured at the receiving end.

thermotropic   In thermotropic materials, liquid crystal phases occur between the liquid and solid phases of certain materials. The solid crystal melts into a liquid crystal. These crystals retain the molecular order to some extent because of the highly anisotropic Van der Waals forces between the molecules. See also *anisotropic*.

Time-Division Multiplexing   See *TDM*.

time transparency   The capability of a network to transport information from the source to the destination in minimal time.

token ring   A LAN in which all computers are connected in a ring or star topology. A token-passing scheme is used to prevent the collision of data between two computers sending messages at the same time. See also *LAN*.

total internal reflection   A phenomenon that involves the reflection of all the incident light on the boundary. It takes place only when light travels from a denser medium to a rarer medium and the angle of incidence is greater than the critical angle. See also *critical angle*.

transmission grating   A grating superimposed on a transparent surface.

transparent optical network   A network involving complex combinations of both optical and electronic devices interconnected in a structured architecture. This infrastructure provides basic communication services to a number of other independent networks, each in turn providing a service to a group of users.

undersea network   A network that connects continents with undersea fiber-optic cable.

unit impulse   A short surge of electrical, electromagnetic, or magnetic energy having infinite amplitude and zero width with unit area.

unshielded twisted-pair cable   See *UTP*.

UTP   Unshielded Twisted Pair. Two insulated copper wires are twisted around each other to reduce cross talk or electromagnetic induction between pairs of wires. There is no shielding. See also *STP*.

virtual channel   The basic unit used in information transfer. It carries a steady stream of cells in a certain order between users.

virtual path   A connection that is set up from end to end across a network.

WAN   Wide area network. A network consisting of computers that spans a relatively large geographical area. Typically, a WAN consists of two or more LANs. See also *LAN*.

wavefront   A surface defined by a locus of points within a two- or three-dimensional medium through which waves pass in phase.

waveguide   A device that confines and directs the propagation of electromagnetic waves, such as radio waves, infrared rays, and visible light. Typical examples include hollow metallic tubes, coaxial cables, and optical fibers.

wavelength chirp   When a laser input signal oscillating in a single longitudinal mode is directly modulated, there is a dynamic broadening of the pulse known as wavelength chirp.

Wavelength-Division Multiplexing   See *WDM*.

WDM   Wavelength-Division Multiplexing. A technique used to increase transmission capacity in which two or more optical signals having different wavelengths are simultaneously transmitted in the same direction over one fiber.

wide area network   See *WAN*.

INDEX

A